FIGHTER ACE

The Extraordinary Life of Douglas Bader, Battle of Britain Hero

DILIP SARKAR

AMBERLEY

This book is for the author Paul Brickhill, whose romanticised bestsellers did so much to inspire my generation of schoolboys, and who made Douglas Bader's a global household name, the advantage of which for the international amputee community cannot be overlooked.

This edition first published 2014

First published 2013
Amberley Publishing
The Hill, Stroud
Gloucestershire, GL5 4EP

www.amberleybooks.com

ISBN 978-1-4456-3819 5 (paperback)
ISBN 978-1-4456-1299-7 (ebook)

Typeset in 11pt on 13pt Sabon Lt Std.
Typesetting and Origination by Amberley Publishing.
Printed in the UK.

CONTENTS

INTRODUCTION

Douglas Bader's life defies fiction. An immensely talented sportsman and aerobatic pilot, he lost his legs in a pre-war flying accident, argued his way back into the RAF and became a national hero during the Second World War. His story was romanticised and made into a global best-seller by the author Paul Brickhill in 1954, and subsequently became a box-office success in 1956 – making Douglas Bader's a household name all over the world. This book is not, however, just another in a long line of narratives peddling a romanticised yarn. It is a serious study which deconstructs the myth and arrives much closer to the truth.

Unsurprisingly this incredible story attracted the interest of various other biographers over the years. The main two, Wing Commander PB 'Laddie' Lucas and John Frayn Turner, both entirely sympathetic to and in awe of their hero, used Brickhill's work, which was inaccurate in various respects, as the basis for their own uncritical books. Consequently Brickhill's original 'gilding of the lily' has been accepted as fact – and still resonates throughout existing published work. In 1996/97, my own *Bader's Tangmere Spitfires* and *Bader's Duxford Fighters* represented a change in tack, however, and the first significant attempts to begin separating fact from fiction. More recently, Paul Mackenzie produced an account entitled *Bader's War*, maintaining this theme. As my final chapter explains, though, certain myths are so cemented in popular culture that a long process of deconstruction is required – especially when dealing with a work of *Reach for the Sky*'s enormous popularity.

Genuinely inspirational though Douglas Bader's story is, the fact is that this has become significantly mythicized. The potent myth arising is inexorably connected with that of the Battle of Britain, the Spitfire, and Britain's popular memory of its part in the Second World War. This is another product of the post-war world, in which Britain lost the Empire, experienced a worrying influx of immigration that changed the country's demography – and is entirely connected with Englishness, rather than Britishness. This, therefore, is a serious attempt to comprehensively separate fact from fiction and explain exactly how this particularly powerful myth was created – and endures. It is not an exercise in denigrating the clear achievements of Group Captain Sir Douglas Bader – which, in fact, are deserving of accurate contextualisation.

Such a work will never again be possible – because nearly all of those witnesses with whom I either interviewed or corresponded are now sadly deceased. This is, therefore, I firmly believe, the last substantive and original word on Douglas Bader.

Dilip Sarkar MBE FRHistS BA (Hons), Worcester, 17 June 2012

I

GROWING PAINS

During the early 1900s, Britain was the world's leading imperial power. In this Edwardian era the British Empire reached its peak, following centuries of overseas territorial expansion.[1] Such pronounced imperialism provided countless foreign opportunities for business and, indeed, adventure for those Britons thus inclined. One such was John Steuart Amos. Taking just a kitbag, Amos set sail from Liverpool docks and worked his passage to India as a ship's carpenter. Given that he had no knowledge of ships or carpentry this was a bold step in itself. India was, of course, the jewel in Britain's Empire. Soon Amos, a bright, resourceful, determined and spirited young man, was commissioned into the Indian Naval Service. He married, having a family of daughters, the eldest of whom was Jessie. According to Brickhill, Jessie Amos, like her father, was 'impervious to fear'.[2] Having married an engineer, McKenzie, Jessie remained in India, living in Kotri, where she bore her husband two daughters: Jessie and Hazel. Jessie McKenzie, it was soon clear, had inherited the Amos spirit. At eighteen she married a civil engineer twenty years her senior: Frederick Roberts Bader – also a strong personality.

A year later the Baders' first son, Frederick, known in the family as 'Derick', was born. Within the year, the family returned to England for Mrs Bader to have a second child, renting a house in St John's Wood, London. Douglas Robert Steuart Bader was born there

8

on 21 February 1910. Three days later mother and baby contracted measles, upon recovering from which Mrs Bader survived a major operation. Just months later, the Bader family returned to India – leaving baby Douglas, considered too young for India's climate and conditions, with relatives on the Isle of Man. It would be nearly two years until he, a stranger, joined his parents and brother. This long period of initial separation from his mother throughout this crucial bonding time was considered by Brickhill to be responsible 'for the loneliness that has been deep within him ever since'.[3] This was undoubtedly pronounced by the lavish attention bestowed upon Derick by the boys' parents, who had, until Douglas's eventual arrival in India, lived the privileged life of an only child. Before long the brothers were at odds, the two-and-a-half-year-old Douglas at first coming off second best to his four-year-old brother, who spitefully pinched skin from his face. Unsurprisingly, the youngest Bader boy was 'sweet-tempered but subdued'.[4] With a tenacity that would one day become an international inspiration, Douglas soon fought back, never crying if he lost. The only time he cried, in fact, was when his parents insensitively left him behind, but took Derick, when they went out visiting friends. None of this represented a normal or healthy emotional entry to the world, the consequences of which, as Lucas wrote, 'were to rumble on and on'.[5]

In 1913, Mr Bader decided upon a career change, studying law, returning with his family to England. In India, the 'Bader Sahibs' had lived very comfortably, after three generations of prosperity, but at their new rented home in Kew, on the outskirts of London, domestic help was limited. Unfortunately Mr and Mrs Bader now had matrimonial problems, which, predictably, these two high-spirited and quickly angered individuals aired loudly in front of their sons. It was not a happy home or calm environment – not least because the brothers' relationship was no better. Indeed this would be a constant problem and battle which, in the bigger scheme of things, Douglas could not win. At five years old he could hold his own physically against his elder brother, until separated by their nanny, but not when any issues were decided by their parents – to Jessie Bader in particular, Derick could do no wrong – and it was their mother, of course, who spent more time at home. Douglas came to consider punishment and admonishment as inevitable, learning from a very early age to face it candidly and stoically. In future years, this would provide him with a hard emotional reserve and response to adversity – Douglas would often need to draw upon it. Nonetheless, his aunt, Hazel, remembered that Douglas otherwise 'bubbled with life', being 'warm-hearted' and 'impulsive'.[6] It was Aunt Hazel, in fact, whose duty it became to escort the brothers on their daily bus journey to school, Colet Court, in Hammersmith Road, London. Derick and Douglas fought constantly, tooth and nail – something Douglas was not afraid to do once at school, no matter the size of his opponent, should the need arise. According to Brickhill, however, there were early signs of sportsmanship and 'generosity' during these violent scuffles, usually with older, bigger boys, because Douglas would 'stop fighting when he had hurt someone'.[7] It is clear that Douglas's early life was one of emotional and comparatively violent conflict. A respite occurred when Derick became a boarder at Temple Grove, Eastbourne. At least then, when Derick was away, home life was quieter – although the status quo was resumed once the elder Bader boy returned.

By 1914, the First World War had broken out. Mr Bader was commissioned into the Royal Engineers and posted to France. From that point onwards he would see little more of his family and was not, therefore, a notable influence on Douglas. In 1917, Major

Bader suffered a head wound and was hospitalised. Recovered, or so he thought, the sapper major returned to the front and survived the war. Afterwards, however, he did not hasten home to his wife and sons but remained in France working for the Imperial War Graves Commission. On 6 May 1922, as a consequence of his old war wound, Frederick Bader died. In 1954, Brickhill wrote that the Major had died at and was buried in 'St Omer'.[8] For reasons that will later become apparent, Lucas added that this particular French town therefore became 'a place-name which, prophetically, was to have a meaning in his (Douglas's) life'.[9] Another biographer, John Frayn Turner, subsequently echoed St Omer as the location of Major Bader's death, making this a significant location in Douglas Bader's life.[10] None of this is true. Major Frederick Roberts Bader actually died in Brussels and was buried in the town's cemetery at Evere, Vlaams-Brabant, Belgium; there his grave can be found to the Waterloo Memorial's left.[11] This is both the first and a perfect example of how one commentator's error permeates subsequent written histories and becomes an accepted 'fact'. Like all events or people subjected to any amount of myth-making, the story of Douglas Bader is punctuated by examples of this – all of which steer us deeper into mythology and further from the actual truth.

When his father died, Douglas was eleven. It is clear that during his formative years Major Bader had been a remote and distant figure to his youngest son, which undoubtedly made this loss easier to bear. Turner argued that this was also because 'children of his age have always been resilient',[12] a generalisation far from true. A direct consequence of Major Bader's death, however, was that his family was now in reduced circumstances – which affected Douglas's education. By then he was in his final year at Colet Court, where he had excelled at sport. Rugby was a natural outlet for his competitive and aggressive spirit. Apparently indestructible, a place for Douglas's talent and enthusiasm was found in teams of older players, among whom he doggedly held his own. He enthusiastically attacked gymnastics and boxing, refusing to be beaten by anything, or, indeed, anyone. Significantly, having had difficulty mastering the parallel bars, Douglas lost all fear of falling; it was, as Brickhill wrote, 'one of the important things that ever happened to him'.[13] Never afraid to accept a dare, this character trait frequently found him on the headmaster's carpet. Uninterested in academic subjects, however, young Bader was considered lazy. Refusing to up his game in the classroom, it was clear that Douglas had inherited his mother's obstinacy. Aversion to the classroom or not, the premature death of his father dictated a change of attitude. By now Derick had moved on to King's School, Canterbury, but Mrs Bader was unable to afford fees for her younger son. The only option was for Douglas to achieve a scholarship – a tall order for a pupil completely at home on the sports field but who found studying an alien concept. Recognising the crucial importance of the situation, Douglas knuckled down, surprising everyone and himself with the end result: a scholarship to St Edward's.

The importance of Douglas having won a scholarship to St Edward's in 1923, therefore being able to continue his education at a public school, cannot be overlooked. At this time, Britain was a hierarchical society. Indeed, this remained the case during the forthcoming 1930s, described by Mowat as 'gloomy ... a devil's decade'.[14] Pugh summarised the situation during the interwar period thus: 'Despite a slight redistribution of income since the Edwardian period, Britain remained a very unequal society roughly divided between the 80 per cent defined as manual working class by their occupation, 15 per cent middle class, and 5 per cent upper class.

While millions of people survived on a typical weekly wage of around £3 10s, and many on less, great fortunes were still being amassed, especially in urban property, finance and the consumer industry.[15] Indeed, Mowat concluded that there were 'several Englands' between the wars, their differences never 'so sharply drawn'.[16] In 1933, the celebrated novelist and broadcaster J. B. Priestly made his English Journey, finding 'four Englands': that of the southern counties and guidebooks, the industrial North with many silent furnaces, the prosperous Home Counties and the 'England of the dole'.[17] The key to advancement was education – but the quality of schooling depended entirely upon the ability to pay fees. The social pyramid's top 5.2 per cent sent their children to independent fee-paying schools, known as 'public schools'.[18] This was a misnomer, the foregoing statistic indicating that these elitist seats of learning were anything but 'public'. Annual fees were over £240,[19] a sum beyond the grasp of all but the wealthiest families and, indeed, exceeding that of a great many families in interwar Britain. To fund such fees for two boys was beyond Jessie Bader's coffers, so Douglas's scholarship for St Edward's was therefore crucial.

Like most public school pupils, Douglas boarded. These traditional British educational institutions were rightly considered 'training grounds for leaders of the nation':[20] between 1920 and 1940, 68 per cent of Conservative MPs were former public school boys; those from working-class backgrounds never exceeded a third and were exclusively Labour.[21] Moreover, of 271 civil servants earning over £1,000 per annum in 1939, 190 had public school backgrounds, as did 56 of 62 bishops, 33 of 37 High Court judges, and 76 per cent of 691 holders of high office in the Church, state and industry.[22] Public schools also provided 25 per cent of all university students, markedly dominating Oxford and Cambridge.[23] A public school background was also required for a commission in the armed forces. The influence of public schools and the grip exerted on society by the social pyramid's top 5.2 per cent is clearly demonstrated by the foregoing evidence – which had everything to do with wealth, not necessarily ability. In 1935, in fact, it was estimated that less than half of children considered to be of 'higher ability' in the population as a whole were receiving a secondary education.[24] Overall, therefore, this division meant that, as Pugh concluded, interwar Britain was 'a very undereducated society'.[25]

During the summer of 1923, for thirteen-year-old Douglas, the prospect of starting at a new public school was not the only major change in his life: Jessie Bader had re-married, to the Reverend Ernest William Hobbs. Consequently the family relocated to their new step-father's large rectory at Sprotborough in Yorkshire. Both Derick and Douglas resented this. They found neither running water nor electricity at the rectory and considered the village almost feudal – a complete contrast to the hustle and bustle of London that they knew so well. In the face of stoic non-co-operation from both step-sons, Revd Hobbs abandoned his insistence that they should help with chores and say grace before meals. It was not a great start. Needless to say, Jessie blamed Douglas who, according to Lucas, realised that 'he was not his mother's favourite son ... very soon began to sense that he wasn't wanted as much as his brother'.[26] Indeed, according to a cousin, Suzanne Goodhew, Douglas's mother 'hated' him.[27] It is said that Douglas inherited the obstinacy and spirit of his mother and maternal grandfather, which may explain his mother's antipathy towards him: perhaps Derick was easier to influence and control than Douglas, or perhaps mother and younger son were too alike? Short-term salvation, however, was at hand.

By this time, Jessie's younger sister, Hazel, had married Flight Lieutenant Cyril Burge – adjutant at the RAF College, Cranwell. It was decided that Douglas would go to stay in Lincolnshire with his maternal aunt and uncle for what remained of the summer holidays. Like winning a scholarship to St Edward's and thereby receiving the key to a great many doors, this would be a defining moment in Douglas's life.

Throughout most of the First World War, British military aviation had been served by two forces: the Royal Flying Corps (RFC), associated with the Army, and the Royal Navy Air Service (RNAS). In 1918, the General Staff (GS) decided that a new air force should be formed, capable of waging war against the enemy's manufacturing resources and independent of the Army and Navy. Major-General Hugh Trenchard was chosen to become Chief of the Air Staff (CAS), overseeing creation of this new service. A former Army and RFC officer, Trenchard's task was to build a force with aerodromes and logistics, absorbing the existing RFC and RNAS squadrons. The RAF, however, was modelled on the British Army. Adhering to tradition and reflecting Britain's hierarchical society, personnel were divided into two social groups. Each of these, James observed, 'was characterized by its own patterns of social intercourse, such as living, eating and drinking together, the use of certain speech patterns, the sharing of off-duty recreations, and by marriage. These groups differ in general and military training, and in their daily working tasks. When men are needed for tasks requiring the exercise of high military or financial or political responsibilities, or of higher intellectual powers and attainments, they are drawn from the higher deference group.'[28] The members of that group are officers – and the RAF's officers were trained at Cranwell. Between the wars, all public schools had Officer Training Corps (OTC), with producing future officers in mind. Those public schoolboys who passed the final OTC examination were awarded 'Certificate A', armed with which, together with an application form signed by at least a colonel, they were awarded a commission as of right.[29]

Cranwell was an old airship station where instructors strove to develop a unique Air Force spirit. Although the selection medical and interview process to become a flight cadet was not rigorous, like a public school, the fees required were substantial: a non-refundable deposit of £150 upon entry, and £100 per annum for two years.[30] Enthusiasm for aviation and even a burning desire to fly, therefore, counted for nothing: only money could guarantee admission – an amount available only to the top 5.2 per cent of Britain's socio-economic pyramid. Admission was one thing but Trenchard insisted that all pilots be officers – and there was a 50 per cent failure rate in flying training.[31] Cranwell was, therefore, an extension of the public school system. Having passed his scholarship to St Edward's, young Bader was already *en route* to achieving the key to this particular door – should he wish to open it. At Cranwell, Douglas, an impressionable young boy with a spirit for adventure, got close to aeroplanes for the first time. Burge sat him in the cockpit of an Avro 504K trainer, the boy spending hours watching clumsy students practising take-off and landings. Although interesting, it was not flying that captivated him about Cranwell but sport. The youngster joined in with the cadets' games, spending less time watching flying and more cricket and athletics. Because of this – not the flying – upon conclusion of his visit, Douglas told the Burges, 'Crumbs, I want to come back to Cranwell as a cadet.'[32] Once at St Edward's, though, he became immersed in sport, his passion, forgetting his ambition to one day return to Cranwell in uniform. Nonetheless, Douglas had been introduced to

Air Force life and very much liked what he saw: the seed had been sown, to germinate in due course.

St Edward's is situated 2 miles north to the city of Oxford, and, like all public schools, can boast many luminaries – including the great actor Sir Laurence Olivier, who was a little older but a pupil concurrently with Douglas, and Guy Gibson – later to win a Victoria Cross (VC) and fame leading the ingenious raid on Germany's great dams – who was there a little afterwards. Yet again, Douglas excelled at games but not in the classroom, where he invested the bare minimum of effort to keep him out of serious trouble. Although teaching staff were frustrated, even with little effort he produced passable results, showing a particular penchant for history and poetry. Maths, though, was a real weakness. Fortunately Douglas's high-spirited behaviour was viewed benignly by the headteacher, the Revd H. E. Kendall, known as the 'Warden', who realised that his heart was in the right place. It was also clear, as Brickhill wrote, that this was 'an increasingly strong-willed boy who could only be reasoned into the mould, never pressed into it'.[33] On both the cricket and rugby pitches Douglas thoroughly excelled, the latter aggressive sport being his particular favourite. At the end of the 1925 summer term Derick, with whom Douglas was now getting along much better, was leaving school, a matter which brought Douglas's continued education and performance into sharp focus for the Revd and Mrs Hobbs: even after the scholarship bursary, St Edward's still cost them a further £100 per annum – which they were no longer able to afford.[34] Mrs Hobbs wrote to the bursar, Mr Walter Dingwell, a history master, to that effect. Although he had never taught Douglas himself, Dingwell must have recognised especial potential in this headstrong but gifted boy – because he became Douglas's anonymous benefactor, paying personally the annual fee until the youngster finished school. This, however, Douglas was unaware of for some time. Had Dingwell not come to the rescue, this could have been a very negative turning point in Douglas Bader's life – without which, nothing that followed would have been possible, so crucial was a public school background to personal advancement.

During his final year at St Edward's, Douglas experienced his first taste of personal authority and responsibility when Kendall made him a prefect – a considerable increase in status, not least because prefects carried a cane and had their own studies. Douglas's strong personality meant that his cane was rarely used, his mere presence alone being sufficient to quell any boisterous scuffle. Henry Kendall had, in fact, become a great influence on Douglas. His approach to headship was to show 'latitude and tolerance in treating the lesser, and inevitable, misdemeanours of youth ... to improve immeasurably the chances of gaining acceptance of the larger principles of life'.[35] Kendall became more than just Douglas's guardian angel, he became a substitute father figure and a great positive influence on him. Kendall liked his 'spontaneous friendliness' and detected a sense of responsibility to be encouraged.[36] Douglas, though, suddenly became gravely ill – with rheumatic fever. Delirious, he wandered close to death. His mother was sent for. St Edward's prayed for him. When a vague consciousness returned, Kendall told Douglas how the school was praying for him. This moved Douglas deeply, it having never previously occurred to him that anyone in particular really cared that much about him. Needless to say, Douglas scored the doctor's advice that as his heart could be affected he must rest a long time. Soon he was out of the 'san' and training again, confounding the doctor who found him fully physically fit and more than able to resume his competitive sporting activities. There can be no doubt that Douglas was supremely physically fit and strong – very intelligent and incredibly positive-willed to match. These attributes and character traits would serve him well in years to come, in ways no one could have predicted at St Edward's.

By 1928, Douglas was captain of both cricket and rugby at 'Teddy's', a role he relished and his first real test of leadership. The requirement for a captain to encourage, inspire and consider the team as a whole made him less selfish with the ball – something he had often been previously criticised for.[37] The games master, Arthur Tilley, noted how whereas some captains were aloof, Douglas infected everyone with his enthusiasm, from dawn to dusk. Fellow team-mates he considered brothers – albeit and understandably less in status to himself – to whom he devoted himself. He demanded a reciprocal arrangement – anyone falling short was out. In those school teams, on the playing fields of St Edward's, was forged the ethos and approach to leadership that remained with Douglas for a lifetime. As Mackenzie argued, by now the 'central elements of his essential nature were already manifesting themselves … the urge to compete and win; the desire to lead; the need to prove himself; the blustery self-confidence that masked a certain loneliness; and the need to show loyalty to all those who demonstrated faith in him, not least authority figures'.[38] As Lucas wrote, Douglas was now 'a leader in embryo'.[39] These qualities and approaches to leadership would be demonstrated repeatedly in the years ahead.

Although Douglas's life revolved around his passion for sport, on the wider stage an important decision required attention: what to do upon leaving school? He had no idea. He considered Oxford but studying, inevitably, failed to appeal. Neither did becoming an engineer and going out to South Africa with Derick. Without clear direction, Douglas firmly placed his head in the sand and concentrated on the present – in which, as a prefect and team captain, he was in his element. A chance visit by an old boy, Roy Bartlett, however, rekindled his interest in becoming a Cranwell cadet. Douglas himself later wrote that 'as soon as I recalled those days my mind was made up. Indeed I cannot truthfully say whether it was the excitement of flying, or watching, as I did that time, the triangular sports between Cranwell, the Royal Military Academy, Woolwich, and the Royal Military Academy, Sandhurst, which struck my mind more deeply. In fact what I wanted to do was go to Cranwell – I think that was the truth.'[40] Towards the end of 1927, the seventeen-year-old Douglas wrote to his uncle Cyril inquiring regarding the possibility of becoming an RAF officer. The advantage of a public school background, without which a commission was unachievable, would now pay off. The importance of this cannot be under-emphasised. As Cox commented, before the Second World War 'the RAF had no formal definition of leadership. To a degree leadership skills were absorbed rather than taught, and the armed forces reflected the social attitudes of the time which were rather more inclined to assume leadership on the basis of social class.'[41] No one, however, could deny that Douglas had shown an exceptional flare and commitment to captaincy, and, as the old oral tradition goes, the Battle of Waterloo was, after all, supposedly 'won on the playing fields of Eton'. Burge's response to Douglas's tentative letter was that he was 'just the type they wanted and he would do everything to help'.[42] Burge was certainly well placed to 'help' his nephew, now serving as personal assistant to none other than the CAS, 'Boom' Trenchard, the 'Father of the Royal Air Force'. Nepotism was, of course, a prominent feature in this society and Douglas would now reap the benefits of having a well-placed uncle.

There was, however, a stumbling block to Douglas's admission to Cranwell: fees. Jessie Hobbs was adamant that Cranwell was not an option, on the grounds that she disapproved of Douglas flying and because affording the necessary fees was impossible. It was at this point that Douglas learned that his education at St Edward's had only been possible because of Mr Dingwall's generous intervention. This embarrassed and surprised him in equal measure, and he lost no time in visiting the bursar to express his appreciation. Like entry to St Edward's, though, there was a glimmer of hope: annually, Cranwell offered six highly prized cadetships, negating the payment of fees. Competition was fierce, the academic standard high. Characteristically, Douglas applied himself wholeheartedly to the process, 'cramming' maths with the help of a master, Mr Yorke. In June, Douglas attended the pre-selection interview at Burlington House, off Bond Street in London – having been briefed on the likely questions and required answers by Burge. It is no coincidence that his score was a seldom achieved 235/250.[43] Rheumatic fever, however, had left Douglas with high blood pressure, requiring rest and a re-examination, which he passed. He was not only in, but had won the fifth of the six cadetships. It was a euphoric moment. Dingwall was so delighted that he even bought Douglas a motorcycle as a reward.

As term ended, Douglas bade farewell to St Edward's, where his time had been both happy and productive. Kendall imparted some final words of wisdom: 'Don't become over-confident. Keep hold on those high spirits of yours.'[44]

2

CRANWELL: GATEWAY TO THE STARS

Douglas Bader's arrival at RAF College Cranwell was inauspicious. En route from Sprotborough, a cow wandered onto the Ankaster straight, causing the motorcyclist to take evasive action. Hitting the verge, his machine cart-wheeled, spilling the rider onto the grass in a dishevelled heap. Shaken but unhurt, the only damage was to his bowler hat, balanced on the front headlamp. The crown had burst, flapping open 'like a tin lid'.[1] A few minutes later Douglas drove through the main gates – and entered service in the RAF. The following day the new recruits assembled on the square, the tattered bowler immediately attracting depreciating remarks from the warrant officer in charge. The hat defied all attempts at repair, so Douglas gave up. A week later uniforms were drawn and the gentleman's civilian bowler was consigned to the bin.

The RAF required officers for specific branches: General Duties (flying), Administrative and special duties, Equipment, Accountant, Medical, Dental, Legal and Chaplains. It was with the first category that Douglas was concerned. Trenchard's vision was that all his officers would be pilots,[2] a skill literally over and above the traditional officer function of leading men into battle on land or sea. Aircrew, however, are a breed apart, as Wells explained: 'From the earliest days of aviation, airmen have been regarded as members of an elite group, largely as a result of the dangers associated with flying. In the early part of the twentieth century, flimsy machines, unreliable engines, and inadequate preparation caused scores of accidents. Aircraft and flying were considered novelties and pilots were often seen as daredevils. In the view of many, it took a special type of man to brave the obvious perils.'[3] Ultimately it proved an impractical imposition for all officers to become pilots, but for Douglas and his new colleagues that was their goal. A former interwar flight cadet described Cranwell and its traditions:

The life of the College is resumed with alacrity and care at the beginning of term. One day the place will be wearing a wan and neglected air, while the next day everything will be bustle and confusion. The night seems to bring forth cadets in the same way a conjurer produces rabbits from a hat. But as they come, so they depart, yielding place for others in a never-ending stream: each one, however, leaves his impression for good or bad on the College. Some may be forgotten; others will be talked of by terms of the distant future. Yet one and all will retain indelible memories of their sojourn at Cranwell, and will regard the College with an esteem and affection which is of more value than the cosmopolitan camaraderie of greater seats of learning. For the associations of Cranwell are enjoyed only by a privileged few, who are closely bound together by their careers.[4]

The final sentence is revealing. Douglas was now entering an extension of the world he had experienced to date, one in which the 'old boy network' would later prove a crucial factor. Lucas confirmed that passing out of Cranwell 'opened most doors in the Service and set them climbing the stairway to the stars'.[5]

The course upon which Douglas now embarked upon was of two years' duration. Appendix III of Air Publication No. 121 described the syllabus:

Year One
English language and literature, General ethnology, The British Empire, Applied Mathematics, including mechanics and draughtsmanship, Elementary physics, History of the RAF, Theory of flight and rigging, Air pilotage and map reading, Drill and physical training, Air Force Law and administration, Hygiene and sanitation, Workshops and engines, Wireless telegraphy, Radio telephony and signal procedure, and Practical flying.

Year Two
Theoretical and practical instruction in internal combustion engines, Aerodynamics, Practical instruction in rigging, Advanced work in the wood and metal workshops, Outline of wireless telegraphy and telephony, Armament, Practical flying, Air pilotage and airmanship, Meteorology, Outline of the organisation of the Navy and Army, War, strategy and tactics.

This represented a full curriculum, with a great deal of classroom-based study – something which, despite his obvious ability, had never appealed to Douglas. In 1928, Cranwell's first-year students flew the Avro 504N biplane, which had a top speed of around 100 mph, progressing the year after to the Armstrong Whitworth

Atlas, which was 42 mph faster than the Avro. The Atlas was also currently in service with operational RAF squadrons policing the Empire. There were also a few Fairey Foxes and, for those showing the aptitude to become fighter pilots, Armstrong Whitworth Siskin IIIs. All were single-engined biplanes. Flight Cadet Bader was assigned to Cranwell's 'A' Flight, commanded by Flight Lieutenant Douglas MacFadyen (later Air Chief Marshal Sir Douglas MacFadyen), his flying instructor being Flying Officer Wilfred Pearson. Douglas's flying logbook confirms that his first flight, 'Air Experience', lasting twenty minutes, was made in an Avro 504 piloted by his instructor on 13 September 1928. Douglas was hooked. On 12 February 1929, Flight Cadet Bader had logged eleven hours and fifteen airborne minutes – and successfully soloed. This indisputable fact is, however, contrary to Brickhill, who claimed that Douglas soloed after just a month with only six-and-a-half hours' flying time. Nonetheless, 'Pissy' Pearson had soon appreciated that this particular pupil was a natural pilot. Douglas responded to Pearson's style of instruction, admiring him enormously. Pearson introduced his pupil to aerobatics, at which Douglas immediately excelled but soon took irresponsible and unnecessary risks, these not actually being that uncommon, in spite of service discipline and regulations. Another cadet, Hank More, removed his parachute, climbed out of his cockpit in flight, crawled forward to the empty front seat, and tied a handkerchief around the control column before returning to his rear cockpit and resuming control. An old Etonian, John Chance, followed suit, as, inevitably, did Douglas.[6] Indeed, MacFadyen had occasion to warn the cadets regarding the dangers of 'bunting' – pulling out of a loop inverted. The manner in which he did this, however, impressed Douglas enormously:

MacFadyen simply appealed to reason and common sense, on the basis of preventing a fatality. This was an example of real leadership, which Douglas immediately recognised. According to Lucas, Douglas saw MacFadyen as a role model to 'emulate', placing him alongside Kendall in esteem.[7]

It was out on the open roads of Lincolnshire, however, that Douglas's bravado was not so easy to curtail. In those days there were few road users – encouraging Douglas and his circle of friends – which included a particular Geoffrey Stephenson – to seek thrills and spills on their motorcycles. Inevitably there were brushes with the police, and this irresponsible behaviour spilled over into College time. These young men were, of course, the equivalent of first-year university undergraduates, not necessarily away from home for the first time, as most had undoubtedly boarded at their public schools, but still experiencing a certain amount of freedom for the first time. At such a young age, it is difficult to get the balance right between work and play, to know where to draw the line. Whatever the trouble, Douglas was invariably either the ringleader or in the thick of it. The last straw for staff came when Douglas, the prize cadet, came nineteenth out of twenty-one in the end-of-first-year examinations. His squadron commander made it clear that if there was no improvement in industry and attitude, he would ensure that Douglas and his like-minded friends were dismissed. Next, Douglas was sent for by the commandant, Air Vice-Marshal Frederick Crosby Halahan, a no-nonsense former RNAS officer and heavyweight boxing champion. Keeping Flight Cadet Bader at attention, the commandant spoke quietly but decisively: essentially his message was simple – the RAF required men, *not schoolboys*.[8] Humiliated, Douglas knew that Halahan was right, and was ashamed. The College had, wrote Lucas, 'lived up to all his aspirations, and more', his time there being 'as agreeable as any he could remember'.[9] Not heeding Halahan's advice, Douglas knew, was simply not an option. Another influencing factor could also have been that Walter Dingwall remained a benevolent benefactor. Every month he sent Douglas an allowance of £12, and, the Cranwellian later discovered, would have personally paid his fees if necessary. Douglas had no idea why Dingwall was so inclined. He always remained in the background, was not prone to demonstration, and, in fact, they never met again after Douglas left St Edward's. Douglas concluded that the old bursar simply 'found pleasure in quiet altruism'.[10] Douglas also knew that failure would throw this generosity and support firmly back in the old man's face. He knuckled down to his studies. Initially the staff viewed this change of heart with suspicion but soon regarded it as permanent – which it was.

As ever, Douglas excelled at sport throughout his time at Cranwell. He won all but one boxing bouts, in which he had sparred in a heavier weight than his classification, and achieved a 'blue' in not only boxing but also rugby, hockey and cricket. A junior cadet, (later Squadron Leader) Rupert 'Lucky' Leigh, considered Douglas 'some kind of god who played every conceivable game and was the best player in every team'.[11] Others disagreed, as fellow cadet (later Air Vice-Marshal) Wilfred Oulton recalled, describing Leigh's 'god' as 'an exhibitionist, not a team player'.[12] Oulton's view is illuminating as it challenges Brickhill's view that Douglas 'lived for the team'.[13] Flying, however, was a solo affair – and at this Flight Cadet Bader equally excelled. Early on at Cranwell, Douglas had developed an interest in learning more about the successful fighter pilots of the First World

War. This, together with his obvious flying ability, particularly in respect of aerobatics, marked him out as a potential fighter pilot. He saw out year two flying single-seater Siskin biplane fighters. With a top speed of 156 mph, this was the fastest machine Douglas had yet flown and he mastered it with ease. Upon conclusion of the course, on 25 July 1930 his logbook was endorsed by Squadron Leader Thomas (for the commandant) with an 'above average' assessment as a pilot. There is only one higher – 'exceptional' – which is rarely, if ever, given to comparatively inexperienced students. Throughout that final year Douglas maintained his improved attitude and industry, coming second on the course, beaten to the coveted Sword of Honour by his friend Paddy Coote. Flight Cadet Bader's final report noted that he was 'plucky, capable and headstrong'.[14]

Douglas himself remembered his time at Cranwell thus: 'Cranwell was half a university for us. It gave us time to read, to think, to listen, to talk and make friends. We drank it all in – the flying, the intimacy of the place, the gaiety, the walks, the messing about on motor bikes, the games, the discipline, the leadership. It was all there. And there seemed to be time for everything and this was reflected in our flying. We absorbed the instruction rather than learnt it.'[15] But was it really 'all there'? These cadets, it must be remembered, were from the population's top 5.2 per cent in terms of education and wealth. They had exclusively attended public schools with those of their own ilk, and Cranwell was an extension of that system. In the services, Non-Commissioned Officers (NCOs) represented the rank and file of society; from such senior NCOs at Cranwell, Douglas 'learnt more about being an officer … than from anyone else'.[16] Was this, however, enough? In positions of operational command, responsible for men of all trades and status, how would these young officers fare? Would they have the ability to empathise with and relate to men of lower socio-economic origins? Would they even feel this necessary in respect of leadership – or was it simply a given that, being superior in rank and social status, their word was to be unquestionably obeyed? Within a disciplined and rank-structured service, an order, of course, is an order – but there is much more to true leadership and man-management than that. Only time would tell how these new officers would fare on their squadrons.

Pilot Officers Bader and Stephenson, to their absolute delight, were both posted as fighter pilots to 23 Squadron at Kenley. Lucas wrote that 'Douglas loved his time at Cranwell, and, in return, Cranwell bestowed its favours upon him. His indoctrination was complete, blind and lasting.'[17] If 'AHE's' words that 'the associations of Cranwell are enjoyed only by a privileged few, who are closely bound together throughout their careers' was not ringing in Douglas's ears as he drove out of Cranwell's gates for the last time that summer of 1930, they should have been. At various significant junctures throughout his subsequent career he would have occasion to be thankful for sharing this close bond enjoyed by the service's privileged elite.

3

'BAD SHOW'

Pilot Officers Bader and Stephenson reported to 23 Squadron on 25 August 1930. 23 had a fine reputation as a fighter squadron during the First World War, after which it was disbanded but re-formed in 1925. The Commanding Officer (CO) was Squadron Leader Henry Winslow Wollett DSO MC* – a thirty-five-victory Sopwith Camel ace of the First World War. Douglas was posted to 'C' Flight, commanded by thirty-two-year-old Flight Lieutenant Harry Day. During the First World War, Day had seen active service with the Royal Marines (RM), later transferring to the Fleet Air Arm (FAA) until being permanently commissioned into the RAF during 1930. He had not, however, been 'a successful First World War pilot' as Lucas stated.[1] From an august military family, with an uncle who won a VC in the Crimea, and an ancestor who fought aboard HMS *Victory* at Trafalgar, Day, like Woolett, was a man of great experience whom Douglas would come to admire. The squadron's base was at Kenley, situated between Croydon and Caterham in Surrey. At this time the RAF was only twelve years old, and during the interwar years was sufficiently select to possess the air of a very select flying club. Kenley had a grass runway and red-brick buildings. The two new pilots were shown into the officers' mess, their rooms in the same corridor.

The squadron flew Gloster Gamecock biplane fighters. In addition to flying, sport was also a prominent feature of squadron life. That August, Douglas was selected to play cricket for the RAF. A month later he passed a trial for the famous 'Harlequins' rugby team. Playing centre-three-quarter, the press frequently referred to him as 'brilliant', the best on the field. Naturally Douglas was soon selected to also represent the RAF at rugby. Brickhill wrote that he was 'a sinewy, beautifully tuned human machine that weighed eleven stone six pounds stripped, and had the temperament of a dynamo'.[2] He also had style. Having replaced his old motorcycle with a modest Austin automobile, he now owned a flashy MG sports car. Life could simply not be any better for Pilot Officer Bader. He later remarked that 'it was truly a man's life ... We all lived in the mess, dined-in four nights a week and spent the weekends playing sport. There were no women on the station. We all knew each other, went out together, played games together, flew together. Life was great, and flying was what we all loved.'

Douglas's logbook recorded 56.10 flying hours upon reporting to 23 Squadron. On that first day, Flight Lieutenant Staniforth checked him out in Siskin J9210. The following day, Douglas flew an operational RAF fighter, Gamecock J8084, for the first time, the sortie comprising, according to his logbook, of 'landings, take-offs, local flying. First solo.' He flew twice more that day, both sorties being described as 'landings, take-offs and aerobatics'. On 23 August 1930, Douglas wrote in his logbook, 'Landed (on nose!) at Sidcup owing to mist and rain.' Fortunately Gamecock J7904 was undamaged, enabling Pilot Officer Bader to take-off and safely arrive back at Kenley ten minutes later. These comparatively primitive biplanes had no brakes, no flaps, a fixed-pitch, single-bladed wooden propeller, no gyroscopic instruments, no trimming tabs, and fixed undercarriage; the Gamecock's top speed was 156 mph. Douglas loved flying the Gamecock, which he described as 'a beautiful, unstable biplane, just right for aerobatics and lovely to handle'.[3] Douglas's obvious natural ability as a gifted aerobatic pilot was immediately recognised. There was an obsession at this time with formation aerobatics, which were perceived to teach and demonstrate flying precision and discipline. Douglas loved it: 'There is no more graceful or exhilarating sight than three or four fighters stunting in formation. To see these aeroplanes looping and rolling with their wings overlapping and only a few feet apart never fails to give me the most tremendous thrill. I think it is the finest form of flying that has ever been invented.' Unfortunately, though, as will later be explained, this fixation with close-formation flying would land the RAF in trouble when war came. Burns, however, argued that 'formation flying was a very important part of a fighter pilot's skills. Upon formation flying depended discipline and cohesion in fighting, for there was no radio, and attacks were carefully orchestrated according to prescribed formulas.'[4] Just how wrong this statement is will be proven in due course.

From April 1931 onwards Douglas's logbook indicates numerous flights practising for the Hendon Air Pageant. Hendon, situated in Colindale, 7 miles north-west of Charing Cross in London, was an important centre for aviation at which the RAF held its first pageant – an air display – in 1920. Such events, representing important public relations opportunities, were held annually thereafter. To participate in the event was prestigious, and 23 Squadron's pilots trained hard to be selected. Woollett put 'Pricky' Day in charge of the exercise, who was an experienced aerobatic pilot. Day developed a new repertoire of five sets of synchronised aerobatics. With only 3 feet separating their wing-tips, in the opening sequence a pair of Gamecocks would dive, pull out and perform two consecutive loops, climb, stall-turn away on opposite sides, dive vertically, turn towards and pass each other, climb, roll off the top of a loop together, dive to opposite sides of the aerodrome, turn, race towards each other once more to start a second set – which included inverted flying. It would be hard to master. Training was intensive. One pilot was killed while flying inverted and Stephenson only narrowly recovered from a slow roll. On another occasion his engine failed, resulting in a forced landing in the grounds of a country estate. Douglas drove over to collect his friend, meeting and being immediately attracted to the owner's daughter, whom he thereafter met on a regular basis.

Day selected Douglas as his No. 2 in the RAF aerobatic pairs competition, with Pilot Officer McKenna and Stephenson comprising the second pair. Stephenson would be reserve when Day and Bader represented 23 Squadron in the RAF pairs aerobatic competition. On 19 June 1931, 23 Squadron's pairs participated in the Andover air show, demonstrating their breath-taking routines. A week later the RAF Display at Hendon took place in glorious weather. An indication of both the event's popularity and the interest in aviation during the interwar years is provided by the volume of people crammed inside the gates: 175,000. Countless others watched from outside and the surrounding area. For the first time the Hawker Fury was revealed to the public, followed by FAA Fairey Flycatchers demonstrating aerobatics. The day's emphasis, however, was on the final ten-minute sequence flown by Day and Bader. Their performance centred on the Royal Box, the 23 Squadron pair won. The next day, *The Times* trumpeted their performance as 'the most thrilling spectacle ever seen in exhibition flying'. It was a coup for 23 Squadron, and, of course, for Day and his twenty-one-year-old subordinate.

Pilot Officer Bader's life with 23 Squadron, however, did not simply revolve around glamorous aerobatic flying. The squadron flew many training flights co-operating with the Army – which was believed by many air power experts to be the aeroplane's second most important function, the first being to bomb the enemy. Given the German night-raids on England during the First World War, searchlight co-operation flights, training anti-aircraft batteries, were also important. Between 26 May and 12 June 1931, 23 Squadron completed annual air firing practice at Sutton Bridge. There pilots fired live ammunition at drogues towed by slow-moving aircraft – which took no evasive action. Again, the reality of the forthcoming war with Germany would graphically demonstrate just how ridiculous such an exercise was. Nonetheless, at that time, given that the machines involved were very similar to those used in the First World War, the air staff believed that future air combat would be little or no different to that fought over the Somme. And so the RAF continued flying lightly armed, slow biplanes – training not for victory but, in fact, defeat.

His life entirely fulfilled, at twenty-one Douglas Bader had already become what would be described today as a celebrity, both in the air and on the sports field. Indeed, his place as fly-half in the full England international rugby squadron looked assured. Overflowing with enthusiasm and confidence, Douglas was also in danger – from himself. As the old adage goes, 'there are bold pilots and old pilots. But there are no old and bold pilots!' Having mastered aerobatics, Douglas now turned, according to Lucas, himself a wartime fighter pilot, 'to the hard stuff ... such euphoria can only be found close to the ground. Low flying, real low flying, right down on the deck; beat-ups of the girlfriend's house; making the picnic party in the country field run for cover; just for the hell of it; flying upside down, in Johnnie Johnson's splendid epithet of Bader at Hendon, "with his head almost brushing the grass" – this is the heroin of flying.'[5] Although Day warned his young stars constantly of the perils associated with unauthorised low flying, he considered that Douglas, even, wrote Brickhill, 'in his wilder moments' only ever flew precisely and with perfect judgement.[6] On 20 August 1931 – exactly a year since Pilot Officers Bader and Stephenson had reported for duty with 23 Squadron – Harry Day led them on a flight from Kenley to Cramlington, near Newcastle, to perform formation aerobatics at another air show. En route, Douglas dropped out of formation and amused himself by hedge-hopping for an hour – well below the regulation height for low flying. Such irresponsibility, however, incurred Day's wrath: Douglas had been warned. Many years later, a Cranwell contemporary, Air Commodore HW 'Tubby' Mermagen, remembered that Douglas 'was a real show off. He could do everything brilliantly – but he did it very low.'[7]

In July 1931, 23 Squadron had begun phasing out its Gamecocks and replacing them with the Bristol Bulldog. This was another biplane fighter with a fixed undercarriage, fixed-pitch propeller and twin machine-guns. With a top speed of 176 mph, the Bulldog hardly represented a great leap forward in design and development. The new machine, however, was heavier than the Gamecock and therefore not as manoeuvrable. Halfway through a slow roll, for example, the Bulldog lost altitude quickly. The conclusion of such a roll could see the Bulldog 400 feet lower than at the starting point. Consequently and sensibly, low-level aerobatics were banned: one pilot ignored this and promptly perished in a fatal flying accident. Following another similarly wasteful and unnecessary death, Day, temporarily commanding 23 Squadron, reminded his pilots that Fighting Area Regulations strictly prescribed the minimum height for aerobatics as 2,000 feet – from which height recovering from the Bulldog's vices was not an issue. Day, though, was sympathetic to aerobatic flying, for obvious reasons, and cautioned that if low-level aerobatics were attempted that should be no lower than 500 feet – and beyond the gaze of senior officers.[8] Characteristically, Douglas ignored all of this. In November he was carpeted by Day for beating up the airfield. It was not just the disregard for safe flying practice and regulations that concerned Day. Some members of 23 Squadron resented Douglas, the Cranwellian, thinking him conceited. Stung by the subsequent rebuke for 'showing off', Douglas 'began to watch what he was saying and shy away from ostentatious aerobatics'.[9] Halahan's intervention in similar vein had done the trick at Cranwell. Day could only hope that his words would have the same effect – but he remained concerned when he left Kenley on leave later that day. For Douglas, though, it seemed that such caution was unfounded. Life for young Bader was just getting better and better: that month he was selected as fly-half for the Combined Services team; his place as an England international rugby player seemed assured. What happened the following month, however, would change his life forever.

According to Lucas, by this time Douglas was 'the best aerobatic pilot in the Royal Air Force'.[10] He was also the victim of his own success. In the wake of his competition-winning Hendon aerobatics, Lucas argued, came an expectation for him to perform, such requests being 'difficult to refuse'.[11] Turner, another sympathetic Bader commentator, suggested that Bader played 'indifferently' during his first Combined Services game and subsequently for the Harlequins, so that 'psychologically ... Douglas was feeling that he had to prove himself to somehow compensate for these two slight failures'.[12] This, however, is pure conjecture on Turner's part. Whatever his state of mind, on the morning of Monday 14 December 1931, 'Pricky' Day authorised Douglas to practise aerobatics. The subsequent flight of an hour and a half increased his total flying hours to 492.20 – just short of the 500 hours Lucas, himself an RAF fighter pilot, considered necessary for maturity.[13] Accounts of subsequent events that day vary. Lucas stated that after this sortie, while Douglas was walking back to the flight hut, another 23 Squadron pilot, Flying Officer G. W. Phillips, invited him and Stephenson (not 'Richardson' as according to Brickhill and Turner) to make up a threesome to Woodley, near Reading, and lunch with his brother there.[14] Burns clearly used Lucas's account as reference, also writing that Douglas and Stephenson accepted Phillips's invitation, the three Bulldogs taking off together.[15] Brickhill, however, wrote that as Douglas was landing he saw Phillips and Stephenson taking off, remembered that they were lunching at Woodley and so 'tacked on'.[16] Mackenzie described how Bader 'tagged along'.[17] Whatever the actual facts surrounding Bader joining the trip to Woodley that day, as Lucas rightly wrote, the consequence of that trip would be 'written indelibly in the annals of the Royal Air Force'.[18]

After lunch, inevitably, the civilian pilots present pressed Douglas to give them an aerobatic display upon leaving. Here again, accounts published to date differ in his response. Brickhill related that Douglas refused on the grounds that his Hendon display had been in a Gamecock, not a Bulldog.[19] This is unlikely. Douglas's logbook records 32.20 hours on the Bulldog, and he was master of it. Brickhill then described that Douglas was stung into performing what was an unauthorised, low-level display, completely contrary to service regulations, because one of the club members accused him of being 'windy'.[20] Turner duplicated this account. Lucas, though, simply stated that Douglas was unable to refuse, making no mention of any barbed comment being necessary to persuade him.[21] Whatever the inspiration or cause for what happened next, the three fighters took off, having agreed to perform a 'Prince of Wales's feathers'. This involved the central aircraft climbing vertically, while those either sides did so slightly to the left and right before peeling away. According to Mackenzie, who, having researched the Court of Inquiry report, is closer to the truth than previous writers, Douglas occupied the left-hand position, breaking in that direction as expected – but then 'quite unexpectedly headed back to the field at low level'.[22] This is crucial. Clearly the three fighter pilots had agreed to perform what was a reasonable aerobatic manoeuvre as a parting gesture to their hosts – but there had been no discussion among them, or other conversation to suggest to Phillips or Stephenson that Douglas was intending to 'beat up' Woodley. Without citing evidence for this view, Mackenzie wrote that before take-off, however, 'it was clear that Bader was going to do something', pointing out that the subsequent Court of Inquiry criticised Phillips – the senior officer present – for not 'holding him back'.[23] My personal view is that the story regarding Douglas being accused of being 'windy' is a fabrication by sympathetic commentators. If that was so, would the allegation have not equally applied to Stephenson? Considering Douglas's proven aerobatic ability, overconfidence and extroverted nature, my interpretation of the evidence is that he decided of his own accord, probably before take-off, that he was going to give the civilians an aerobatic demonstration to remember. Douglas was not coerced into doing this, it was his own impetuosity, conceit and overconfidence that, in a few seconds, would change, and nearly claim, his life.

Douglas's intention was to roll over the airfield at around 125 mph and virtually at zero feet. As he swept across the grass his fixed undercarriage was only 10 feet above the ground, his head just 18.

The Bulldog, Lucas pointed out, was never rolled any faster – so characteristically Douglas was right on the edge.[24] This was reckless indeed. A roll subjects an aircraft further to the forces of gravity, meaning that it will lose height. To counter this, the pilot needs to increase thrust – forward speed. Speed was, therefore, critical – and yet the Bulldog, in this attitude, had insufficient more to give. The little Bulldog rolled right, successfully, the pilot now inverted, his head almost brushing the grass. As the aircraft continued to right itself, speed, as the machine defied gravity, slightly reduced – in this scenario enough to be catastrophic. The reserve of power was not enough to permit correction. An irretrievable slide began – the recklessly slight safety margin gone. Douglas's left wing-tip touched the ground, completely destroying the aircraft's forward trajectory and stability. The biplane was immediately completely uncontrollable, in a fraction of a second the damage done. The airscrew and engine tore loose, bounding across the field, the left wing collapsed, buckling below the fuselage. The right wing literally collapsed onto the open cockpit while the top wing was ripped straight off. Shocked onlookers rushed to the scene, the crash site shrouded in dust and smoke. Meanwhile Pilot Officer Bader, his mangled aircraft crumpled ignominiously around him, lay conscious but gravely injured.

Douglas's right knee was covered in blood, the rubber bar sticking through it, the stain on his white flying overalls increasing with every pump of his heart, his foot contorted in an abnormal angle. His left leg had been flung backwards, his seat collapsing on top of it. Quickly men gathered about the wreckage, a steward offering Douglas a shot of brandy – which he immediately declined on the basis that he never drank alcohol – ever. Soon afterwards he passed out. Those onlookers gathered about then began cutting Douglas out of the wreck, laying him on the grass and removing his shoes while the injured aerobatic star passed in and out of consciousness. An ambulance arrived and while Douglas was in it, en route to hospital, an Australian student pilot, Jack Cruttenden, held the femoral artery closed, preventing Douglas bleeding to death. In such circumstances of serious injury, the body goes into shock, nature protecting the mind from pain – Douglas felt none. In fact he was soon struggling to get up, even hitting Cruttenden a glancing blow on the chin when prevented from doing so! In short order Douglas was being examined by a doctor at the casualty department of the Royal Berkshire Hospital in Reading. The bones of both legs were nearly severed, the right at the knee, the left shin shattered. Douglas's pulse faded, requiring a heart stimulant. The doctor feared the worst, telling the ward sister, Sister Thornhill, to prepare a warm bed, so as to 'ease the shock … I don't think there's much we can do'.[25] The consultant agreed: operating in Douglas's current state was no option; perhaps if he survived the next few critical hours, but of that there was no realistic prospect. By a coincidental stroke of good fortune, however, Leonard Joyce, considered by many the best practising orthopaedic surgeon in Britain at that time, was operating at Reading that day. Sister Thornhill alerted the great man who was soon at Douglas's bedside. Acknowledging that the young pilot was fit and strong, Joyce agreed to wait and see if the patient recovered sufficiently from shock to survive an operation – that being so, he would do so personally. Information gleaned from the ward suggested to Kenley that Douglas was dying. Harry Day fired off telegrams accordingly to Douglas's mother, Jessie Hobbs, and his uncle, Cyril Burge, the latter only an hour away at Aldershot.

By 2 p.m. Douglas's pulse and breathing were – incredibly – strong enough for Joyce to operate. From X-rays it was clear that the right leg had to be amputated immediately. Over the shattered left leg Joyce deliberated. Thorough surgery, due to Douglas's critical condition, was impossible. Joyce amputated the right leg, rapidly sealing the wound in the hope of preventing infection. According to Brickhill, after the procedure Douglas was 'close to death'.[26] By 9 p.m., post-operative shock had nearly sapped all of Douglas's strength – Joyce knew he was dying and unlikely to survive the night. Cyril Burge was informed and at 2 a.m. summoned to Douglas's room; the time, it was believed, had come. As Burge arrived, however, he was asked to wait: Douglas's pulse had suddenly become marginally stronger. And so it went on, all night and the following day. Mrs Hobbs arrived but was so overcome with emotion that sedation was necessary. Although still unconscious, Douglas still lingered in this world the following morning – when Joyce told Burge that, providing he survived another twenty-four hours and infection was kept at bay, he might live, and the left leg might even be saved. Twenty-four hours later the patient was indeed still breathing – and opened his eyes for the first time since the operation.

Joyce was summoned immediately, breaking the news of amputation. Douglas heard but comprehension was slow to follow. Joyce then examined him, confirming that the right leg, or what was left of it, was free from infection – but not so the left, which showed irrevocable signs of septicaemia and gangrene. While Joyce and Sister Thornhill left to discuss the matter with Douglas's mother and uncle, the patient could contain his curiosity no longer, peeking beneath the bedclothes at his severed right leg. Again nature had its own way of protecting the human mind from the enormity of such a realisation in such critical circumstances; at this time news of amputation appears to have had little impact, it was simply too much to take in. Joyce was now in a cleft stick: it was unlikely that Douglas would survive another amputation – but given the infection death was in any case inevitable. The only option was to amputate and hope for the best. Before long Douglas was back in theatre, Joyce removing the infected left leg 6 inches below the knee. Then Douglas's heart stopped. Adrenalin was immediately administered. The heart restarted. The pulse weak and erratic, Douglas was nonetheless alive. Eighteen hours later he briefly regained consciousness, before slipping back into the netherworld. Six hours later he surfaced once more – the pain from his left leg so intense that not even morphine soothed it. And so it went on, hour upon hour, Douglas drifting in and out of a morphine-induced semi-consciousness, in dreadful pain.

Everyone expected Douglas to die. His mother and uncle remained at the hospital, awaiting the inevitable. Then, the following morning, as Douglas lay in a rare moment of lucid consciousness, a defining moment occurred. Outside his room young nurses hurried by, going about their business. A matron rebuked them, telling them to be quiet, because 'there's a boy dying in there'.[27] This jolted Douglas's fading spirit back into action. Dying? He bloody well wasn't! As Brickhill wrote, 'It was the challenge that stirred him.'[28] And that was the crux of it. Douglas Bader was possessed of the most incredibly strong spirit, an iron will beyond the comprehension of most. Already throughout his young life he had demonstrated the presence of this intense will – which now faced its toughest test. In that moment in which the matron's comment had stung his consciousness into action, Douglas was actually dying. Now he had a battle to fight – the kind of thing he thrived upon. He now focussed his mind, fighting the unseen power that tried to lure him back to the nether world – permanently. The pain, however, was such that more morphine was administered. Unconsciousness was inevitable – this time for two whole days – and so began a battle between Douglas and his nurses against death. When he surfaced again more morphine put him out for another two days and nights – throughout which he had but momentary periods of consciousness. Shock was the problem, but Douglas's supreme physical fitness eventually overcame. The coma subsided and he returned to the real world. He remained, however, in tremendous pain and was unaware that his left leg had also been amputated. Strangely, it was his missing legs, particularly the left, which hurt so much. No one had the heart to tell Douglas that he was now a double amputee – until visited by Squadron Leader Woollett, the CO of 23 Squadron. Complaining profusely of pain from his left leg, Douglas commented that it might be best if it was amputated. Casually, Woollett answered that it had, in fact, been cut off. Douglas heard and understood, but, due to the morphine, the impact remained lost on him. Back at 23 Squadron, the general feeling was that the loss of both legs for Douglas, the gifted aerobatic pilot and sportsman, was so tragic that death in the accident would have been kinder.

There was never any question that Douglas Bader was entirely responsible for his own misfortune. Later, he wrote in his logbook 'X Country Reading. Crashed slow-rolling near ground – Bad show.'[29] Indeed, as he flippantly remarked many years later to Laddie Lucas, 'I just made a balls of it, old boy. That's all there was to it.'[30] In 1996, Lady Bader observed that 'he knew that it was his own bloody silly fault, and that was that'.[31] Air Vice-Marshal Wilfred Oulton, however, summed up the feelings of the service as a whole: 'I was very sorry, but not surprised.'[32]

4

'GREENLANDS': GATEWAY TO THE WILDERNESS

The catastrophic crash at Woodley was not unnaturally the defining moment of Douglas Bader's life. While he lay in hospital during those early days, throughout which he had relentlessly fought for his life, no one could have guessed that the loss of both legs would actually become a positive, enabling the disabled Douglas Bader to inspire and give hope to fellow amputees the world over. All of that, though, was a long way off as Douglas battled through those first days. The fight against death itself, however, may have been over, but as a double amputee the remainder of his life would in so many ways be an on-going uphill struggle. A man of lesser spirit and tenacity would have given up the ghost and slid into oblivion after Joyce's operations – but not Pilot Officer Bader. Already Douglas's fight against adversity and his incredible spirit was inspiring – the first person to be so moved was his nurse, Dorothy Brace. The more he fought, the greater inspiration she drew from this physically shattered but clearly exceptional young man.[1] Nurse Brace would be the first of countless people, all over the world, to be captivated and impressed by the now legless Douglas Bader.

On Christmas Eve 1931, Douglas was moved into 'Greenlands', the private nursing home in the grounds of Reading Hospital. Joyce, however, remained concerned that his young patient could still die. By New Year Douglas remained alive, his stitches removed. Rapidly his health improved and the morphine was gradually reduced. Remarkably, he was unconcerned regarding the loss of his legs. It had been a gradual process, through a morphine-induced haze, grasping the reality of what had happened. By now he had simply accepted it. Bedridden and nursed, though, his every need was met. Douglas had yet to experience the physical reality of having no legs. Not once did Douglas complain, enduring all with an optimistic good humour – winning him the admiration and respect of all involved. On 15 January 1932, Douglas rose from bed for the first time since the crash. He manoeuvred into Brace's tactically placed wheelchair, pushing himself to the nearby window. There he sat for two hours before becoming tired and returning to bed; of his thoughts there is no record. A week later the dressings were removed from his stumps, after which he wheeled himself happily around the grounds. A fortnight later Joyce gave him a 'pylon' – a wooden leg – to try on the left stump, permitting Douglas to start using crutches, but hid from him the fact that another operation would soon be required to cut the remaining bone to fit a proper artificial leg. His first experience of this new mode of transport was excruciating: the technician forgot to put a sock over the stump before fitting the pylon. Measurements were taken and a plaster cast of his stump. A new, custom-made pylon was created, into which the stump fitted neatly. It was quite a contraption, however, featuring a hinge replicating the knee and secured in place by a tight leather corset. Unfortunately the knee was weak – it took three days of maximum effort before Douglas could manage even three solo steps. It was a start. The next milestone came when he lurched from his room and took a bath – unaided.

Brickhill wrote that 'soon he was independent of outside help and spent hours stomping around the garden', in the 'limited world' of which 'the loss of his legs still did not seem all that serious'.[2] What was serious was that another operation was required. In the urgent and initial life-saving operations performed by Joyce, the leg bones had been simply sawn through. They now needed shaping to fit comfortably into the armatures of artificial legs – which Douglas, of course, was most anxious to have fitted without delay. This surgery was equally crucial if Douglas was to regain independent mobility. Joyce removed 2 inches of bone from what was left of the right leg, bevelled the sharp edges and stretched muscle to create a pad beneath the bone. The left fibula lost an inch, another muscular pad created. Afterwards the pain was intense, not even morphine completely providing respite. Two days later Douglas was deteriorating. One week later the patient had beaten the odds again and emerged from delirium – a period Turner summarised simply as one of 'pain and inconvenience'.[3] Joyce then treated haematoma, during which Douglas gripped the iron bedstead so tightly that he twisted the frame. Ten days later the fluid had finished draining, the healing process well underway. Again as Brickhill wrote, 'the physical battle was over. Then the mental battle started.'[4] This was not strictly the case. Certainly Douglas had fully accepted the loss of his legs and the initial operations were now complete. This was a juncture when the wider implications of immobility started sinking in. Moreover, another hard physical slog now lay ahead as Douglas learned to walk on artificial legs. Once more, his determination to do so proved inspirational.

It has been suggested that having accepted his situation, Douglas regarded the challenge ahead as exciting. Typically, he was massively enthusiastic about achieving his latest goal – throwing every ounce of effort at it. He had read promotional literature provided by manufacturers of artificial limbs, and consequently decided that a reasonably normal life awaited him once he had mastered such things. Rugby, of course, was out of the question, but cricket, batting with a 'runner', seemed likely, as did general walking around, socialising, driving and – flying. That was the ultimate objective: getting back into the cockpit. Flying required mainly eyes and hands, the operation of rudder pedals needing only small foot movements which Douglas felt were not beyond him. Fortunately the brakes on British aircraft were hand-operated. Piece of cake! They must surely let him fly again. There was no doubt in Douglas's mind about it. There appeared no practical reason why this should not be so. The burning ambition to fly again motivated and sustained him – but there were an increasing number of dark moments. His dreams were those of an active and able-bodied young man, depression overwhelming his consciousness upon waking. When a pilot was killed on 23 Squadron, Douglas yelled at his nurse, Brace, that the dead man was luckier than he. Although he exuded a spirit of optimism and confidence generally, it was his nurse, Brace, to whom Douglas confided his worst fears: rejection by the service he loved so much, without even a pension, given that the accident was his own fault. The consequences of his error of judgement at Woodley, both in having 'made a balls' of the slow roll and even considering executing it in the first place, could not, he knew, be undone. Brickhill, however, gives us a significant clue regarding Douglas's feelings regarding the events of that day, claiming that Douglas cautioned Brace never to do 'anything in temper'.[5] That, for sure, had been the hardest lesson of all for Douglas himself to learn. Indeed, Turner commented that 'strangely enough, Douglas derived strength and mental balance from the very knowledge that it had been his own fault'.[6]

Inevitably a Court of Inquiry was held regarding the accident. According to Brickhill, the findings 'slid adroitly round the question of blame, considering that whatever had happened, Bader had suffered more than enough'.[7] Lucas and Burns, however, fail to comment. Mackenzie, though, consulted the official file at The National Archives (TNA) and noted that the court rightly rejected a suggestion that Douglas was drunk at Woodley because he never drank alcohol.[8] Mackenzie confirmed that Flying Officer G. W. Phillips, the senior officer present, was 'blamed by higher authority for not holding him back: a judgement which assumed, of course, that this could be done'.[9] It was also against regulations for service aircraft to land at civilian aerodromes, and yet the evidence available clearly confirms that the flight from Kenley to Woodley was a pre-arranged 'jolly' to enjoy lunch with Phillips's brother at the flying club there. To circumnavigate this problem, Phillips claimed that the three-ship formation of Bulldogs had landed at Woodley because a map had fallen onto the floor of his cockpit, causing him concern that this could affect the safe operation of flying controls. It is clear that the court treated Phillips's evidence with contempt: he was court-martialled.[10] No action was taken against Douglas, however. This was undoubtedly a relief, and his mood generally began to improve.

Encouraged, Douglas was soon getting about the grounds in his wheelchair once more, and on the single pylon. A trip to the cinema in Reading, though, saw Douglas the object of ignorant curiosity as people unabashedly stared at the man without legs. He would have to get used to it. A month later, in mid-April, the

RAF decided that Douglas was well enough to leave 'Greenlands' and be admitted to the service's own hospital at Uxbridge. To Douglas this was welcome news. The RAF was home, and Uxbridge was a part of it – it was literally another step forward on his pylon to resuming his formerly happy and fulfilled life in the service. The nursing staff, though, had become quite attached to Douglas, whose determination and courage had affected them all. After sad and sincere farewells, Douglas was driven off in a service car to embark upon another stage of his uncertain journey into the future.

5

'DAMN THAT! I'LL NEVER, *NEVER* WALK WITH A STICK!'

At Uxbridge Douglas was reunited with like-minded and similar 'types', although the resumption of an inflexible service time-table was initially irksome. In May 1932, Douglas's mother spent two weeks nearby, visiting him daily and taking her double-amputee son out for country drives. On one such jaunt across Windsor Great Park, Douglas persuaded her to let him drive. Although the car's gear-selector lever was on the steering wheel, Mrs Hobbs operated the clutch pedal and off they went. Provision of an umbrella, with which to personally depress the clutch pedal, saw Douglas in complete control. The driver was delighted. Inevitably, this newly discovered ability led to high jinks.

Although forbidden to have automobiles, another patient, Flying Officer Peel, kept a Humber near to the hospital. Peel was confident that he could operate the clutch in spite of his left leg being encased in plaster, suggesting to Flying Officer Victor Streatfeild and Douglas that they should slope off for a drive after doctors' rounds. Once more Douglas was behind the wheel in Windsor Great Park. The car's throttle lever was on the steering wheel, leaving his pylon to operate the clutch. In Slough, though, the traffic was heavy, requiring great concentration from Douglas and generating a sweating brow. Brickhill wrote how 'he ploughed remorselessly on, butting, weaving and honking; carving a kind of bow-wave of squealing brakes on other cars and pedestrians jumping like startled springboks out of the way'.[1] Some interpret behaviour of this kind as amusing and praiseworthy. It is not. It is selfish and irresponsible. While satisfying his own lust for excitement and attempting to regain his lost adventure, the fact is that Douglas Bader drove Peel's car with total disregard for the potentially dangerous and negative consequences for other road users. This reckless attitude had already lost him two legs and would be evident on various occasions in the future.

Late that afternoon, the three invalids stopped for tea at a roadside café near Bagshot called The Pantiles. They were served by a pretty waitress, there being an immediate mutual attraction between Douglas and the girl – in spite of his lack of legs. The following day Douglas ensured that a drive with his mother stopped at the same place for tea, where he equally contrived to be served by the same girl. Her name was Thelma Edwards, the daughter of a senior RFC officer and whose cousins were both RAF pilots. That, of course, Douglas did not know – and nor could he have realised that he had, in fact, met his soul mate and the woman who would, in due course, become his first wife. Douglas was now even more impatient to gain access to and become mobile on artificial limbs.

Just five months after his terrible accident, Douglas was told to attend the Ministry of Pension's hospital at Roehampton to be measured for his artificial legs. There was a link with aviation here, too. A British aviator, André Marcel Dousetter, had crashed at the London Aviation Meeting held at Hendon on 23 March 1913. The control column had slipped from the pilot's hand, plunging his Gnome-Blériot into the ground. One of Desoutter's legs was so badly broken that amputation above the knee was necessary. The unfortunate pilot's brother, Charles, used his extensive knowledge of aircraft manufacture to design and build a jointed leg of Duralumin alloy – which was half the weight of the standard wooden pylon. Desoutter, in fact, resumed flying with his new limb, and Desoutter Brothers Limited began commercially producing artificial legs at their premises in London's famous Baker Street. After the First World War, demand for these alloy limbs increased, dictating a move to a bigger factory in Hendon. Workshops were also provided at Roehampton, for on-site measurement and fitting of such limbs to patients. After moulds were taken of his stumps, Douglas's enthusiasm was tempered by the news that it would take at least two weeks to make his new 'pins'.

While awaiting news from Desoutter, Brickhill described how during the next fortnight Douglas, 'unlicensed and uninsured, drove the Humber a lot in defiance of Air Force and Civil regulations'.[2] More accurately, Douglas repeatedly broke the law and disregarded the safety of others. This was not admirable or clever. Nonetheless, it was clear that Douglas could still drive, and Peel's Humber provided the means and excuse to visit The Pantiles and chat up Thelma Edwards. He had other girlfriends, in fact; one that had bordered upon being serious before his accident, another who wrote frequently from South America. Others took him driving. But Thelma was different. Douglas knew that his future was uncertain, on which grounds he resisted the urge to rush headlong into asking her out on a date. His new legs, he thought, were the key to this and so Douglas anxiously and impatiently awaited Desoutter's call. He also had a garage at Kenley change over the brake and clutch pedals. His vision was to arrive at The Pantiles in the MG, and walk over to Thelma, legs and all. Eventually the long-awaited call came, but achieving his vision would be an agonising journey indeed for Douglas.

At last Desoutter called. Douglas went to Roehampton and saw his new, shiny and factory-fresh artificial legs for the first time. The only problem was that it had been necessary to reduce their length by an inch, to improve balance; Douglas was unimpressed. Two assistants, Walker and Tulitt, helped the amputee strap on the limbs, which entailed doing up a leather corset-like harness. The instep was hinged and fitted with rubber pads, with which the toe was also jointed. It was necessary, however, to lift the leg higher than normal when walking to lift the toes clear of the ground. Douglas first tried the left leg with a crutch, the inflexible foot catching him out. After a few more steps he was sufficiently confident to try the articulated right leg. The various straps were tightly done, making Douglas feel that he was in a truss. The moment came for him to walk unaided. His right stump was painful, the whole experience alien. Uncharacteristically Douglas declared that the prospect of walking was impossible. Having believed for months that he would simply strap on artificial legs and walk out to a near-normal life, he was crushed. But then, as in the hospital when he overheard the nurse's remark that he was dying, a comment by Desoutter stung him into action. Bluntly, Desoutter told him to face up to the fact that he would never walk without a stick. To Douglas this was unthinkable; the gauntlet had been thrown down. Accepting the challenge, Douglas passionately replied, 'Damn that! I'll never, *never*, walk with a stick!'[3] Subsequent events proved that he meant it.

So began another trying journey, as Douglas learned new techniques to walk on his new legs. Without the spring provided by toes and muscle, he found it best to kick forward, to generate momentum. It was easier to move the left leg, because he still had use of his knee, but the right was problematic. Every time Douglas needed to move his right leg, Walker and Tulitt had to pull him forward, until he was able to engage the left leg. And so he kicked and jerked his way down the room, thinking carefully about each step and indicating when he needed pulling. The fact was, Douglas needed to forget everything he remembered about walking naturally. Reducing the length of the right leg by half an inch helped transfer weight easier. Determined to walk unaided that very first day, Douglas pushed Walker and Tulitt away and staggered several steps before collapsing onto the parallel bars. Desoutter was both delighted and impressed. He had never before seen even a single amputee make so much progress on day one – and started to believe that Douglas really would walk without a stick. Some years later, Douglas himself commented regarding this agonising process,

The biggest disappointment was the initial difficulty of trying to operate the artificial legs when I first got them. Having always been of an athletic nature and knowing nothing about artificial legs, I thought during my convalescence that once I got them I should wander around after a day or two quite normally. When I went for my first fitting of these legs, actually put them on and tried to stand up in them, I never thought that I would be able to move. With a strong man either side of me, having been levered to my feet, I stood there as far as I was concerned nailed to the ground – with no conscious balance if I let go of my two supporters. After a certain amount of time, trouble and a great deal of sweat I began to get some inkling of how to operate the artificial knee of the right leg. After battling away for several days, during the course of which I spent a good deal of time on the ground, my mind and reflexes gradually acquired the method of movement needed. Then, as always, it came with a rush and did not seem so difficult.[4]

Over the next few weeks, Douglas made great progress, learning to walk, turn – which was initially very difficult – negotiate stairs and rise from a chair. Eventually the time came for him to take his new legs away – it was an incredible moment. For the first time Douglas put his clothes on over the legs and harness – and stood in front of a mirror admiring his apparently normal reflection. Walking out of Desoutter's hut and driving his MG back to Uxbridge was an incomparable achievement.

Mobile though he now was, clearly life could never be the same again for Douglas. Later, he wrote of how mobility difficulties impact upon the most basic domestic tasks, which the able-bodied take totally for granted:

My morning routine is to get up, get on to the floor and go along by the hands and backside method to the bathroom where there is a chair or stool beside the bath. With one hand on the edge of the bath and one on the stool you seat yourself on the latter. With one hand on the stool and one on the edge of the bath, you raise yourself and sit on the edge of the bath and then with a hand on each side of the bath you lower yourself into the bathtub. Having slipped off the edge once and hurt yourself, you remember to put a wet face flannel on the nearest side of the bathtub on which you are going to sit before getting into the bath. This stops you slipping. You only need to forget it once and you will remember it for the rest of your life. The same thing applies to getting out. You seat yourself on the face flannel on the edge of the bath and then on the stool. If you have left your legs in the bathroom the night before, they are there for you to put on and walk away from the bathroom in the morning.

It is in overcoming the ordinary day-to-day requirements, like that above, that a disabled person achieves normality. If you cannot wash yourself and have a bath and do all the essential daily requirements of life without assistance, you are inevitably restricted – and the aim of every disabled person is to be completely independent. If you have achieved that, you have achieved normality. You can travel all over the world, visit out of the way places and lead a similar life to anyone else without ever being a nuisance to other people or yourself. To my way of thinking, a disabled person who achieves independence is no longer disabled.[5]

Douglas's determination to master his new legs – and as quickly as possible – was typical of him. Being a gifted ball player, the ability to think quickly and alter balance also helped, together with his physical strength and fitness. Also, while a gymnast at Temple Grove he had learned early in life to have no fear of falling. Equally, if not more important than all of the foregoing, was his personal attitude to life and adversity. Douglas was an individualist and knew that only he, through sheer effort and determination – could overcome this new challenge. Self-pity, complaint and inaction were not options to him. In fact, he was simply unable to understand people with such mentalities. As Lucas wrote, 'It was this acceptance of this essential quality of self-help which subsequently developed in him an intolerance of the moaners and whimperers, those who sought sympathy or who were reluctant to act for themselves. Difficulty and hardship swelled an already generous heart; but his open generosity was not extended to embrace groaners.'[6] Without such a positive, determined, and downright stubborn psyche, Douglas would never have overcome immobility and achieved independence – but he did, in record time and with only one operable knee. This was the beginning of what really made Douglas Robert Steuart Bader such a unique inspiration to people the world over.

Back at Uxbridge, Douglas received a rousing welcome as he lurched into the mess. He did not, however, intend to visit The Pantiles until such time as he felt master of his new legs. His stumps, though, were soft and soon became painful, so Douglas knew that it would take time for the skin and muscle to toughen up – until that time his periods of mobility would be comparatively short. Nevertheless he did what he could, tackling long flights of hospital stairs and other manoeuvres. He fell frequently, exhausted. As Brickhill observed, 'Hour after hour he doggedly kept at it when other men would have given up to rest or despair.'[7] The stumps were a continual source of pain and frustration, requiring further adjustment by Desoutter to Douglas's legs – the mastery of which he became obsessed by. Eventually he sensed that at last it was getting easier, that certain actions were becoming automatic, natural – like riding a bicycle. Douglas's modified MG was brought over by a mechanic, the doctors having decided that driving would be good therapy, and he passed a disabled driver's test at the local police station. Douglas was now ready, at last, to visit The Pantiles and chance his luck with Thelma Edwards. The sortie was successful – Thelma remarking only upon the fact that Douglas had not been there for some time but, to his satisfaction, made no mention whatsoever of the fact that he now had legs. As these visits continued, their friendship grew, but still no move was made on either side. Douglas also visited 23 Squadron at Kenley and swam in the pool at Harry Day's Surrey home. Life could certainly have been worse, but Douglas still needed to know whether he had a future in the RAF.

Towards the end of summer 1932, Douglas was invited to spend a weekend with Sir Philip Sassoon, the Under-Secretary of State for Air. Sassoon had been the Member of Parliament for Hythe for some twenty-seven years and entertained his influential circle of friends at one of his homes, either at 45 Park Lane, London, Trent Park or at Port Lympne. It was to the latter that Douglas was invited. Unbeknown to him Sassoon, who had been present in the Royal Box at Hendon when Day and Douglas had won the aerobatic pairs competition, was an ally and admirer – who had asked to be kept personally updated regarding the young amputee's progress. Sassoon was also Honorary Air Commodore of the Auxiliary Air Force's 601 'County of London' Squadron, which, coincidentally, was undertaking its annual camp at nearby Lympne airfield. Another young officer from 23 Squadron, Peter Ross, was also invited. Their host arranged that on the Sunday morning Bader and Ross could fly in 601's Avro 504. When this treat was announced, Douglas was absolutely delighted and could hardly believe it. Climbing into the cockpit was easier than Douglas anticipated. Needless to say, from his back-seat position it was Douglas, not Ross, who flew the aeroplane – up to Kenley where he made a perfect three-point landing. After lunch, Douglas flew back to Lympne, making another perfect landing.

Of flying without legs, Douglas later wrote,

Flying an aeroplane presents no difficulty unless it is equipped with foot brakes. Before the war all British aeroplanes were equipped with a rudder control which was either a bar pivoted in the middle (so that pressure by either foot swung the bar) or there were two complete foot pedals which moved up and down. You pushed with your right foot for right rudder and vice-versa. Now, if you place your foot on a bar and push you can do that from your thigh and your shin without having to depress your foot in relation to your shin. The brakes of aeroplanes in those days were operated from the control column or joystick by means of a lever, rather like that on the handle of a motorcycle. When you depressed the lever and the rudder bar was central, both brakes went on. You obtained differential braking by moving the rudder bar on whichever side you wanted the brake, i.e. right rudder, right brake.[8]

Another legless fighter pilot, Colin 'Hoppy' Hodgkinson, confirmed that 'flying without real legs caused no real problems, because their involvement was largely restricted to aileron control'.[9] After his trip to Kenley and return to Lympne, Douglas was elated and felt sure that the RAF would allow him to fly again. Indeed, when Sassoon asked to be informed when Douglas had his medical board, the prospect seemed assured.

While flying proved easy, cricket did not. With alacrity Douglas had accepted an invitation from Kendall to play for the St Edward's Old Boys' XI, which he did in high spirits after his weekend at Lympne. It was a frustrating experience, more realisation setting in that things had changed for good. A batsman has to move either forward or back quickly, responding to the ball's predicted pitch, and this Douglas found impossible to do. Instead it was another matter of developing a new technique – instead of stepping to the ball he had to await its arrival, finding it easier to pull, rather than cleanly drive. He scored a respectable eighteen before being caught by the wicketkeeper. Fielding, though, was a disaster. Lacking the speed necessary for the outfield and agility in the slips, he also fell over whenever he threw a cricket ball. Douglas knew that he would never play the sport seriously again, which, being unable to even contemplate football or rugby now, was a blow. During several weeks' sick leave with his mother in Sprotborough, Douglas was able to reflect and contemplate his future. One thing remained constant in his uncertain world: he *had* to fly!

Soon afterwards, Douglas was ordered to attend the Central Medical Establishment (CME) at Kingsway for assessment. He passed with an A2H rating, which, without legs, could not have been higher. Interestingly, it was noted that his blood pressure was lower, due the lack of legs, because the heart had less distance to pump blood around – meaning that without extremities he would be less inclined to black out in dives and steep turns. An A2H rating, however, meant that Douglas couldn't fly solo or overseas. He could live with both prospects for now, confident in his ability to overturn such decisions once given an opportunity to prove himself. Next stop was the Central Flying School (CFS) – for a formal flying assessment – at Wittering. This great news, however, was tempered by the fact that Wittering, in Cambridgeshire, was a long way from The Pantiles. Thelma had, in fact, already mentioned to Douglas that she was leaving her waitressing job and going to live with her parents in London. This prospect made him realise how attached he had become to the girl – whose name he still did not know! Motoring over to The Pantiles for one last time, Douglas finally asked the girl out – learning that her name was Thelma Edwards. Introducing himself, Douglas was surprised to discover that she already knew much about him – on account of the fact that her father was a retired Wing Commander and three of her cousins, the Donaldson brothers, Jack, 'Teddy' and Arthur, were all RAF officers. Contact details in the bag, Douglas went off happily to Wittering.

At first, Douglas was thrilled to be there. After a few dual flights in an Avro 504, the instructor, Flight Lieutenant Leach, authorised Douglas to go solo over lunch – but the offer was retracted when the station doctor mentioned too loudly to Douglas over lunch that he must be frustrated at not being allowed to solo. Douglas was crestfallen, salt being rubbed into the wound given that the one-legged Freddie West, who had won a Victoria Cross (VC) in the First World War, was soloing at Wittering daily. A consolatory weekend's leave at least allowed him to take Thelma out at last. Douglas drove over to London, climbed the ninety-six stairs to the apartment she shared with her mother and stepfather, Lieutenant Colonel Addison, and so the courtship formally began. They enjoyed each other's company at the Monseigneur Club at the corner of Lower Regent Street and Piccadilly, the Café de Paris, and the Ace of Spades on the Kingston bypass.[10] In spite of unwittingly standing on his girlfriend's foot, Douglas even danced passably – even if onlookers did wrongly assume him to be drunk when he stumbled and fell while negotiating two steps returning to their table. After a drive in the country the following day, when Thelma tactfully put that she admired his mobility,

Douglas knew that she was the one. A kiss or two sealed the relationship – Douglas Bader was now part of a couple. What endeared Thelma to him more than anything was that when they first met, he had been on crutches with a single pylon. Naturally, however, the Addisons were concerned, Thelma's mother inquiring of her daughter whether she had considered that she could simply become a nurse to a man without legs – '*Not* with *Douglas*!' came the spirited and accurate response.[11]

Douglas's flying at Wittering was immaculate. The Chief Flying Instructor (CFI), in fact, soon decided that Pilot Officer Bader being there and 'mucking about not being able to go solo' was a pointless exercise.[12] Douglas agreed. The CFI reported to the medical board that Douglas could clearly still fly – resulting in a rapid return call ordering the legless pilot to attend the CME again. There Douglas was surprised not to have to appear before a board of doctors, instead being ushered into the presence of a Wing Commander. Assuming it to be a mere formality, Douglas entered the room confidently. The words uttered by the officer before him were more crushing than the accident at Woodley: Pilot Officer Bader could not be passed for flying duties because King's Regulations failed to provide for such a circumstance. Unsurprisingly Douglas was stunned. When his initial astonishment and anger subsided, he began to suspect that the decision had already been made before even he went to Wittering. Indeed, later he discovered that during his time there an article had appeared in a Sunday newspaper questioning the wisdom of providing a legless man with a flying course. This, the author considered, was a waste of the taxpayers' money and unfair on the mothers of sons who had to fly with the individual concerned. Whether this publicity influenced the RAF's decision is unknown, but Mackenzie suggested that it may have, and that this, coupled with Douglas's 'record of hazardous flying' made his reinstatement as a service pilot 'an unacceptable risk'.[13] Whatever the truth, it was a furious Douglas Bader who drove over to 12 Avonmore Mansions, Kennington, to see Thelma Edwards.

In November 1932, Douglas was posted to RAF Duxford in Cambridgeshire. There 19 Squadron flew Bulldogs and the Cambridge University Air Squadron (UAS) received instruction. Pilot Officer Bader was given command of the station's Motor Transport (MT) Section. Air Force pilots are commissioned into the General Duties branch of the RAF; Douglas refused reclassification as an Administrative or Equipment officer. Signing chits, organising lorries and drinking tea all day was unendurable for Douglas. Fortunately, however, a Cranwell contemporary of Douglas's, Flying Officer Joe (later Air Vice-Marshal) Cox, was the Cambridge UAS instructor and invited Douglas to fly with him as a 'passenger' in an Armstrong Whitworth Atlas. On one occasion, the Atlas landed with Cox's hands held above his head, confirming to those pilots assembled on the ground that the legless Douglas Bader was doing the flying. A perfect landing ensued – watched by the Station Commander who immediately pounced on the intrepid airmen. Although suitably advised on the tarmac, nothing further was heard of the matter. Unfortunately, Douglas then clashed with the Station Commander over a road traffic accident in which four of his lorries collided. Pilot Officer Bader's report exonerated the drivers and criticised the service for fitting solid rubber tyres, contributing to skidding. The Wing Commander told Douglas in no uncertain terms that it was not for him to advise the RAF on their lorries or anything else; Douglas knew full well what advice he would really like to give the Wing Commander regarding the

MT Section! Solace was not even found when a friend, Adrian Stoop, took Douglas and Thelma to watch the Harlequins: soon after the game began Douglas became uncharacteristically quiet, later announcing to Thelma that he would never watch another rugger match again. As Lucas wrote, 'These were sombre days.'[14] The greatest blow, however, had yet to come.

In April 1933, Pilot Officer Bader was summoned to see Duxford's Acting Station Commander, Squadron Leader Sanderson, the CO of 19 Squadron. Faced with an unenviable task, Sanderson gave Douglas sight of a letter from the Air Ministry. It pulled no punches. The Ministry 'regretted' that as a result of Pilot Officer Bader's last medical board it was no longer possible to employ him in the General Duties Branch. Douglas was to be retired on the grounds of 'ill health'. The only good news was that he would get a service and disability pension. What had been inevitable stunned Douglas. That he could no longer remain a pilot in the RAF was now a stark reality. Although Burns wrote that Douglas 'resigned from the RAF', this was not, in fact, the case.[15] Mackenzie questioned, 'Why was it necessary to give him the push?', and pointed out that 'while most General Duties officers were active pilots, this was not universally the case'.[16] Moreover, there was a precedent for a legless man being a service pilot: Captain Drummond had flown in the RFC with two artificial legs. Given that Douglas had the personal support of the Under-Secretary of State for Air, this end result can only be considered rather surprising. One explanation has already been offered, that Douglas's reckless flying now made him an unacceptable risk, meaning that in spite of losing his legs the powers that be did not consider him to have learned his lesson – this being borne out by further clashes with authority. There were certainly powerful forces at work here.

Douglas's immediate concern was that the RAF and flying was the only life he knew, the only skills he had to sell being connected with both the service and that activity. Unemployment could, therefore, be his future. In turmoil, Douglas drove over and discussed the situation with Thelma. He rejected her suggestion of remaining in a ground job, emphasising that he was not much of a catch, with no legs, no career or money. Stoically Thelma's response was that they would somehow manage. This, then, constituted a proposal and acceptance of marriage. On 30 April 1933, Douglas was formally retired from the RAF – but at least he was not alone.

With an annual pension amounting to £200, Douglas needed a job, and began scouring newspaper columns. He took a room at 86 Boundary Road, St John's Wood, close to Avonmore Mansions, and began to realise what a sheltered and literally accommodating life being a serving Air Force officer had been. It was a privilege he had taken for granted. Situations-vacant columns provided no inspiration, the Officers' Employment Bureau no leads. Then the latter suggested that he should speak with the personnel managers at Unilever and the Asiatic Petroleum Company. The former company offered him a job, which was good, but as this required going out to West Africa was an impossibility because of his stumps, which would suffer in such a climate. A similar response was received at the latter, Douglas's inability to work overseas clearly being a major hindrance to promotion. Then a stroke of luck at last: A. P. Grey, the overseas personnel manager, suggested to Douglas that the Petroleum Company's new, home-based aviation section might be of interest to him.

After an interview with the departmental head, Walter Hill, Douglas landed a job with a £200 per annum salary. Over the next few weeks, working at the company's offices at Great St Helen's, off Bishopsgate, Douglas learned much about prices and the logistics of supplying fuel to Australia. The tedium involved was incomparable, however, to the excitement of life as an RAF aerobatic pilot. Nonetheless, on 5 October 1933, Douglas and Thelma secretly married at Hampstead Register Office. Two days later their engagement notice appeared in *The Times*. It would not be until four years later that the Baders enjoyed a church wedding, behaviour that Lucas described as 'typical Bader' while noting the 'the interim period was a period of rather more shade than light'.[17]

6

THE WILDERNESS

According to Lucas, Douglas disliked administrative detail and 'quickly became adept at off-loading the bumph'.[1] Like a squadron, however, an office is a team. This behaviour was not, therefore, admirable and again reflected the selfish side of Douglas's personality. Brickhill wrote of how once more Douglas found his thrills behind the wheel of the MG, negotiating the Great West Road 'at his usual 70 mph'.[2] This continued recklessness and disregard for the safety of other road users unsurprisingly nearly ended in disaster. On one occasion Douglas overtook a lorry but the efficiency of his brakes was adversely affected by water retention in the brake drums after hose-washing, contributing to a collision with an oncoming Humber. The resulting repair bill was £10 for the Humber and £68 for the MG – which Douglas was permitted to repay at £1 a week. Fortunately, Douglas's work at the Petroleum Company was considered acceptable, in spite of his aversion to paperwork and efforts to avoid it, leading to an annual raise of £50. Douglas's brother, Derick, was then killed in an accident while working in South Africa. Fate, it seemed, was unkind to the Baders. For nothing but amusement, Thelma persuaded Douglas to visit a fortune teller, who told him that one day he would be famous and decorated by the king, although difficult times were ahead and he would suffer with his feet and legs. Douglas was certainly intrigued by this, because the woman had not noticed his gait upon arrival and a previous client was one David Beatty, the hero of Jutland, whom she predicted would one day become an admiral. That was all very well, but the present remained a largely unhappy place.

Then Douglas discovered golf. The Baders were invited to walk the course while two friends played. Instead, Douglas took a club and ball with which to mess about on the fairway. His first attempt to drive the ball saw him overbalance and end up on his backside. As determined as ever, after twelve attempts he hit the ball. Forty falls later he had hit it three times – with an immense feeling of satisfaction. Here, perhaps, was a ball game in which he could, with practice, compete with the able-bodied. Of golf he later wrote,

Golf is undoubtedly the game that a physically handicapped person can play on equal terms with others. The great thing about golf is that you can play it anywhere. Whether you have one arm or no legs, or whatever, the handicapping system is such that you can always have a good game and a lot of fun. I would say that it is probably the game that is played most by disabled people in preference to any other. I have met some splendid one-armed players and ones with legs missing. When I first started this game I used to swing the club very fast and fell over every time, but after a bit discovered that swinging slowly and gripping the club lightly enabled me to keep my arms clear of my body and therefore avoid upsetting my balance. I still over-balance occasionally but so does everybody else. Only on rare occasions does one get a stance, for instance, in the left-hand corner of a bunker, which is more difficult for a disabled man than the ordinary chap, the reason being that you cannot take weight on your above-knee leg when it is bent.[3]

In short order, Douglas's handicap had been reduced to a very respectable nine. The game became, in many ways, his salvation and an outlet for that determined and irrepressible spirit. Indeed, by the Baders' first wedding anniversary Douglas was playing a straight eighteen holes. Soon afterwards he played twenty-seven, then eighteen twice in one day. The significance of these achievements must not be overlooked.

While Douglas's future during the mid-1930s was uncertain, so too was that of the wider world. Internally, in the First World War's wake, Britain experienced privations caused by the Great Depression which caused widespread unemployment and emphasized the disparity in the distribution of wealth. Mowat accurately, given that in 1932 there were 2,750,000 unemployed in Britain,[4] described the 1930s as 'gloomy ... a devil's decade'.[5] Society, Branson and Heinemann argued, remained 'stratified into layers divided by rigid class barriers'.[6] Depending on which side of the socio-economic divide the decade was experienced from, Calder argued that it was 'the best of times, the worst of times'.[7] Nonetheless, twentieth-century consumerism was born between the wars, in addition to the growth of mass entertainment – the cinema emerging the most popular.[8] Many of the films people in Britain watched were made in America, projecting an idealised impression of the American nation and popular culture. Far away from Hollywood, however, a new danger stirred in Germany. The Treaty of Versailles in 1919 had severely restricted the size of Germany's armed forces and weapons, incensing that defeated nation. The United States President, Woodrow Wilson, believed in the heady notion of 'self-determination' for all nations, leading to the creation of various new states in Central Europe. Various of these, however, included large ethnic German minority populations. As nationalism emerged in

Germany after the First World War, all of these problems, coupled with the effects of the Great Depression, failure of democracy and fear of communism, led to the growth of fascism and the National Democratic Socialist Workers Party – the Nazis. On 30 January 1933, Adolf Hitler, leader of the Nazis, became Chancellor of Germany. A month later, Hitler was in complete control of the country, destroying Germany's federal system, and proclaiming himself *Führer* of the new Third Reich. Hitler rapidly set about re-armament, it soon becoming clear that his ultimate goal was aggressive territorial expansion. For the second time in the twentieth century, the world was heading for war, more terrible than the first. This, though, would be Douglas Bader's salvation.

Although reduced to a shadow of its former self in the immediate wake of the First World War, it was always intended that Trenchard's RAF could be easily expanded if necessary. The first half of the 1930s saw Britain and certain other nations 'hell bent', according to Dean, 'for collective security and prepared to accept incalculable risks in that cause'.[9] In 1932, the year before Hitler came to power, Britain abandoned what was a minuscule re-armament programme. In 1934, Britain revisited re-armament but, given the restricted spending involved, Dean charged that 'even now Britain was not taking its problems seriously'.[10] It was not just a reluctance to re-arm, however, that had contributed to this sorry state of affairs: the infamous Wall Street Crash had plunged the world into financial crisis, giving Britain's government serious social and domestic issues to resolve. Against this calamitous backdrop, Nazi Germany re-armed. British military spending between the years 1931 and 1935, however, Churchill later considered to be those 'of the locust'.[11] In 1934, though, the British Prime Minister, Stanley Baldwin, told the House of Commons that Britain would 'in no conditions ... accept any position of inferiority with regard to what Air Force may be raised in Germany in the future'.[12] Nonetheless, the resulting re-armament plan was woefully inadequate and considered a façade. By 1935, British intelligence considered that Germany would be ready for war by 1939, and that consequently the threat posed by Germany could no longer be ignored. On 25 February 1936, Expansion Scheme 'F' was approved by the treasury: 124 squadrons (1,736 aircraft of all types) by April 1937. Germany's target was 2,000 front-line aircraft. Scheme 'F' also led directly to the creation of the RAF Volunteer Reserve (RAFVR), which planned to recruit and train 8,100 aircrew by the end of 1938. From the regular service, 4,000 more pilots and 1,264 observers were required during the years 1936–39. All of these events and figures would ultimately impact on Douglas Bader's uncertain future.

In spite of the difficult prevalent financial conditions, the interwar period was an exciting time for aviation. For example, there were many inspirational record-breaking flights of endurance. In April 1919, Major Keith Park and Captain Stewart completed a non-stop circuit of the British Isles in a Handley-Page 0/400. The route, measuring 1,880 miles, was flown at an average speed of 66 mph in 28.33 hours. In 1927, the American Charles Lindbergh flew solo across the Atlantic in his tiny, single-engined monoplane *Spirit of St Louis*. Amy Johnson flew solo to Australia and South Africa, while Francis Chichester flew solo in his diminutive De Havilland Moth from New Zealand to Australia. In 1939, Alex Henshaw flew his single-engined Percival Mew Gull non-stop from England to Cape Town. Imperial Airways pioneered new passenger flights to the Far East while Hillman Airways provided a service between Britain and Europe. Most exciting of all, however, was the Schneider Trophy competition. Given that seven-tenths of the world's surface is covered by water, Jacques Schneider, son of a wealthy French arms manufacturer, could not understand why marine lagged so far behind land-based aviation. He saw the seaplane as being possessed of enormous potential, with water providing cheap airports. As an incentive for aircraft designers to invest in seaplane development, Schneider presented his iconic trophy for an international air race over a measured water course. Whichever country won the coveted trophy three consecutive times kept it. This was, of course, a period of emerging nationalism on a global basis, the Schneider Trophy becoming an emotive competition evoking intense national pride. Throughout this time, however, Douglas remained office-bound, helping to compile air route schedules, providing information regarding routes, distances and airfield locations all around the globe. This work provided an occasional opportunity to travel to European countries, such as Sweden, Denmark and Poland, meeting customers both actual and potential. Such excursions were a welcome change from the monotony of Douglas's office but a poor exchange for flying fighters – in which area of aviation dramatic advances were being made.

The advances in aviation design and technology wrought by the Schneider Trophy competition would have far-reaching effects on military aviation – and fighters in particular. On 12 September 1931, Britain won the Schneider Trophy for the third consecutive time – and kept it. The winning entrant, at a speed of 340.08 mph, was the Supermarine S.6B, a low-winged, bullet-shaped, single-engined seaplane built on the banks of the River Itchen at Woolston, near Southampton. The experience gained throughout the contest by the S.6B's designer, Reginald Joseph Mitchell, would soon be put to great use in producing a fighter with which to defend Britain's shores. When Mitchell won the trophy in 1931, the air defence of Great Britain was entirely dependent on biplanes, including the Bulldog previously flown by Douglas, together with the Hawker Demon and Fury fighters. The new Hawker Hart bomber, though, had a top speed of 174 mph – 10 mph faster than the Bulldog. The air power doctrinal thinking of the time concentrated almost exclusively on the theory that bombers would always get through and that little or nothing could stop them. If fighters could not catch them, the bombers would indeed get through. Air Marshal Hugh Dowding became Air Member for Supply and Research in 1930, and recognised, due to Mitchell's work, the superiority of monoplane designs. Dowding wanted to see the marine-based experience gained throughout the Schneider Trophy contest applied to land-based fighter aircraft. In April 1935, therefore, the Air Ministry issued its 'Requirements for Single-Engine Single-Seater Day and Night Fighter (F.10/35)'. Designers were asked to create an aircraft very different to – and much more advanced than – the biplanes currently in service with the RAF. The main points were that the new fighter:

Had to be at least 40 mph faster than contemporary bombers at 15,000 feet.

Have eight forward-firing machine-guns.

Had to achieve no less than 310 mph at 15,000 feet at maximum power, with the highest speed achievable between 5,000 and 15,000 feet.

Have the best possible climbing performance to 20,000 feet.

Had to be a steady firing platform.

Had to include the following features and equipment:

Enclosed cockpit.

Cockpit heating.

Night flying equipment.

Radio Telephony (R/T).

Oxygen for two-and-a-half hours.

Easily accessed and maintained guns.

Retractable undercarriage and tail wheel.

Wheel brakes.

Dowding's intention was that the resulting machine would be 'a real killer fighter'.[13] Such an aircraft was badly needed. The previous year, the RAF's annual air exercise had been, argued Orange, 'a fiasco'.[14] Only two of the five bombers which simulated an air attack were intercepted – and the air defences of the period were only capable of simultaneously intercepting five raiders at any one time. Dowding's 'real killer fighter' was, therefore, urgently required – and in numbers. On 6 November 1935, Hawker's response to F.10/35 flew for the first time. It was designed by Sydney Camm and called the 'Hurricane'. On 6 March 1936, Mitchell's fighter made its maiden flight at Eastleigh. It was called the 'Spitfire'. Both aircraft would become legendary, and Douglas Bader, although he was yet to know it, would become synonymous with both.

In 1937, Douglas and Thelma enjoyed the church wedding service that they had promised themselves when they actually married four years previously. During a honeymoon celebration with friends in the Royal Tank Corps' mess, Douglas uncharacteristically drank five glasses of champagne. The result was, according to Brickhill, 'the first and last hangover of his life'.[15] Sharing their own home at last, Thelma noted that Douglas's bouts of depression, which sometimes lasted several days, were becoming both rare and short. Her husband's golf handicap was a respectable nine, and he was even starting to play squash. Then the Munich Crisis came in 1938 – and Thelma's cosy bubble burst. Having re-armed Germany and in so doing ignored with impunity many clauses of the Versailles Peace Treaty, Hitler's confidence grew. On 12 March 1938, Austria was annexed into the new Reich – forbidden by Versailles – this being ignored by Britain and France. The Sudetenland of Czechoslovakia included a large number of ethnic Germans, giving Hitler the opportunity to make inroads into that territory. Britain's Prime Minister, Neville Chamberlain, knew full well that Britain was unprepared for war, and so to buy time pursued a policy of appeasement. Britain and France, therefore, ceded the Sudetenland to Germany – at the infamous Munich Conference on 30 September 1938, to which the Czechs were not invited. Many people still failed to wake up to the danger to world peace that Hitler posed, not wanting to believe that there could be another war. A month before Munich, however, 19 Squadron received the first Spitfires delivered to the RAF – and Douglas Bader must have read about this new, sleek fighter, possibly even seeing one, with envious eyes. When Munich came Douglas knew that there was going to be a war. He also realised that the RAF would need all the trained pilots it could muster. Having already proved at Lympne, Duxford and Wittering that he could still fly, in spite of whatever King's Regulations did or did not say, Douglas wrote to the Air Ministry offering his services. The polite refusal stated that without legs he was still considered a permanent accident risk. Once more he was offered an administrative role, which again Douglas declined.

Flying was an integral part of Douglas's very being – especially the most exciting aspects of it. During his previous service he had expressed this through aerobatics. Combat flying was an altogether different dimension and one without parallel. Suddenly the burning ambition to resume the cockpit of a service aircraft rose to the fore again and this time would not go away. Naturally, after six happy but difficult years, Thelma was against her husband flying again. Thelma's mother, Olive, shared her daughter's angst and concern, although Colonel Addison – a professional soldier – understood Douglas's mindset. Douglas, of course, remained in contact with various RAF contemporaries, who talked excitedly of the future and new fighters. Men with whom he worked at Shell were also preparing to do their 'bit'. John Longley, formerly of the Cambridge UAS, was going on a flying refresher course; another had joined the VR; others joined the Territorial Army (TA). As Lucas wrote, 'it was wholly uncharacteristic for him to be out of it'.[16] More than that, it was intolerable. Douglas resolved to continually pressurise the Air Ministry, garnering support from friends still in the service and refusing to take no for an answer. Lucas described how

several of the instructors (at Cranwell) in Douglas's time were (now) in positions of influence. Men of the calibre of Boyle, Constantine, MacFadyen and Coningham had obviously been marked out and were on the way up. Additionally there were several among his old contemporaries, close friends like Geoffrey Stephenson and Rupert Leigh, who were in a position to be useful and certainly try to help. Stephenson, a staff officer at the Air Ministry, beavered away for him behind the scenes. Best of all, his first Commandant at Cranwell, Frederick Halahan, was also at the Air Ministry. An air vice-marshal, he carried some responsibility for personnel – not aircrew, but that didn't matter. The important thing was that he was there, in Kingsway, at the centre of things.[17]

It was from this point onwards that the words of the otherwise anonymous Cranwell cadet 'AHE' must have been ringing in

Douglas's ears: 'For the associations of Cranwell are enjoyed only by a privileged few, who are closely bound together by their careers.' Indeed, Douglas himself resolved to harness the 'Old Boy Network' to his absolute advantage.

Although the British Prime Minister, Neville Chamberlain, had returned from Munich brandishing his famous piece of paper signed by Hitler and supposedly guaranteeing 'peace for our time', the storm clouds of war continued to gather over Czechoslovakia. By now Hitler's army and Luftwaffe had fought successfully in the Spanish Civil War on behalf of the fascist General Franco, providing an opportunity to test new weapons and tactics. Hitler wanted to unleash a short, sharp war on the Czechs as a signal to other European states that Nazi Germany was not to be resisted. Ultimately this proved unnecessary. Appeasement at the Munich Conference gave up the Sudetenland to Hitler – and more importantly the confidence that Britain and France would not go to war against Germany over Czechoslovakia. On 16 March 1939, therefore, German troops invaded Czechoslovakia; a week later Slovakia placed itself under German control. There was now no question whatsoever regarding Hitler's true intentions, convincing Douglas further still that his place was in the cockpit of a Spitfire.

At this time, Geoffrey Stephenson was serving at the Air Ministry and, according to Brickhill, 'friendly with the personal staff officer to the new Air Member for Personnel, Air Marshal Sir Charles Portal, and soon, by arrangement under the "Old Chums Act", Bader wrote to Portal'[18] – the man pivotal to Douglas achieving his ambition. 'Peter' Portal had Air Council responsibility for selections and postings. Any decision about Douglas's unique case could only be made by him – so Stephenson's influence in engineering this contact should not be underestimated. As Lucas said, going to the top had 'always been Bader's practice',[19] but having help on the inside was no bad thing. Stephenson's suggestion was that Douglas should be admitted to the new Auxiliary Air Force (AAF) reserve.[20] Portal was largely unmoved, responding to the effect that even a flying capacity in the reserve was impossible during peacetime. There was, however, hope: 'If war came,' Portal wrote on 31 August 1939, 'we would almost certainly be only too glad of your services in a flying capacity after a short time if the doctor's agreed.'[21] From that point onwards, the prospect of another world war became Douglas Bader's salvation. Indeed, according to Brickhill 'part of him began almost praying for war'.[22] Those prayers were answered during the early hours of Friday 1 September 1939, when Hitler invaded Poland.

It was obvious now that Hitler's intention was territorial expansion by aggressive means. Appeasement had bought time for Britain to prepare for war at the eleventh hour but the policy had otherwise failed. It was equally obvious to Douglas that Britain and France would have to go to war over Poland. While Thelma fretted, Douglas eagerly awaited further news. On 2 September he sent Thelma to stay with her parents – anticipating an imminent declaration of war against Nazi Germany and rapid the arrival of German bombers over London. Such was the fear of air attack, in fact, that between June and the first week of September 1939, some 3,750,000 people were evacuated, such movements in the first week of September alone affecting up to a third of Britain's population.[23] It was fully expected that Germany would immediately attempt to deliver the dreaded 'knock-out blow'. News from Poland was dire: the Polish Air Force had been destroyed, largely on the ground, on the campaign's first day, on which the Luftwaffe achieved total aerial superiority. Hitler ignored an ultimatum from Britain and France to withdraw his troops, leading to the long-awaited declaration of war on 3 September 1939. Chamberlain broadcast the far-reaching news to the nation and Commonwealth at 11.15 a.m. that Sunday morning. Twelve minutes later the sirens wailed – causing Londoners to fear that Armageddon had arrived. Fortunately this was a false alarm – because Duxford's Spitfires were scrambled with no ammunition! Douglas Bader, though, was not among those who scurried to the shelters. Instead he sat down and wrote to Portal again. He also began 'telephoning and writing peremptory notes to Stephenson and another friend, Hutchinson, at the Air Ministry'.[24] Several weeks passed, during which Douglas promptly had his name removed from the list of those Shell employees exempt from military service, until the Air Ministry responded. That communication took the form of a simple telegram, instructing Douglas to attend Adastral House for a selection board.

Upon arrival, Douglas was shown into the office of none other than Air Vice-Marshal Halahan – his old Cranwell commandant. Once more a ground job was offered and declined. Douglas's spirited response that only returning to a fighter squadron was acceptable to him led to Halahan providing his former pupil with a letter for the doctors. It read, 'I have known this officer since he was a cadet at Cranwell under my command. He's the type we want. If he is fit, apart from his legs, I suggest you give him A1B category and leave it to the CFS to assess his flying capabilities.'[25] Douglas's fitness was subsequently not found wanting and he was referred to the CFS. There is no doubt, of course, that, as Mackenzie commented, Halahan 'had pressed his thumb into the scales',[26] tipping them in Douglas's favour. He was ecstatic, although, needless to say, Thelma was understandably far less enthusiastic about the prospect of him flying into war. The days passed with no further word from the RAF of which he yearned so desperately to be an active part again. Tellingly, Brickhill described how Douglas soon began 'bullying' Stephenson and Hutchinson 'to make someone do something immediately'.[27] Unfortunately this kind of behaviour was a less admirable Bader personality trait. Nonetheless, on 14 October a telegram arrived from the CFS, now based at Upavon in Wiltshire, ordering Douglas to attend for a test four days later. He packed and drove there the following day. Not having flown for seven years, unsurprisingly, even for Douglas, nagging doubts regarding his ability to pass the test gnawed away at him during the journey. He need not have worried – Cranwell was about to look after him once more.

The first person Douglas met at Upavon was Joe Cox – with whom he had flown at Duxford after his fateful crash and before leaving the service. They were old chums, and Cox was now a senior instructor at the CFS. Posted to the Refresher Squadron's 'A' Flight, Douglas found the commander to be an old Cranwell chum: Squadron Leader Rupert 'Lucky' Leigh. Junior to Bader at Cranwell, Leigh considered his senior 'to be some sort of god'. This was fortunate indeed: Douglas's flying test was to be taken by Leigh in a North American Harvard monoplane – which had footbrakes. Nonetheless, Brickhill confirmed Douglas's feeling that 'Under the "Old Chums Act" it was in the bag unless he made some unthinkable blunder'.[28] He did not, and Leigh operated the footbrakes, justifying this on the grounds that Douglas would not be flying the American-built Harvard operationally and all British service types' brakes were operated by way of a handbrake. Douglas passed the test with a recommendation from Leigh that he return to the CFS for a refresher course. Douglas could have hoped for no better outcome. He went home to await further orders, which again came not quick enough – soon Douglas was pestering Stephenson and Hutchinson at the Air Ministry again. At the end of November, however, the long-awaited letter from the Air Ministry arrived: Flying Officer Bader was not being commissioned into the VR but back into the regular service and in a flying capacity. This was even more than he had dared hoped for.

Restored at last to the active list, on 27 November 1939, Flying Officer Bader reported to Upavon for his refresher course – with 500 flying hours recorded in his logbook, all on biplanes. The first flight of his resumed career was as a passenger in an Avro Tutor flown by Flight Lieutenant Clarkson. The second was solo – including an *inverted* circuit of the aerodrome. This beggared belief, and failed to impress the Chief Flying Instructor (CFI), Wing Commander Pringle, who asked Leigh to 'be good enough' to ask Bader 'not to break *all* the flying regulations straight away'.[29] On 2 December, Douglas flew with Leigh in Harvard N7184. Although he could never solo on this type, due to its footbrakes, because operational RAF fighters were now monoplanes it was imperative that Douglas gained experience of this new type. Two days later, he soloed on a monoplane for the first time – not a fighter but a Fairey Battle. With an enclosed cockpit, retractable undercarriage and a variable pitch propeller, even this comparatively lumbering light bomber was a very different machine to the biplanes Douglas had flown previously. Another Harvard flight with Leigh followed on 10 December. Then, on 20 December 1939, Flying Officer Bader flew one of the new fighters, Hawker Hurricane L1873, for the first time. In his logbook Douglas wrote, 'Circuits, landings and low-flying'; he could not have had a better Christmas present. By conclusion of the course, Douglas recorded a total of 5.20 hours on the Hurricane.

At this time, Wing Commander Alfred B. Woodhall was Station Commander and Sector Controller at Duxford:

One day, Douglas Bader flew over from the CFS in a Hurricane. I was delighted and amazed to see him as I had not done so since his crash. He was in terrific form, and, as it happened, the Air Officer Commanding (AOC) also came to visit us. I introduced Douglas to the AOC, Air Vice-Marshal Leigh-Mallory, and over lunch Douglas used all his considerable charm to persuade 'LM' to take him into one of his operational fighter squadrons. After lunch, with the AOC watching, Douglas put on a most finished display of aerobatics, and this finally decided LM. Douglas impressed us all with his terrific personality and his amazing keenness and drive. I have never known his equal. Flying was his supreme passion and his enthusiasm infected us all.[30]

At Upavon it was decided that Douglas had proved himself and could be posted to a fighter squadron. Rupert Leigh described him as 'an exceptionally good pilot' who should be posted to a fighter squadron; Joe Cox agreed: 'When flying with this officer it is quite impossible to even imagine that he has two artificial legs. He is full of confidence and possesses excellent judgement and air sense ... I have never met a more enthusiastic pilot ... he lives for flying.' The CO, Wing Commander George Stainforth, endorsed Douglas's logbook as 'Exceptional'.[31] While no one could deny Douglas's achievements or question whether he met the standard required of a fighter pilot, not all of the foregoing comments appear justified. How Cox, for example, could write of his pupil's 'excellent judgement and air sense', given Douglas's repeated contempt for flying discipline and regulations, is difficult to understand. Squadron Leader Geoffrey Stephenson had recently left the Air Ministry – where he had been well placed to assist Douglas's return to the service – and was now commanding 19 Squadron, equipped with Spitfires, at Duxford. With a green light from Upavon, Douglas lost no time in haranguing Stephenson to engineer a posting to his new squadron. Douglas's visit to Duxford, described by Woodhall, timed for when the AOC was lunching there, was no coincidence. Stephenson – a squadron commander – had access to the AOC that day and deftly used the occasion to further his friend's cause. On 7 February 1940, the effect of string-pulling became evident: Flying Officer Bader was posted to 19 Squadron. The Cranwell 'Old Chums Network' had undoubtedly looked after one of its own.

After years in the wilderness, Douglas's ambition had been achieved: he was once more a fighter pilot in the RAF. Ironically, his new career resumed where his previous commission had terminated: RAF Duxford. It was to that famous fighter station that Douglas now drove – no doubt feeling happier than he had in a very long time.

7

SPITFIRES

The Fighter Command 12 Group Sector Station at Duxford in early 1940 was, according to eighteen-year-old fitter Bob Morris, 'a young man's dream ... what an absolute thrill to see Spitfires!'[1] Flying Officer Douglas Bader doubtless shared this view upon reporting to fly the iconic Supermarine fighter with 19 Squadron. The Spitfire was thus described in *The Aeroplane*:

From the mediocrity of the F.7/30 came the brilliance of the Spitfire, a much smaller aeroplane with greater power ... Structurally the Spitfire is a straightforward stressed-skin design. The elliptical cantilever low wing, which tapers in thickness, is built up on a single spar with tubular flanges and a plate web. Forward of the spar the wing is covered with a heavy-gauge light aluminium sheet which forms the torsion box with the spar. Aft of the spar the covering is of thinner gauge sheet with light-alloy girder ribs. The wing tips are detachable for ease of maintenance and repair. Split flaps are between the ailerons and the fuselage.

The fuselage is an all-metal monococque, built on four longerons with transverse frames and a flush-riveted light-alloy skin. The front frame forms the fireproof bulkhead and is built as an integral part with the centre portion of the main wing spar. To help in maintenance the tail portion of the fuselage with fin and tailplane is detachable.

The tail unit is of the cantilever monoplane type. The fin is integral with the rear fuselage. The tailplane is of metal with smooth metal covering. The elevator and rudders have light alloy frames and fabric covering. There are trimming tabs on elevator and rudder.

The undercarriage is fully retractable outwards into the under-surface of the wings. There are two Vickers cantilever oleo-pneumatic shock absorber legs which are retracted hydraulically. An emergency hand system is fitted to lower the wheels should the hydraulic system be damaged.

The rather uneven spacing of the guns is explained by the fact that the Spitfire was originally designed for only four guns, and not until it was in an advanced stage were eight guns decided upon. If it had not been for this then the installation would have been neater.

Probably the Spitfire could never have come to life had it not been for the relative failure of the F.7/30. For the Spitfire's thin wing we thank the F.7/30's thick wing. For the Spitfire's smoothness, the F.7/30's corrugations and roughness. For the Spitfire's sweet lines the F.7/30's angularities. For the Spitfire's simple basic structure, the F.7/30's complex structure of tubes and stressed skin.[2]

The Spitfire was undoubtedly stunning in appearance, akin to a flying bullet. Its elliptical wings provided a unique signature, the Spitfire soon exciting the general public as its iconic shape and sound was seen and heard in British skies. Douglas's new squadron, 19, had actually been Fighter Command's first to receive the Spitfire, on 4 August 1938. Among those first Spitfire pilots was Flight Sergeant George Unwin:

Before the Spitfire arrived we flew Gloster Gauntlet biplanes, which were good so far as biplanes went. But of course the Spitfire was in a completely different league. We were naturally very proud to have been chosen to be the RAF's first Spitfire squadron and it was our job to learn to fly it operationally and iron out any teething troubles along the way. There were a few accidents. Flight Lieutenant Clouston and Pilot Officer Ball collided, but neither was hurt. Clouston forced-landed on Newmarket racecourse, causing quite a stir! On 9 March 1939 I had to make a forced landing at Sudbury in Essex due to a broken coolant pipe, which caused the engine to partially seize up. I decided to land on a large playing field and was doing fine with undercarriage down until the schoolchildren who were playing on the various pitches saw me descending – I was apparently on fire and trailing smoke. They ran towards me and on to the path I had selected for a landing. I was then at less than 100 feet and decided to stuff the Spitfire into the thick hawthorn hedge in front of me. The impact broke my straps and I gashed my right eyebrow on the windscreen but was otherwise unhurt. For this I received an AOC's Commendation. It was the first of many an exciting adventure flying Spitfires – the speed and power after our old Gauntlets was quite something to behold, and the aircraft's aerobatic ability was excellent. This was the fighter that we wanted to go to war in.[3]

As Douglas later wrote of his arrival at Duxford, 'Now, modern types consisted of low-wing monoplanes, with retractable undercarriages, wing flaps, constant-speed variable-pitch propellers, blind-flying instruments and radio telephony. None of these things existed when I crashed in 1931.'[4] He was not to fly a Spitfire for a few days, however. Stephenson was away and the squadron operated daily from the coastal station at Horsham St Faith, flying convoy patrols, leaving no serviceable Spitfires at Duxford. Monotonous though such patrols over the North Sea could often be, it was of course essential to protect convoys bringing crucial supplies to island Britain. While his fellow pilots performed this very necessary task, Douglas, not yet being operational, remained at Duxford, making his first flight with 19 Squadron in a Miles Master. He described this machine as being 'nothing like a Hurricane or Spitfire, for it had a wide undercarriage, was without vice, and was easy to fly. But you sat behind a Rolls-Royce liquid-cooled engine, the Master went quite fast and it was fully aerobatic.'[5] It was indeed, as 19 Squadron armourer Fred Roberts remembered: 'Bader's first flight with us was in the station Master, and he beat up the aerodrome in every way.'[6] Ernie French was a member of 'A' Flight's ground crew: 'When Flying Officer Bader arrived at Duxford from the CFS at Upavon, there was no publicity. He simply joined our Squadron as an ordinary pilot. My first sight of him was arriving in his MG. He often took me and other airmen flying in the two-seater Master, making me sit in the front cockpit and joking "French, make sure you start her up before you get in!" These were cross-country flights and he would point out his digs in March and other landmarks.'[7]

Douglas's first impression of the Spitfire was that it

looked good and was good. But my first reaction was that it was bad for handling on the ground, made taxiing difficult since it was not easy to see ahead. It was necessary to swing from side to side to look in front. The view at take-off was restricted in the same way until you were travelling fast enough to lift the tail; only then could you see over the nose. Once accustomed to these minor inconveniences, they were no longer apparent, and once in the air you felt in the first few minutes that here was the aeroplane *par excellence*. The controls were light, positive and synchronized; in fact the aeroplane of one's dreams. It was stable; it flew hands and feet off; yet you could move it quickly and effortlessly into any altitude. You brought it in to land at 75 mph and touched down at 60–65 mph. Its maximum speed was 367 mph. You thus had a wide speed range that has not been equalled before or since.[8]

Given the technological differences between the biplanes and the new fighters, Douglas's transition to the Spitfire was not without difficulty. Flying Officer Bader made his first Spitfire flight, in Mk I K9853, on 12 February 1940: 'I sat in the cockpit while a young pilot officer, with little experience, showed me the knobs. He omitted to tell me one important thing about the undercarriage operation which embarrassed me in due course, fortunately without damage.'[9] That 'young pilot officer, with little experience' was, in fact, Pilot Officer Frank Brinsden, who was serving with 19 Squadron before it received Spitfires:

I feel free to elaborate on this comment as Douglas raised the matter and I was there. Any 'young pilot officer with little experience' on 19 Squadron assigned to brief Douglas Bader would actually have been flying Spitfires since October 1938. By early February 1940, when Bader came on the scene, that pilot officer would have been qualified to fly operationally by both day and night. Is such a pilot officer therefore likely to have omitted from the briefing the rather important matter of raising the undercarriage? In any case the crew room had an ample supply of Pilot's Handling Notes and anyone who embarked upon his first solo in such a (for that time) radical aircraft without fully understanding its controls was a complete bloody fool! It must be remembered that the biplanes with which Bader had previously been familiar had a fixed undercarriage. Although he had flown a handful of hours in a Hurricane, retractable undercarts remained relatively new to him.[10]

It was both typical and offensive that Douglas should blame his own mistake on another. It would not, though, be the only one he would make. Michael Lyne was a Cranwell graduate and young pilot officer on 19 Squadron:

By March 1940 the weather was better but we now had Flying Officer Douglas Bader to contend with. He was very brave and determined but having a hard time getting to grips with the Spitfire, a far more advanced machine that the biplanes he had flown previously. He particularly experienced problems in cloud. More than once my friend, Watson, and I were lent to Bader as a formation by the CO, but emerged from cloud faithfully following our leader only to find ourselves in a steep diving turn![11]

Ernie French was assigned as engine fitter on Douglas's Spitfire:

I was consequently with Flying Officer Bader on the airfield whenever 19 Squadron was 'available'. At 'readiness' he would come to the aircraft out at dispersal and remain in the cockpit, so I gradually got to know him and realised that he was someone out of the ordinary. I looked after his aircraft for several months; we would sometimes fly from Fowlmere or Horsham St Faith, and I was with him throughout this time. You got to know little things about him, like he'd never take his plane off without one of his wife's silk stockings tied to the gunsight! Another little thing I remember was one day when we were available he said to me 'French, I want you to get hold of some webbing. I want it strung across the cockpit, my side of the gunsight, fairly tight'. I couldn't think why, but he was trying it out to steady his body during firing, by using his chin, being unable to brace himself using his feet on the rudder pedals. Prior to trying this out, he had found that when firing his guns he was thrown slightly forward by the recoil. The webbing idea worked perfectly![12]

Douglas was not only having a hard time with the Spitfire, but also fitting back into squadron life as a comparatively junior officer – his rank not being commensurate with either his age or contemporaries. Douglas was nearly thirty; his Cranwell contemporaries were largely squadron leaders, whereas his years out in the wilderness meant that he was a flying officer – senior only in rank to a pilot officer. So here was Douglas

Bader, the Cranwell graduate, pre-war officer and famous aerobatic champion, a very junior officer in a fighter squadron commanded by his best friend, an exact contemporary. Those pilots of equal or junior rank were twenty-odd-year-olds – even his flight commander in 'A' Flight, the quiet and intellectual Flight Lieutenant Brian Lane, was only twenty-three. Douglas's antipathy is reflected in Brickhill's account that on 13 February 1940, he flew with Lane, 'an un-blooded veteran of twenty-five'.[13] Lane was actually only twenty-three – but nonetheless had been a fighter pilot since 1936. Before the war he flew Hurricanes, since when he had accumulated many hours on Spitfires. Lane was, therefore, infinitely more experienced on the new monoplane fighters and current operational procedures than Flying Officer Bader, and, in due course, would prove himself not only an able fighter pilot but more so a truly exceptional leader. While on finals, upon conclusion of that sortie with Lane, Douglas's Spitfire hit and removed the roof of Duxford's cricket pavilion, removing his tail-wheel in the process. Brickhill described how afterwards Lane (who he does not identify by name) 'came across laughing, and said "I'm awfully sorry, ol' boy. Most extraordinary thing – d'ya know not long ago I landed a chap in a tree just the same way." He never forgot the blunt details which Bader told him about his character in the next few minutes.'[14] This, like the story about Brinsden having failed to correctly explain the Spitfire's undercarriage control, is completely untrue. Brian Lane was a quiet intellectual – not a reckless flippant. There is no record whatsoever of a 19 Squadron Spitfire hitting a tree. This was actually only Douglas's *second* flight in a Spitfire – on the first he had 'embarrassed' himself by being unable to lower the undercarriage. This accident was entirely due to pilot error caused by inexperience on type and failing to cope with the reduced visibility during landing caused by the Spitfire's long nose. Unfortunately Burns, as ever, took his lead from Brickhill, and wrote that the anonymous flight commander had demonstrated 'a clear sign of lack of understanding of what formation flying entailed, and a lack of basic awareness that stemmed from poor basic training'.[15] Again, this is completely untrue – but is a 'clear sign' of limited research. The fact of the matter, in spite of Brickhill extolling the virtues of Flying Officer Bader's formation flying skills and Burns fashionably blaming Flying Officer Bader's leader, is that this particular flight was another Bader cock-up.

During a dummy interception of Wellington bombers, Douglas hit a tree while chasing a low-flying bomber. Characteristically he blamed his leader, complaining to his CO, 'That silly clot led me into a tree.' Stephenson's response was, 'Well, you're the silly clot. It's up to you to see where you're going. He can't fly the aeroplane for you.'[16] Brinsden previously made the point, rightly, that even the most junior pilot officer on 19 Squadron upon Douglas's arrival was operational by both day and night. Any suggestion that 19 Squadron's pilots were poorly trained, led and inexperienced is completely without foundation. Young they may have been – but these men were the most experienced Spitfire pilots in the entire RAF. The fact is that Douglas was clearly unable to accept responsibility for his own mistakes – which made poor copy when writing a best-seller. Blaming these errors on other airmen, however, is not admirable. Douglas was simply unable to play second fiddle to anyone – and certainly not a young twenty-odd-year-old. This arrogant, negative aspect of his personality, coupled with senior years and an elitist Cranwellian background, made Douglas unable to cope with being 19

Squadron's 'sprog' pilot. He did not see that as his place – that was commanding a fighter squadron, like his Cranwell chums.

At this time, the fast monoplane fighters remained comparatively new and, apart from the odd skirmish with lone German bombers, were largely untested in combat. The RAF's tacticians did not envisage Britain ever being within range of single-engined enemy fighters operating from bases in Germany, and assumed that only bombers, with their longer range, would be engaged. Such raiders were slower than Spitfires and Hurricanes and any evasive action possible would be incomparable to the British fighters' aerobatic capabilities. It was also believed that due to the high speeds achieved by the monoplane fighters, fighter-*versus*-fighter combat would be impossible. The tacticians therefore assumed that bombers were the only threat, and RAF fighters should intercept them in closely grouped V-shaped sections of three, called a 'vic', each flight being subdivided into two such sections, a whole squadron four. In this way, each section would bring twenty-four guns to bear simultaneously, instead of the eight of a single Spitfire or Hurricane. The 'Fighting Area Attacks' arising consisted of six set-piece attacks involving whole squadrons lining up on enemy bombers in an orderly queue and attacking only from astern or below. So much faith in these tactics did the Air Ministry place that individual squadron commanders were forbidden to experiment with alternative ideas.[17]

So it was that during early 1940, in addition to providing convoy patrols, 19 Squadron rehearsed the Fighting Area Attacks. Douglas, however, disagreed with the Air Fighting Manual and considered the air exercises completely unrealistic. For years he had read the memoirs of First World War fighter aces, and firmly believed that height, sun, getting in close and independent action would win the day – not the rigid formation attacks endorsed by Fighter Command. Instead of attacking in an orderly fashion from the same direction, Douglas argued that fighters attacking from all angles would be more deadly. Future events confirmed that the tacticians were wrong – but only because Hitler's unprecedented conquest of France placed southern England within range of his single-engined fighters. This meant that there would be an enormous amount of fighter-*versus*-fighter combat – which, contrary to the experts' belief, *was* possible. Fighter combat was largely, therefore, ignored by the tacticians. Douglas's take on fighter tactics, however, did not just concern fighters. He believed that once battle was joined, each pilot should act independently and attack as he saw fit – not be bound to a set-piece, rehearsed attack that in reality would be impossible due to the enemy's evasive action and return fire. In this area of argument, he was more right than wrong. Douglas remonstrated with Stephenson over tactics, but whatever 19 Squadron's CO thought, he had no brief to deviate from the stipulated tactics – which relied upon teamwork and not the individual. As ever, Douglas remained convinced that he was right. The inability for independent action and his disagreement with Stephenson, though, exasperated him further still. He had much to thank Stephenson for, but was becoming increasingly unhappy on 19 Squadron. Indeed, Douglas openly told his CO, 'Look, I don't feel happy flying behind these younger chaps. I'm more experienced and older, although I've not so many hours on Spitfires.'[18] The fact was, as Mackenzie rightly argued, Douglas was unhappy as a team player – unless he was the leader of it.[19]

Again, though, 'the associations of Cranwell' were to rescue him. Another significant officer at Duxford was also a Cranwellian,

Squadron Leader H. W. 'Tubby' Mermagen, CO of 222 Squadron. Brickhill wrote that 'in the mess one night Mermagen buttonholed Bader and casually said, "I want a new flight commander. I don't want to do the dirty on Geoffrey, but if he's agreeable, would you come?"'[20] Burns, as ever, followed Brickhill's lead and duplicated this tale,[21] as inevitably did Turner.[22] Lucas makes no mention of how Douglas became a flight commander so soon – having 'bent' several precious Spitfires. Unique first-hand testimony from Mermagen himself, however, detailed what really happened: 'When I was commanding 222 Squadron at Duxford, which had recently exchanged twin-engined Blenheims for Spitfires, Douglas Bader, a personal friend, was serving alongside us in 19 Squadron. However, he was finding it difficult to serve under Geoffrey Stephenson, with whom he had once shared equal rank at Kenley before his accident. Bader knew that I had a flight commander suspected as being "lacking in moral fibre" and whom I wished rid of. Bader therefore asked me if I would approach the AOC, Leigh-Mallory, regarding the possibility of him being transferred to 222 on promotion to acting flight lieutenant and becoming a flight commander. The AOC agreed.'[23] Douglas, of course, had already personally met the AOC, at the meeting ironically arranged by Stephenson. Wing Commander Woodhall had been present on that occasion and commented that 'as a spectator, I was intrigued to see the impact that Douglas had on the AOC – and vice-versa. Air Vice-Marshal and Flying Officer, rank did not enter into it, they were two of a kind – born leaders. They were both men who were respected by all and were affectionately esteemed by most. Their attraction for each other was immediate and their friendship was, I am sure, established at that first meeting.'[24] Woodhall – Duxford's Station Commander – was also impressed by Flying

Officer Bader during that far-reaching visit to Duxford: 'I had not seen Douglas since his crash, and his maturity appealed to me very strongly. Such was his zest for living and flying that one forgot his artificial legs. He ignored them, and so did everyone else. His prowess at golf and squash was such that very few people on the station were a match for him in either game.'[25] Woodhall supported Mermagen's formal recommendation that Douglas replace his existing flight commander.

By this time, the Spitfire's original fixed-pitch propeller – as fitted to the old biplanes – had been replaced by the De Havilland two-pitch airscrew. 'Pitch' refers to the angle at which the propeller blade cuts into the air. The effect of changing pitch is akin to changing gear in a car. This development also caused Douglas difficulty, as Michael Lyne described: 'On 31 March 1940, Douglas was leading our section of three Spitfires on a convoy patrol. We went off downwind on the shortest run at Horsham. Douglas, however, forgot to put the airscrew into fine pitch for take-off and cartwheeled across the main road and into a ploughed field. Watson and I stuck with him until the last minute but then pulled up and away on emergency power. I remember only just clearing the hedge and seeing clods of earth flying high overhead from my leader's Spitfire. Bader broke a pair of artificial legs in the accident, in fact, and had to send away for a new pair.'[26] The Spitfire concerned, K9858, was written off. It was an extremely stupid mistake, drawing a rebuke from Squadron Leader Stephenson – and a 'snarled' response from Flying Officer Bader.[27] It is surprising, therefore, that on the same day, Squadron Leader Stephenson wrote in Douglas's logbook 'Ability as a Spitfire Pilot Exceptional'.[28] If Douglas bemoaned his own humble position in 19 Squadron, his personal behaviour must have been exasperating for his old friend Stephenson – the CO. Able officer though Stephenson was, he was unable to cope with his old friend's overwhelming personality in these circumstances. The easier option was to give the petulant Flying Officer Bader what he wanted – for a quiet life. This could explain why, instead of taking Douglas to task for both his flying mistakes and attitude (his open criticism of Fighter Command tactics, for example, was hardly good for squadron morale) – it was easier to humour him. Glowing reports were more likely to resolve the situation: Douglas would move to another squadron on promotion, and all would again be well. No written evidence exists to support this view, but the circumstantial evidence certainly supports the probability.

Although Douglas was concerned that bending another Spitfire could (and should, perhaps) have jeopardised the rapid promotion and transfer he sought, unsurprisingly, given Woodhall's account, the AOC's approval was assured. When interviewed by Leigh-Mallory, Douglas made no excuse for the accident – how could he? The AOC agreed – there was none – but still promptly promoted Douglas to acting flight lieutenant, posting him to 222 Squadron. The evidence, however, of how this came about contradicts the myth. The fact is that Douglas's loyalty should have been to Geoffrey Stephenson and 19 Squadron. The only purpose served was Douglas's own ambition to climb the ladder up to where he thought he should be. To use Brickhill's expression, Mermagen did not 'do the dirty on Geoffrey' – but Douglas Bader did not hesitate to do so in pursuit of his own ambition. Posting Douglas to 19 Squadron, though, had been a mistake. He should not have been allowed to join a squadron commanded by such a close friend – which put both in a very difficult position. The RAF at that time was a relatively small world and so arguably wherever Douglas was sent the likelihood is the squadron commander would have been known to him – but his relationship with Stephenson was a particularly close one. Douglas's reaction to the situation in which he found himself in 19 Squadron made a difficult one unworkable. As Frank Brinsden said, 'Although we all admired Douglas, I wasn't the only pilot not sorry to see him go.'[29] Clearly, 19 Squadron had simply been a stepping-stone to better things: on 16 April 1940, Flight Lieutenant Bader took command of 222 Squadron's 'A' Flight.

Squadron Leader Mermagen had actually formed 222 Squadron at Duxford as a 12 Group night-fighter unit equipped with twin-engined Bristol Blenheims. On 9 March 1940, however, the Squadron converted to Spitfires – much to Mermagen's pilots' delight. Reg Johnson joined 222 the following month:

> I was a member of 'B' Flight and soon learned that 222 Squadron was addicted to tight formation flying, for which I had no training whatsoever. A study of the pre-war career of our CO, Squadron Leader Mermagen, might explain this, particularly in having to fly so tightly that our wings overlapped. He led us off in squadron formation, three behind three, we even looped in formation. Once, we even rolled as a Squadron! Mermagen was an exceptional pilot but such training was to prove unsuitable for the Battle of Britain which lay ahead.[30]

Any aerial threat was still expected to come from bases in Germany, the range involved dictating that intruders would only be bombers. Indeed individual Fighter Command squadron commanders were forbidden to deviate from the Air Fighting Manual or experiment. Nonetheless, Douglas continued to expound his own contrary theories on air fighting. He also remained unable to behave responsibly in the air; Brickhill: 'On his own he tested his nerve and skill with illegal low aerobatics, though the Duxford Wing Commander at one stage said ineffectively, "I *wish* you wouldn't do that. You had such a *terrible* accident last time."'[31] This beggars belief. Douglas had well proven his exceptional ability as an aerobatic pilot, and his flying indiscipline had already cost him his legs; moreover, the struggle back to re-join the service after those unhappy years in the wilderness should have made him realise how lucky he was to be back in the air. The fact is, that Douglas was *the* maverick to whom the old adage that 'there are old pilots and bold pilots, but there are no old bold pilots' applied like no other. He had now, though, made progress in his ambition to catch up his contemporaries – but still had a way to go: in early May Rupert Leigh, promoted to squadron leader, brought his own Spitfire Squadron, 66, to Duxford. For now, though, commanding 'A' Flight of 222 Squadron on the usual round of convoy patrols and training flights would have to do.

In September 1939, the British Expeditionary Force (BEF), commanded by Lord Gort VC, was deployed to France. The Belgian king, however, who desired to remain neutral, refused the 'Tommies' permission to enter his country and fortify his border with Germany. Consequently the BEF dug in along the Franco–Belgian border – and awaited Hitler's next move. To the south, the French peered through the periscopes of their much-vaunted Maginot Line in anticipation of Germany's attack on their country. The situation and feeling was perfectly described by Brian Lane, Douglas's former flight commander on 19 Squadron:

It was a queer war. Everybody said so. The experts said it was going to be a war of attrition. Maybe that was their word for it, but it was still a queer war. The Luftwaffe's expected blows on this country did not fall. Göring contented himself instead with raids by single aircraft against the convoys round the coasts. So for month after month we patrolled the shipping, no doubt frightening away many Huns but never so much as catching sight of one.[32]

A small number of Fighter Command's pilots had engaged the enemy, however. On 16 October 1939, thirty Ju 88s of I/KG 30 attacked shipping in the Firth of Forth, damaging several ships of the Royal Navy. It was the first air attack on Britain of the war – hardly the dreaded knock-out blow expected – from which two raiders failed to return. Both were shot down into the sea by Spitfires of 602 Squadron – the Supermarine fighter's first combat success. Five days later, the Hawker Hurricane recorded its first kills when three mine-laying He 115 seaplanes were despatched off Yorkshire. So far, the tacticians looked like being proved correct. Only Hurricane-equipped fighter squadrons had been sent to support the BEF in France, but it was not until 26 March 1940 that 73 Squadron recorded the type's first success against the Me 109, claiming four destroyed and two unconfirmed in a skirmish over Saarlautern and Trier.

Lane's 'queer war' continued until 9 April 1940, when Germany invaded Norway. The Royal Navy was unable to prevent this seaborne landing, and British air cover, flying from aircraft carriers, proved both inadequate and ineffective. Abruptly, on 10 May 1940 the great storm finally broke when Hitler invaded Belgium, Holland, Luxembourg and France. Douglas heard the news of Hitler's attack on 10 May 1940 from Rupert Leigh, and was consequently 'nearly on fire with joy'.[33] Douglas and Duxford's other fighter pilots, though, would be disappointed: while the newspapers and radio were full of news covering the fighting in France, their monotonous routine remained unchanged. Two days later Liege fell, and panzers crossed the Meuse at Dinant and Sedan. The Belgian king called for help, the BEF pivoting forward from its prepared defences on the Belgian–French border. Gort's troops advanced for 60 miles over unfamiliar ground and in anticipation of meeting the German *Schwerpunkt* – point of main effort – which was expected to follow the same route as in the First World War. It did not. Holland was certainly attacked – the Dutch Air Force being wiped out on the first day – but the main enemy thrust was cleverly disguised. As Allied eyes were firmly focussed on the Belgian–Dutch border, *Panzergruppe* von Kleist achieved the supposedly impossible and successfully negotiated the Ardennes, much further south. German armour shockingly poured out of the forest, by-passed the Maginot Line and rendered its concrete forts useless. The panzers then punched upwards, towards the Channel coast – ten days later the Germans had reached Laon, Cambrai, Arras, Amiens and even Abbeville. Indeed, Erwin Rommel's 7th Panzer covered ground so quickly that it became known as the 'Ghost Division'.

On 21 May, Spitfires at last saw action off the French coast, pilots of 54 and 74 Squadron claiming a number of enemy bombers offset against the loss of two Spitfires: the pilot of one safely returned to England, the other was captured. Both Spitfires and pilots were precious, and these operations across the sea were dangerous indeed. So much faith, in fact, did Air Chief Marshal Dowding have in his Spitfire force that he had refused to send any to France, appreciating the crucial importance of preserving them for Britain's defence. 22 May saw 222 Squadron receive orders to move – not south, but east. Douglas was exasperated. While the battle raged over France, Mermagen led his Spitfires to the east coast station of Kirton-in-Lindsay for more convoy patrols. As the situation on the Continent deteriorated hourly, however, it became clear that the hard-pressed Hurricane squadrons required further support from home-based fighter squadrons. Dowding therefore began moving various Spitfire squadrons to operate temporarily from bases in southern England, thus increasing the time their limited fuel permitted them to remain on patrol over the French coast. On 25 May, Douglas's friend and Cranwell contemporary Squadron Leader Geoffrey Stephenson led 19 Squadron from Duxford to the 11 Group Sector Station at Hornchurch – still north of the Thames, but closer to France. Pilot Officer Michael Lyne:

To us the Mess had a new atmosphere, people clearing kit from the rooms belonging to casualties and the Station Commander insisting on closing the bar and sending us to bed early to be ready for the battles awaiting us.

On 26 May we were called upon to patrol over the beaches as a single squadron. I will always remember heading off to the east and seeing the columns of black smoke from the Dunkirk oil storage tanks. We patrolled for some time without seeing any aircraft. We received no information from British radar. We had received excellent VHF radios shortly before, but they were only of use between ourselves, we could not communicate with other squadrons should the need arise.

Suddenly we saw ahead, going towards Calais where the Rifle Brigade was holding out, about forty German aircraft. We were twelve. Squadron Leader Geoffrey Stephenson aligned us for an attack in sections of three on the formations of Ju 87s. As a former CFS A1 Flying Instructor he was a precise flier and obedient to the book, which stipulated an overtaking speed of 30 mph. What the book never foresaw was that we would attack Ju 87s at just 130 mph. The CO led his Section, Pilot Officer Watson No. 2 and me No. 3, straight up behind the Stukas which looked very relaxed. They thought we were their fighter escort, but the leader had been very clever and had pulled his formation away towards England, so that when they turned in towards Calais he would protect their rear. Alas for him we were coming, by sheer chance, from Dunkirk rather than Ramsgate.

Meanwhile Stephenson realised that we were closing far too fast. I remember his call 'Number 19 Squadron! Prepare to attack!' then to us 'Red Section, throttling back, throttling back.' We were virtually formating on the last section of Ju 87s – at an incredibly dangerous speed in the presence of enemy fighters – and behind us the rest of 19 Squadron staggered along at a similar speed. Of course the Ju 87s could not imagine that we were a threat. Then Stephenson told us to take a target each and fire. As far as I know we got the last three, we could hardly have done otherwise, then we broke away and saw nothing of the work by the rest of the Squadron – but it must have been dodgy as the 109s started to come round. As I was looking round for friends after the break I came under fire from the rear for the first time – and did not at first know it. The first signs were mysterious little corkscrews of smoke passing my starboard wing. Then

I heard a slow 'thump, thump', and realised that I was being attacked by a 109 firing machine-guns with tracer and its cannon banging away. I broke away sharpish – and lost him.

I made a wide sweep and came back to the Calais area to find about five Stukas going around in a tight defensive circle. The German fighters had disappeared so I flew to take the circle at the head-on position and gave it a long squirt. It must have been at this stage that I was hit by return fire, for when I got back to Hornchurch I found bullet holes in the wings which had punctured a tyre.

Alas my friend Watson was never seen again. Stephenson forced-landed on the beach and was taken prisoner.[34]

The incident perfectly illustrates how and why Fighter Command's predicted tactics were so wrong. Once Me 109s were introduced into the equation, the Manual of Air Fighting became meaningless – attempting to apply its teachings in such a scenario was suicidal. Douglas, in spite of his bull-headed refusal to toe the party line, had been absolutely right in his rejection of Fighter Command's approved tactics and perception of future air combat. The following day, 222 Squadron, still languishing at Kirton, received a delivery of armour plate – rapidly fitted to its Spitfires' cockpits, it would be needed soon enough.

German strategy on the Continent was undoubtedly inspired. With the Maginot Line effectively by-passed, the French Army largely collapsed; further north, the Belgians had done so rapidly. The BEF was soon in danger of envelopment. By 26 May it was clear that the situation, so far as the Belgian and French Armies were concerned, was hopeless. The reluctant decision was made, therefore, for Gort to withdraw on and be evacuated from

Dunkirk. The man entrusted with providing a protective airborne umbrella to this depressing operation was Air Vice-Marshal Keith Park, AOC 11 Group. For what he was about to do, there was no precedent. At 0300 hours on 28 May, Flight Lieutenant Douglas Bader was awoken by his batman: at 0400, 222 Squadron was to fly to and operate from Martlesham Heath – in 11 Group. Park was concentrating even more Spitfire squadrons in the south-east, ready to operate across the Channel. Mermagen and his pilots did not know this, however, as they took off, bleary eyed, and flew to their destination, near Felixstowe in Suffolk. Biggin Hill's 92 Squadron was already there and had seen action – losing the CO, Squadron Leader Roger Bushell, on the unit's second patrol. Just as Flight Lieutenant Brian Lane had assumed command of 19 Squadron in the air after Stephenson's capture, Bushell's senior flight commander, Flight Lieutenant Robert Stanford Tuck, found himself in temporary command. Upon landing, Douglas marched up to Tuck and demanded to know 'the score'. Tuck's response was to rebuke Flight Lieutenant Bader for not having tucked the loose end of his silk scarf into his tunic – which, in the event of bailing out, could have snagged on something. Indeed, Tuck's first impression of the 'obstreperous man' was that he was 'too cocky' and 'ought to be taken down a few pegs'.[35] Doubtless many would have agreed with Tuck's assessment.

Initially, so as to extend the length of aerial protection provided, Dowding insisted that his Spitfire squadrons operate singly. Park, however, realised that maintaining a constant aerial umbrella throughout the long hours of daylight was impossible, and weak patrols had already proved ineffective. Instead he favoured strong patrols, squadrons operating in pairs or wings, a 'wing' being a formation of at least three squadrons. The following year, Fighter

Command was re-organised so that every Sector Station had a three-squadron wing with a dedicated Wing Leader. It must, however, be understood that the use of 'wings' at this time was very different – and a temporary expedient without precedent. There was no officially designated Wing Leader, that position in the air generally being occupied by the most combat-experienced squadron's senior pilot. This was more a convoy scenario, of fighters travelling together and arriving over the designated patrol-line *en masse*; once battle was joined, however, cohesion was lost immediately. While Dowding's Hurricane squadrons continued to be decimated in France, thirty-six fighter squadrons had been preserved for home defence. Of these, sixteen – 200 aircraft – were put at Park's disposal.[36] A First World War fighter pilot, the AOC 11 Group, unlike his counterparts, had also learned to fly the new monoplane fighters; over Dunkirk, from his personal Hurricane, 'OK1', Park was able to observe first hand what was happening. This experience, coupled with analysing his pilots' reports, convinced him that patrols in even greater strength were necessary, even though this increased the length of time between them. The effect, argued Orange, was that 'aircraft losses were reduced, there were more successful combats and bomber formations were broken up, thus reducing the effects of their attacks'.[37]

So it was that 92 and 222 Squadrons flew together on 28 May, with Tuck and the former squadron leading. Mermagen's pilots flew in the stipulated vics of three, while, according to Burns, Tuck led 92 in 'loose pairs, well-spaced'.[38] It was clear from what happened to Squadron Leader Geoffrey Stephenson when he tried to attack by the book over Calais two days earlier, that Fighter Command's tacticians really had got it wrong – as Douglas had charged. The presence of the German single-seater fighter, the Me 109, had changed everything. As Douglas had predicted, in practice the formation attacks stipulated by Air Ministry had proved useless. Although the Spitfire, hitherto preserved by Dowding for home defence, was only now meeting the Me 109 for the first time, the RAF pilots were learning quickly. The Me 109E and Supermarine Spitfire were arguably equally matched, although at this early stage the German machine had certain technical advantages – such as a variable, as opposed to two-pitch, propeller and fuel injection, meaning that the enemy fighter's engine was unaffected by gravity and, unlike the Rolls-Royce Merlin, did not cut out in the dive, losing precious speed. That said, the RAF fighters were now enjoying the benefit of 100 octane fuel, the Merlin III providing an extra 12 pounds of boost for a short period and in an emergency; Spitfire pilots had many occasions over Dunkirk to be grateful for this expedient. The 109 also enjoyed the benefit of both two nose-mounted, rifle-calibre machine-guns and a pair of wing-mounted 20mm Oerlikon cannons. While the latter's slower rate of fire required greater accuracy, this was offset by longer effective range and great destructive power. The addition of armour plate to enemy aircraft increasingly proved that rifle bullets were inadequate – but it would take time before the Spitfire could respond with cannon-fire.

It was in the tactical arena, however, that the Germans had a distinct advantage at this time. In August 1936, Nazi Germany intervened in the Spanish Civil War, on behalf of the fascist General Franco. On Spanish battlefields the Wehrmacht was able to test and evaluate new weapons and tactics. Indeed, the conflict in Spain became an essential proving ground for the new monoplane types, which began arriving there in the summer of 1937. It was immediately apparent that the Me 109 was superior to the He 51 biplane fighter previously in use, aerial supremacy rapidly being achieved and maintained by the German fighter pilots. With a full complement of 109s, the *Kommandeur* of 3/ JG 88, Werner Mölders, was instrumental in working out the mechanics of combat tactics for the new monoplane – in the process achieving fourteen personal aerial victories. Mölders discovered that fighter combat was a fast and furious affair requiring flexible formations. Pilots needed to keep a sharp lookout – because trouble arrived suddenly. A formation was required capable of breaking and reacting aggressively to any threat. Mölders decided that the best and most practical formation was a pair of fighters – the *Rotte* – comprising a leader, whose job it was to attack and whose tail was protected by his wingman. Two such pairs, in fact, formed a *schwarm*, which flew in a roughly line-abreast attitude, the aircraft occupying the fingers of an outstretched hand. Unlike the tightly grouped RAF vic of three, though, which required pilots to concentrate as much on formation flying as searching for the enemy, the *schwarm* was widely spread out. In this way, the German pilots could concentrate on searching the sky without fear of colliding with their neighbour. Upon either being attacked or when 'bouncing' the enemy, the *schwarm* broke into the two fighting pairs. This worked perfectly, and remains, in fact, the basis of fighter combat even in our jet-powered age. Not only, of course, had the Germans worked these tactics out in Spain: the theory had also been put into practice over Poland in 1939, and in 1940 above France and the low countries. With the BEF now preparing to evacuate from Dunkirk, the Allies' various military deficiencies were only too evident. Terraine, however, argued that it was not simply the new panzers and *blitzkrieg* tactics that won the day:

> The German fighters – over 1,200 of them but above all the Me 109s – ruled the sky, and in so doing achieved, for the first time against a major enemy, the saturation of a battle area by air power, and that is what won the Battle of France ... The Allies had lost the battle to the achievement of complete air superiority by the German Air Force, enabling the Stukas to perform, the panzers to roam where they willed; this was an achievement above all of the fighter arm, in particular the Messerschmitt 109.[39]

No Me 109s, or indeed any other enemy aircraft, were encountered on Douglas's first patrol over the French coast. During the return flight, 222 Squadron was diverted to the Kentish coastal station at Manston. After re-fuelling it was off to Duxford, from where Mermagen was ordered to take his pilots to Hornchurch. From that Sector Station the Spitfire pilots of 54 and 65 Squadrons had already been in action for several days, their place in the line now being taken by 222 and 41 Squadrons. In the mess that night, Douglas spoke to some of the outgoing pilots of their experiences – and learned that all, without exception, actually agreed with his assessment of the area attacks insisted upon by Fighter Command. The suicidal impracticality of these had become immediately apparent, leading to their instant rejection. The problem now faced, though, was that new formations and tactics literally had to be worked out on the job – and a very dangerous one it was, considering the massive advantage in combat experience enjoyed by the enemy's fighter pilots. The Spitfire pilots were also disadvantaged in that they were operating across the sea; these were difficult times indeed.

On 29 May, 222 Squadron was up again, as Mermagen remembered: 'At 6.30 a.m. that day I led the Squadron, in fact a wing of several squadrons, on its first patrol of the Dunkirk beaches. The sortie lasted two hours and forty-five minutes – a long flight in a Spitfire.'[40] During that operation, 222 Squadron ran head-on into a gaggle of twin-engined Me 110s, which broke for cloud out of the Spitfires' guns' range. Mermagen, however, managed to hit one, chalking up 222's first combat victory. The next two days saw Mermagen's pilots patrol uneventfully. Of events on 1 June, Douglas later wrote,

We were all flying around up and down the coast near Dunkirk, looking for enemy aircraft which seemed also to be milling around with no particular cohesion. The sea from Dunkirk to Dover during those days of the evacuation looked like any coastal road in England on a bank holiday. It was solid with shipping. One felt one could walk across it without getting one's feet wet, or that's what it looked like from the air. There were naval escort vessels, sailing dinghies, rowing-boats, paddle-steamers, indeed every floating device known in this country. They were all taking British soldiers from Dunkirk back home. The oil-tanks just inside the harbour were ablaze, and you could identify Dunkirk from the Thames estuary by this huge pall of black smoke rising straight up in a windless sky. Our ships were being bombed by enemy aeroplanes up to about half way across the Channel and troops on the beaches were suffering the same attention. There were also German aircraft inland, strafing the remnants of the BEF fighting their way to the port.

I was flying along at 3,000 feet when an Me 109 appeared straight in front of me at about the same speed and going in the same direction. Like me, he must have been a beginner, because he stayed there while I shot him down, and I didn't get him with the first burst.[41]

Mermagen recalled their return from this particular sortie:

When we landed, Douglas stomped over to me and enthused 'I got five for certain, Tubby, old boy!' Now this was the first time we had met Me 109s, which were damn good aeroplanes, and everything happened very quickly indeed. To be certain of having destroyed five enemy aircraft in such circumstances was impossible. I said 'You're a bloody liar, Bader!' We credited him with one destroyed. Nevertheless, Bader was generally easy to keep in order, as it were, and had already proved to be an excellent flight commander.[42]

Douglas was also credited, in fact, with damaging an Me 110. 222 Squadron was up again later that day, Douglas writing of that sortie, 'Attacked two He 111s. Killed one rear gunner and damaged machine.'[43] Of this operation, Douglas wrote,

A day or two later I saw a Dornier bombing one of our ships. He was about a mile away and I rushed at him with the throttle wide open, giving myself just enough time for a hurried burst which silenced the rear-gunner. I had to pull up very quickly to avoid a collision. Thinking about it later that evening I got the message which every fighter pilot assimilates early in his career – if he hopes for a career at all. It is this: overtake your target slowly and relax before you start shooting; you will never get him in a hurry.[44]

Interestingly, Douglas recorded the enemy aircraft involved in his logbook – a note made at the time in an official record – as an He 111, but later referred to it as a 'Dornier', not that this mattered to those on the ship being bombed!

By 4 June, the evacuation was over. While the Fall of France was an unmitigated disaster of immeasurable proportion, the fact remained that 340,000 troops had been rescued. In spite of recent attempts by certain academics to marginalise the achievement and spirit of Dunkirk, this was an incredible achievement. Moreover, the Spitfire, in difficult circumstances, had acquitted itself well. During this vicious air fighting, Fighter Command lost 106 aircraft and 80 pilots; 130 German aircraft were lost. Indeed, Peach argued that over Dunkirk 'the balance in the air shifted to the RAF and its Spitfires'.[45] From a personal perspective, Douglas had now seen combat – and scored his first successes against the enemy. The RAF's experience over France had also confirmed his belief that the tacticians had got it wrong. Fortunately these deficiencies had been discovered just in time for a certain amount of positive adjustment before the enemy's crucial aerial assault on Britain itself. Douglas was even more convinced now that the experience of First World War fighter pilots held true: he who has the height advantage controls the battle, he who has the sun behind him achieves surprise – and he who gets in very close hits his target.[46] Flight Lieutenant Bader was not, of course, the only pilot to have realised this – but he doubtless expounded his theories loudest.

Burns cited the number of flying hours recorded in his hero's logbook – 767.25 – as evidence confirming Douglas to be 'one of the most experienced fighter pilots at that point in the war'.[47] Lucas argued that Douglas's flying time 'made him an experienced pilot at this stage of the war'.[48] But 'experienced' on what? The vast majority of those flying hours were on *biplanes* in peacetime – but it was experience on Spitfires and Hurricanes that counted now. Douglas, however, had accumulated but a handful of Hurricane hours at the CFS, and had only flown Spitfires for three months. His modest tally of enemy aircraft destroyed over Dunkirk was both equalled and exceeded by many other pilots. For example, the logbook of Flight Lieutenant Brian Lane, Douglas's former flight commander in 19 Squadron and dismissed by Brickhill as inexperienced, provides some interesting statistics – which are not atypical and rather put Flying Officer Bader's actual status in perspective. When Lane converted to Hurricanes in January 1939, he had a total of 468.52 flying hours – mostly on Gauntlet biplanes. By the time of Flying Officer Bader's arrival on 19 Squadron, in addition to his many Hurricane hours, Lane had added 53.20 hours on Spitfires. Upon conclusion of the Dunkirk fighting, Lane had a total of 780.30 hours – well over 300 of them on Hurricanes and Spitfires.[49] Lane was also credited with three enemy aircraft definitely destroyed, plus a 'probable', and received a DFC for his efforts. Pilot Officer Alan Deere of 54 Squadron destroyed at least six German aircraft over Dunkirk and was also awarded the DFC; there were others with similarly impressive scores. Douglas's experience, however, contrary to Burns' assertion, did *not* rank him among these men – although he yearned to be leading the pack.

On 12 June 1940, Air Vice-Marshal Leigh-Mallory visited the Sector Operations Room at Duxford. It is no surprise that Leigh-Mallory favourite Douglas flew the Spitfire required for a radio-test demonstrated to the AO. The following night, though, Douglas crashed another Spitfire; Mermagen: 'On that occasion Douglas came in far too high and far too fast. He went through a hedge. I drove over to pick him up and he was ranting, shouting that the flarepath was incorrectly laid out. I thought "Well, look at that, what a total lack of humility, he's blaming someone else now!"'[51] The Spitfire was badly damaged. Nonetheless, Mermagen was a fan: 'Douglas carried out several operational sorties under my command and displayed exceptional leadership qualities; he was a fine Spitfire pilot. He used to come stomping into dispersal saying "Come on chaps, get out of the way, I want a cup of coffee", barging everyone else aside, but the chaps loved him for it, he was a real morale booster.'[52] Mermagen's observation that Douglas was 'a fine Spitfire pilot' is surprising – more so is the 'Exceptional' rating that he officially gave his legless flight commander on 23 June 1940.[53] By now, however, Douglas had been earmarked for better things – in spite of his various blameworthy flying accidents. Wing Commander Woodhall:

Soon after the Fall of France, Leigh-Mallory rang me to say that 242 (Canadian) Squadron was reporting to Coltishall and would be under the operational control of my Duxford Sector. He told me that the Squadron had had a tough time in France, and that the ground crews had only just been evacuated via Cherbourg thanks to the resourcefulness of their adjutant, Flight Lieutenant Peter MacDonald MP. Their own CO had left them to their own devices after the pilots had landed in England, and the Squadron, led by Flying Officer Stan Turner, had landed at Coltishall with nothing but the uniforms they were wearing. Tools, spare kit, baggage, the lot, had been abandoned.

'LM' said, 'I've got to find them a new squadron commander but he's got to be good, because these chaps are Canadians and they've had a rough time. They are browned off with authority and need a good leader – any suggestions?'

At once I said, 'What about Douglas Bader?'

LM replied, 'I thought you'd say that. I think you are right.'[54]

Mermagen:

By the time Bader was promoted to command 242 Squadron, a Canadian unit suffering from poor morale, he was known personally to the AOC, Air Vice-Marshal Leigh-Mallory, who knew of his record and had particular respect for the way in which he had dealt with both the crash and amputations. I had spoken to Leigh-Mallory on several occasions, confirming that Bader was an 'above average' Spitfire pilot, a most mature character and quite an outstanding personality in Fighter Command. I feel certain that my high opinion of Douglas Bader helped him achieve such rapid promotion which he rightly deserved and as proven by his later service record.[55]

Mackenzie, however, questioned whether Mermagen 'still believed that Bader was the best of subordinates as a flight commander', emphasising that 'the accolades the 222 Squadron CO provided to a higher authority helped speed Bader's promotion, and therefore posting'.[56] That was certainly so, but Mermagen's foregoing opinion undoubtedly confirmed the genuinely high regard in which he held Douglas. The evidence thus far examined indicates that much of Douglas's flying experience was dated, and that he had comparatively little experience on the monoplane fighters; what he unquestionably was, nonetheless, was, as Mermagen said, at the age of thirty, 'a most mature character' and 'an outstanding personality'. It has also been acknowledged that Douglas was at his best when leading the team – he had, at last, got one: his own fighter squadron. Likewise, if it was a strong leader 242 Squadron required, it now had one. In that regard, Douglas Bader truly was *exceptional*.

Now Acting Squadron Leader Bader, Douglas had caught up with his Cranwell contemporaries – in an incredible four months since arriving to fly Spitfires with 19 Squadron. Indeed, just eight weeks ago he had been a lowly flying officer! During his years in the wilderness such a scenario had been unimaginable. Now Douglas could really get to work – and drove off on 23 June 1940 from Kirton to Coltishall, relishing the prospect: 'The AOC told me that the 242nd (Canadian) Squadron was a pretty brassed-off bunch; they lacked discipline and he thought that I might be some use in getting the thing straight. So I rushed off, thinking that this would be absolutely splendid!'[57]

8

242 (CANADIAN) SQUADRON

Driving through the night, confounded by the lack of signposts and uncooperative locals who viewed his inquiries as to Coltishall airfield's location with suspicion, Douglas arrived at the main gate tired and frustrated. It was not a good mixture, leading to an inauspicious start, which was far from 'splendid': 'When I got to the station where this squadron was I had some difficulty getting in, because the chap on the gate said "What's the password?". I replied, "You stupid prick, I don't know!"'[1] According to Brickhill, Douglas 'exploded' but was forced to simmer by the barrier for twenty minutes until the duty officer 'ruled that he was admissible'.[2] It could justifiably be asked what Acting Squadron Leader Douglas Bader expected? The country was at war and he was attempting to gain access to a service installation. It was entirely his responsibility to have obtained and be aware of the necessary password. Arguably, therefore, it was not the stoic sentry who behaved like a 'prick'.

The following morning, Douglas was delighted to find that Coltishall's resident Spitfire squadron, 66, was commanded by an old friend: Squadron Leader Rupert 'Lucky' Leigh. Breakfast was followed by an interview with the Station Commander, Wing Commander 'Bike' Biesiegel, who briefed Douglas on his new command. 242 Squadron had been formed at Church Fenton on

30 October 1939, the first Canadian squadron to do so. It had arrived at Coltishall only a short time before Squadron Leader Bader, having been severely mauled during the Battle of France. When the *blitzkrieg* began, the squadron had been operating with 1 Squadron at Châteaudun, from which it rapidly withdrew to Le Mans. By the campaign's conclusion what was left of 242 Squadron was at Nantes, without effective leadership, cohesion, or even its ground personnel, which were somewhere between Le Mans and the coast with the adjutant, Flight Lieutenant Peter 'Boozy Mac' MacDonald. There had certainly been a crisis of leadership in France, so far as this particular fighter squadron was concerned. The CO, a French Canadian, had a background in Training Command – not as a fighter leader. Unfortunately this political appointment was far from atypical even during those desperate days. In the face of Hitler's onslaught inspirational leadership was required – but neither the CO nor his flight commanders had the ability to provide it. The outcome was inevitable: only nine pilots survived the crucible of France. Douglas clearly had work to do, in order to restore morale and gain 242 Squadron's confidence – for all his faults, it was exactly this kind of challenge that brought out the best in Douglas Bader.

I found myself ... in conjunction with my adjutant, an elderly gentleman of the finest class who had been member for the Isle of Wight for the past plus 500 years, and had fought in World War One, he took me into a dispersal hut where these chaps were lying about on beds, wearing Mae Wests and flying clothes, and all reading comic strips. He said, 'Gentlemen, this is your new Squadron Commander, Squadron Leader Bader' – and for some extraordinary reason, because I had been trained at the RAF College Cranwell, I thought they might stand up. In fact some of them lowered their comics, looked over the top, obviously didn't care for what they saw, put the comics back up and went on reading! There was one chap lying with his back to me. He actually turned over, had a look, then turned back again and went on reading! I then told the adjutant that I wanted to see all of the pilots in my office.

During the interval, of an hour and ten minutes, 242 Squadron's new CO took off in Hurricane P2967 on what he described in his logbook as 'Practice on type'.[3] More accurately this was a breathtaking display of low-level aerobatics – intended to impress upon the disgruntled pilots that, even without legs, their new CO was no passenger and that things had changed.

'They arrived and I gave them what I thought was a reasonable three-minute talk. When finished I said "Has anybody got anything to say?" There was a long silence, then, from the back of the room a voice said "Horseshit!" Again, they hadn't taught me at Cranwell what to do in such a situation. As I was getting rather red around the neck and face, and was about to make a bloody fool of myself, the same voice added "Sir!"'.[4] A lively discussion then ensued, in which Douglas was enlightened as to why morale was so poor: even the pilots' clothes, left behind in France, had yet to be replaced, and neither had they been paid for some time. Immediately recognising the urgent need for strong leadership in all aspects, Douglas firstly sent his pilots clothes shopping in Norwich, personally guaranteeing payment, then established a new command team: Flight Lieutenant Eric Ball was brought in from 19 Squadron to command 'A' Flight, and Flight Lieutenant

George Powell-Sheddon, an ex-Cranwellian, came from the Fighter Command Pool to command 'B' Flight. There was already another young British officer flying with 242 Squadron, Pilot Officer Denis Crowley-Milling. An Old Malvernian who had joined he RAFVR, 'Crow' remembered that

> when he received command of 242 Squadron, Douglas Bader was approaching thirty whilst the rest of us were around twenty or twenty-one. After France we were in a bad state, but less than a month after Douglas took command the Squadron was fully operational – and our morale was high. Fear was always there, of course, but Bader was afraid of nothing. Through personal example and constant encouragement he helped us all conquer our anxieties. You always felt perfectly safe when flying with Douglas Bader. For me, his arrival at Coltishall was the start of eighteen exciting months of operational flying together, an unforgettable experience which helped shape my subsequent career.'[5]

As Lucas wrote, 'A super-charged injection of air was sweeping through the Squadron.'[6]

In addition to 242 Squadron's pilots' problems, its Hurricanes had suffered too: although eighteen new aircraft were on charge, no spare parts or tools were on the inventory. Douglas's next port of call was the Squadron's Engineering Officer, Warrant Officer Bernard 'Knocker' West. For the next few days, Douglas berated Coltishall's Stores Officer, but his forthright demands for equipment fell upon deaf ears. After a week of this, West informed his CO that stores had cited an obscure regulation confirming a three-month wait before fresh equipment could be ordered.

Justifiably on this occasion, Douglas was absolutely furious. In response, on 4 July 1940, he sent an unprecedented signal to 12 Group HQ: '242 Squadron now operational as regards pilots but non-operational repeat non-operational as regards equipment.'[7] He then lurched into the Station Commander's office and showed the flimsy to him. A heated scene ensued, and West could not believe his eyes when he read the signal shortly afterwards. What Douglas failed to tell his boss, but not Mr West, was that a copy had also been sent to Fighter Command HQ. The response came that evening from the latter. An unhelpful squadron leader concluded by pointing out that Dowding himself was 'furious' – before having the phone virtually rammed down his ear.[8] Two days later Douglas was carpeted before the AOC himself: Air Chief Marshal Sir Hugh Dowding. Suffice it to say that Douglas got his way: the obstructive Stores Officer found himself removed from his cushy HQ post and 242 Squadron's much-needed equipment was soon arriving.

Of Douglas's dismissive view of administration, however, 'Woody' Woodhall wrote,

Douglas was very apt to cut corners and ignore regulations or interpret them his own way in order to get on with the war. On one occasion when he had offended against some rule, I was given orders from a higher authority to reprove him. He was ordered to report to my office, and when he stumped in and saluted with his usual cheerful grin he noticed that I was wearing my cap and did not tell him to sit down, indicating an official interview. Douglas stood to attention and with an impish grin said, 'Woody, you're not going to be rotten to me, are you?' What could I do but laugh, then tell him to sit down? Needless to say the reproof was passed to him as a joke – but the fact that it *was* passed on proved quite effective. The administrative and operational tasks and problems increased daily, and hampered as we were by a set of peacetime rules and regulations, designed as they were in the main to prevent petty pilfering, it is not surprising that everyone trying to do his job had to cut the red tape in order to get on with the war. In this Douglas Bader and I saw eye-to-eye, and I can state that we backed each other up loyally in this matter of tape-cutting. LM, our AOC, was always on our side too, which was very comforting![9]

David Evans was a member of 242 Squadron's ground crew:

When Douglas Bader arrived at Coltishall, there was a little resentment and the feeling generally was 'Who the hell is this newly promoted squadron leader without legs, who has seen little action, coming to tell us how to do it after we had been in the Battle of France?' By example, however, Squadron Leader Bader gained our respect – but he was undoubtedly an autocrat. I always felt that Squadron Leader Bader bullied our Engineering Officer, Warrant Officer West, a bit to keep the aircraft serviceable. At the time Coltishall was a grass airfield, and the squadron was soon flying endless convoy protection patrols. I was a flight mechanic and in view of this constant flying keeping our Hurricanes serviceable was an exhausting undertaking. We used to work a pattern of shifts, 0800 until noon on the first day, 1630–0800 the following, and finally 1430–1630. We had the use of a Nissen hut at dispersal but it was such a lovely summer that more often than not we would just kip down beneath the mainplanes. Many of the ground personnel were Canadians who had enlisted in the RAF with a view to flying – an ambition some later achieved through Squadron Leader Bader's encouragement, help and recommendation. Certainly our CO couldn't tolerate inefficiency or incompetence and made this very plain to all and sundry. I wonder whether this is why he fast gained a reputation of being rather bloody-minded and arrogant. I would prefer to think it more a case of single-mindedness as his priority was to beat the Germans – which was after all the object of the exercise. I will always recall Squadron Leader Bader working his way backwards on his backside along the port mainplane until reaching the cockpit, when he then went into a practised routine of swinging his right leg up into it. He was a very brave man – make no mistake.[10]

Hard taskmaster though Douglas was, he was in his element: and would defend any member of 242 Squadron to the hilt, if necessary. 'I felt they were *mine*, all the pilots and troops. I used to get furious if anyone said anything about them or did anything to them, and I arranged with Norwich police that they never put my chaps on a charge but sent the matter to me to deal with. I was tough with them myself, but always closed ranks if anyone else tried to interfere. I suppose I was unreasonable in my attitude to the squadron, but it was an obsession with me and I would not brook interference.'[11] Incredibly, this stance even extended to the Station Commander. When several of 242 Squadron's ground crew contravened blackout restrictions, Biesegel's punishment was making them sleep in a hangar. This, however, was done without reference to 242 Squadron's CO, who, furious, stormed into the Wing Commander's office and called him 'a bastard'. Such insubordination was, and is, unthinkable. In the face of such a determined verbal assault the Station Commander backed down – no one, it seemed, could resist the sheer force of Douglas Bader's incredible personality.[12]

On 29 June, Douglas had begun an intensive programme of flying training. Naturally, the emphasis was on aerobatics – but not to thrill crowds at Hendon; there was now a deadly purpose to those loops and rolls, as Douglas wrote: 'If you have been used to controlling an aeroplane upside down, side-ways or in a vertical dive or upward zoom you have become used to being in those odd positions with the ground instead of the sky above your head and your mind remains clear. You find yourself in all these positions in combat and you don't get flustered. As a result you can shoot in whatever position you may find yourself.'[13] Over a period of eight days, 242 Squadron practised aerobatics for ten hours and twenty minutes, a punishing schedule requiring utmost concentration. On 6 July, 242 Squadron spent the day practice firing at Sutton Bridge – achieving a record score and evidencing the fact that 242 Squadron had been restored to a disciplined, motivated fighting unit. As Douglas himself later said, 'It did not take long for me to get this Squadron back into first-class shape.'[14] Fortunately, after the Fall of France, Hitler had paused – providing a lull during which, up there in 12 Group, Douglas had been able to concentrate entirely on re-organising and inspiring his squadron – unfettered by action with the Luftwaffe. This provident break enabled Squadron Leader Douglas Bader to perform what undoubtedly amounted to an exceptional feat of dynamic leadership.

The matter of air fighting continued to obsess Douglas, and he expounded his theories at every opportunity. Having seen action over Dunkirk, he was even more convinced that his ideas were right – and that Fighter Command was wrong; Wing Commander George 'Grumpy' Unwin:

The tacticians who wrote the book really believed that in the event of war it would be fighter *versus* bomber only. What they could not foresee was Hitler's modern ground tactics that would take his armies to the Channel ports in an unprecedented period of time – thus providing bases for his fighters in the Pas-de-Calais and putting southern England within their limited range. Our tight formations were all very well for the Hendon Air Pageant but useless in combat. Our CO in 19 Squadron, Douglas Bader's friend Geoffrey Stephenson, was a prime example: without modern combat experience he flew exactly by the book on our first sortie covering the Dunkirk evacuation – and was in effect shot down by it.[15]

Indeed, contrary to the pre-war belief that air warfare would be dominated by the all-conquering bomber, it was actually the Me 109 single-engined German fighter which had dominated the battlefields of France. Far from fighter combat being impossible due to the high speeds achieved by monoplanes, the Battle of France and Operation DYNAMO confirmed it just as common an occurrence as during the First World War. In his early opinion that this would be so, Douglas had been exactly right. While it could be considered that his forceful comments on this subject while a flying officer without actual combat experience on 19

Squadron had been insubordinate and undermining, as a squadron commander with aerial victories under his belt he was now in a position of both command and credibility. In short, Douglas Bader was in his absolute element – the wilderness years forgotten.

On 18 June 1940, the British Prime Minister, Winston Churchill, had stirred the nation's spirit with his usually inspirational rhetoric, making perfectly clear what lay ahead:

The Battle of France is over. I expect that the Battle of Britain is about to begin ... The whole fury and might of the enemy must very soon be turned on us. Hitler knows that he will have to break us in this island or lose the war. If we can stand up to him, all Europe may be free and the life of the world may move forward into broad, sunlit uplands. But if we fail, then the whole world, including the United States, including all that we have known and cared for, will sink into the abyss of a new Dark Age, made more sinister by the lights of perverted science. Let us therefore brace ourselves to our duties, and so bear ourselves that if the British Empire and its Commonwealth should last for a thousand years, men will still say, 'This was their finest hour.'

The Battle of Britain predicted by Churchill began on 10 July 1940 – just one day after Squadron Leader Bader declared 242 Squadron fully operational.

9

THE SYSTEM

Before continuing with the main narrative, at this juncture it is necessary to explain the system of air defence and background which really underpinned the remainder of Douglas Bader's war – and had far-reaching consequences.

When Britain belatedly began re-arming in 1935, air defence was co-ordinated by the Air Defence of Great Britain (ADGB). In 1936, the single command was divided into Fighter and Bomber Commands. Fighter Command was created on 6 July 1936, its headquarters located at Bentley Priory, near Stanmore, to the north of London. On 14 July, the new command's first AOC-in-C was appointed: Air Marshal Sir Hugh Caswell Tremenheere Dowding.

Born at Moffat on 24 April 1882, Dowding was commissioned into the Garrison Artillery in 1899. By 1912 he was at the Military Staff College, Camberley, at which time he learned to fly privately. By 23 July 1915, he was commanding 16 Squadron of the Royal Flying Corps, serving in France and engaged upon observation duties. It was then that Dowding first came into conflict with Major-General 'Boom' Trenchard. Dowding was technically minded, and complained when his squadron received a batch of wrong-sized propellers. Trenchard objected to his subordinate's 'pernickety primness'; Dowding fitted the propeller and was nearly killed in the subsequent test flight. While Trenchard considered the incident typical of Dowding's self-righteous stubbornness, the latter thought it 'typical of Trenchard's technical stupidity'.[1] After further clashes, Dowding was posted home on New Year's Day 1917, and replaced as leader of 9 Wing by Lieutenant-Colonel Cyril Newall. By the Armistice, both men were Brigadier Generals, albeit temporary ones – but Newall was Trenchard's deputy.

It was Trenchard, of course, who became the first Chief of the Air Staff (CAS) upon foundation of the RAF in 1918. Echoing the prevalent air power doctrine of the day, in 1921 Trenchard said that 'it is on the destruction of enemy industries and, above all, in the lowering of morale of enemy national caused by bombing that the ultimate victory lies', adding that 'the aeroplane is the most offensive weapon that has ever been invented. It is a shockingly bad weapon for defence.' In fact, Trenchard thought so little of defensive fighters that he considered them necessary only 'to have some defence to keep up the morale of your own people'.[2] The British Prime Minister Stanley Baldwin emphasised these points to the House of Commons in 1932: 'The bomber will always get through. The only defence is offence.' Like most other people he believed in the dreaded 'knockout blow'.[3] Dowding disagreed. Resisting Trenchard's obsession with offence, he steadfastly maintained that 'security of the base must come first'.[4] Completely opposed to Trenchard's view, he wrote that 'the best defence of the country is fear of the fighter. If we were strong in fighters we should never be attacked in force. If we are moderately strong we shall probably be attacked and the attacks will gradually be brought to a standstill ... If we are weak in fighter strength, the attacks will not be brought to a standstill and the productive capacity of the country will be virtually destroyed.'[5] Dowding's argument, however, was not that the fighter force should be expanded at the expense of the bomber force – it was simply that a powerful bomber force would be useless unless the fighter force was strong enough to keep that force safe. In an age when air power thinking and, it must be said, careers were dominated by bombers endorsing Trenchard's views, Dowding was unusual in that he took a keen interest in defence – his belief that 'security of the base must come first' was absolutely unshakeable.

On 14 January 1935, Dowding became Air Council Member for Research and Development. This was a new post, formed in response to Dowding's own concerns as head of Supply and Organisation, that Britain was lagging behind compared to certain other nations – not least Hitler's Germany. From that point onwards, Dowding was heavily involved in the development of the key things associated with the aerial defence of Britain in 1940: the new monoplane fighters and Radio Direction Finding (RDF) – more commonly known as radar. The RAF air exercise in 1934, in fact, had shown the weakness of the existing 'early warning system' which relied upon the eyes and ears of the Observer Corps. The 'early warning' of approaching aircraft could only be given, therefore, providing they ventured within sight and/or earshot. In his new post, Dowding far-sightedly backed research being undertaken in the area of RDF. In 1935, the scientist Robert Watson-Watt confirmed that radar worked, and identified three areas where radio waves could help: the detection of aircraft, identification of friendly aircraft, and communication between fighters and a ground controller. This was inspired – and became the cornerstone of the radar-based system of Early Warning, Interception and Control. Without these things, it is doubtful that Britain could have defended itself at all in 1940 against modern aircraft – and Dowding had played a key role in the procurement of these weapons. No one, therefore, was better placed to become

Fighter Command's first Commander-in-Chief. His immediate aim to help create the ideal air defence system.

At this time Britain was divided into two groups: 11, with responsibility for London and the South, and 12, protecting the industrial Midlands and the North. 13 Group was soon added, covering the North of England and Ireland, but 10 Group, presiding over the South West of England and South Wales, would not become operational until 8 July 1940. Between the wars, any aerial attacks were expected to approach from the east, over the North Sea. Although 11 Group included the prestigious capital, it was actually 12 Group which was expected to meet the brunt of any attacks, as enemy aircraft approached from Germany – and therefore represented the most crucial responsibility. Air Marshal Leslie Gossage was given command of 11 Group, while 12 Group went to Air Commodore Trafford Leigh-Mallory. A Cambridge history graduate, Leigh-Mallory was wounded in 1915, serving with the King's Liverpool Regiment, before volunteering for the RFC and flying observation aircraft over the trenches. Indeed, he both became and remained, according to Robert Wright, 'an expert' in army co-operation.[6] By the First World War's end, Major Leigh-Mallory was a squadron commander, decorated with the Distinguished Service Order (DSO); he had no experience whatsoever of fighters, and nor did he gain any between the wars and before, incredibly, being selected as AOC 12 Group. This was undoubtedly a career appointment. In 1933, Group Captain Leigh-Mallory had attended the Imperial Defence College – the most senior staff college – indicating that he was destined for high office. Although he had no fighter experience, the fact is that at that level of command, few did. There would, however, be far-reaching consequences for an expert in army co-operation – and not fighters – being entrusted with a fighter group at a crucial moment in Britain's history.

In July 1938, Air Commodore Keith Park – a tough New Zealander – reported to Fighter Command HQ as the AOC's Senior Air Staff Officer (SASO). Wounded at Gallipoli in 1916, Park transferred to the RFC and became a fighter pilot – an ace with the Military Cross (MC) and Bar to his credit. As a fighter leader, Park had gained valuable experience and earned respect. By 1920 he had been permanently commissioned into the RAF and was a flight lieutenant commanding the surplus aircraft store at Hawkinge. A certain Squadron Leader Sholto Douglas suggested that he and Park, together with a third pilot, should make ready three of those aircraft and perform a truly daredevil low-level fly-by at that year's Hendon display. Park agreed. The crowd were thrilled but Trenchard less so – who rebuked Douglas, another career officer. According to Park's biographer, Vincent Orange, Douglas and Park 'were never on close terms after this incident'.[7] Although both Douglas and Park were both on the first intake at the RAF's new staff college at Andover, the rift was not healed – but Park did engage favourably with another key wartime RAF personality: Charles Portal. These alliances and squabbles, in equal measure, would later have significant consequences.

After a tour of duty in Egypt ended prematurely due to ill health, in 1926 Park was appointed to the staff of Air Marshal Sir John Salmond, chief of ADGB. Park commanded the 'Operations, Intelligence, Mobilisation and Combined Training' department. Next stop was command of a fighter squadron, 111. In 1929, more staff duties followed, this time at HQ Fighting Area, Uxbridge; his Fighting Area commander was Air Vice-Marshal Dowding. Further flying appointments had followed. In 1937, Group Captain Park became commander of RAF Tangmere, a famous fighter station near Chichester. On 1 July 1938 he was promoted to air commodore – and became Dowding's SASO at Fighter Command. There can be no doubt that outside of Germany, Air Commodore Keith Park was one of the most experienced officers of air rank where fighters were concerned. Park immediately understood Fighter Command's planned method of operation, and helped his boss improve it.

By this time, the advent of radar and improved air-to-ground communications had permitted a complete overhaul of the system of fighter control and interception. Although one of the many myths surrounding the Battle of Britain is that Dowding single-handedly envisioned and created 'The System', that is untrue – although Dowding, when Air Member for Research and Development, had provided the necessary tools and understood how best to use them. Indeed, that experience perfectly placed Dowding as the right man to oversee the re-organisation of Britain's air defences. Much, though, was based upon conjecture, as Overy argued: 'There was so little experience to draw on about the kind of air war most powers expected to fight ... As powers became more aware of what potential air enemies were preparing to do, the initial guesswork was often modified or abandoned.'[8] The resulting 'guesswork' became known as the 'Dowding System'. So crucial is an understanding of it in relation to this book, that the whole system is described below – extracted from a 1943 Air Ministry pamphlet.

Fighter Command

At the time of the Battle of Britain, Fighter Command was organized into four Fighter Groups. Each group was, for purposes of tactical control, subdivided geographically into a number of sectors. A sector consisted of a main fighter station and airfield, sector headquarters and operations room, also one or more satellite or forward airfields upon which were based a number of squadrons varying in accordance with the situation and the need for good dispersal.

No. 11 Group's area covered South-East England and, consequently, it was this group which bore the brunt of the fighting, although other groups extensively reinforced the air battle from time to time and, in addition, fed into No. 11 Group a regular supply of fresh squadrons to relieve those worn down by intensive air fighting.

Operations Rooms

The heart of each headquarters at command, groups, and sectors, was its operations room. This varied somewhat in size and complexity depending upon the scope and function of the headquarters and upon the amount of detail regarding our own squadrons that it was necessary for the commander to have before him; but the ultimate object of all operations rooms remained the same, namely, to ensure the utmost rapidity in the issue of orders. For time was the essence of the problem; with machines of war moving at the rate of 5 miles a minute, the issue of written orders was out of the question and the only possible course was to cut the length of orders to a minimum and to use direct telephone, whether landline or radio. To effect this, the operations room had, first, to portray physically the movements of enemy aircraft and, where necessary, of our own fighters, over the whole country and the sea approaches thereto (or such part as was appropriate to the headquarters concerned); secondly, to show how soon and in what strength our own squadrons could leave the ground; and, thirdly, to provide an adequate and reasonably secure network of communications both by landline and radio telephony.

Air Raid Intelligence

The essential basis of any air defence system is, of course, a good air-raid intelligence system. In this country, during the Battle of Britain, as now, such a system comprised a chain of radio location stations sited around our coasts. The function of these stations was the detection of all aircraft approaching this country over the sea. This early warning was vital since the German Air Force was in occupation of airfields just the other side of the Straits of Dover, which could be crossed in four or five minutes. It was supplemented over the land by the Observer Corps, whose function was to take over and 'tell on' the tracks of all aircraft as they crossed our coasts and proceeded inland to their targets.

During the Battle of Britain, information received by radio location was transmitted to Fighter Command headquarters and after passing through a 'filter room' was telephoned direct to one of the plotters in the Command operations room and simultaneously to those at the group and sectors affected. Information received from the Observer Corps followed the reverse course, being passed through observer centres to fighter groups and sectors and repeated by the group tellers to Fighter Command and adjacent groups.

Display of Information

In all Fighter Command operation rooms was a large table map upon which this air-raid intelligence could be accurately plotted as tracks, after such tracks had been identified as hostile, friendly or doubtful. Seated round the table map were a number of plotters, each one connected by a landline to the appropriate reporting centre. From these centres the plotters received minute-to-minute information of the progress of enemy aircraft towards and over this country, together with their numbers and height. The plotter displayed, on the table map suitable symbols indicating the identity, numbers, height and track of the aircraft concerned. Thus each R.A.F. commander, from the Commander-in-Chief in his operations room at Fighter Command down to the sector commander in his operations room at a fighter station or airfield, -had continually before him the same moving picture of the enemy as the situation continually changed at the speed of modern flight. Naturally the area that had to be covered by the picture presented to a Sector Commander was much smaller than the area required for the command or group operations room, but in so far as their responsibilities were severally affected, it was the same picture.

During the heavy attacks in September it was found that in No. 11 Group Headquarters operations room the table got too congested, so all detail regarding enemy raids and the fighter squadrons detailed to intercept was transferred to a slotted black-board on the wall known as the Totalisator, leaving the map clear except for the raid numbers and symbols for our squadrons in the air.

Each operations room contained an elevated dais which might extend much of the way round the room; a gallery was sometimes added between the dais and the floor of the room. On the wall was shown complete meteorological information including wind and clouds and, at groups and sectors, the strength and degree of readiness of our own squadrons. In sector operations rooms arrangements existed whereby the minute-to-minute position of our own fighters was also plotted on the table map.

Transmission of Information and Orders

In the centre of the dais sat the Controller with his assistants responsible for the issue of orders. In the gallery or on the dais sat the tellers who passed on the information appearing on the table map to plotters in other operations rooms. Accommodation on the dais was provided for representatives of the Observer Corps, A.A. guns and searchlights and the Ministry of Home Security. Very complete intercommunication was provided; for instance, the Controller in a group operations room could, by moving a switch, speak directly to any of his sectors, and the Controller in a sector operations room could speak through R/T with any of his squadrons in the air or at their dispersal points on the ground.

At Fighter Command headquarters was the main operations room. In addition to the Commander-in-Chief Fighter Command and his staff, it contained the Commander-in-Chief A.A. Defences and the Observer Corps Commandant, or their representatives, liaison officers from the Admiralty, Bomber and Coastal Commands, as well as a Home Security official. It fulfilled many functions. Information from the various sources was co-ordinated and analysed and the reported formation identified as friendly or hostile and, if the latter, was allotted a number. Where any doubt existed as to the responsibility, raids were allotted to groups. The air raid warning system was operated through certain trunk exchanges in direct telephone communication. The Commander-in-Chief Fighter Command exercised general control over the opening of A.A. gunfire and the exposure of searchlights, through the Commander-in-Chief, A.A. Command. He also controlled the balloon barrage through his group commanders. Group commanders decided which sector should meet any specified raid and the strength of the fighter force to be employed. Sector Commanders detailed the fighter units.

Responsibility of Commanders

This system enabled R.A.F. commanders at each different level immediately to dispose their 'air forces to meet any situation as it could be seen threatening or developing before his eyes on the table map. It enabled the Commander-in-Chief to reinforce groups with fighters from an adjacent group as and when he saw where the weight of the enemy's attack was likely to fall. It enabled a group commander to organize his squadrons in the various sectors at the appropriate states of preparedness to leave the ground and to. order his readiness squadrons off the ground at a moment's notice. It enabled a sector commander to carry out interceptions with incoming raids; since he could see on his table map the minute-to-minute position, course and height both of the incoming enemy formation and of his own outgoing intercepting fighters. He could thus, by R/T, issue orders to his formation leaders in the air, giving the compass course to steer and height at which to fly so as to ensure the best chance of interception.

When once visual contact in the air with the enemy raid had been made, the executive control of the fighters passed automatically from the sector commander in the operations room to the man on the spot, the leader of the fighters, who, in turn, issued to his pilots by radio telephony his executive orders for the conduct of the ensuing air battle. Interception depended finally on being able to see the enemy, so although the system worked well by day, it was not sufficiently accurate to effect interception at night against raiders not illuminated by searchlights.

When the battle was joined, it was the function of the sector commander or his representative in his operations room to 'listen-in' and observe radio silence during the fighting, unless it appeared that other enemy fighters or bombers were approaching the area, when the formation leaders were duly informed. Immediately the battle was over, it became the function again of the sector commander to take control and assist his pilots to regain their home base or nearest airfield if necessary, particularly when, as often happened, squadrons became much split up during a dog-fight or when bad weather intervened and petrol was low.

Group, and, in a less degree, sector commanders had many factors to keep in mind: the necessity for holding some squadrons in reserve to meet further attacks that might develop at short notice; recalling squadrons at the right moment to land for re-fuelling and re-arming; petrol endurance; probable expenditure of ammunition. All these had constantly to be weighed up and decisions made very rapidly.

The whole technique of operating fighters in defence of Great Britain and the facilities provided in Fighter Command operations rooms were the result of a steady process of development over many years. Arrangements are never static. Improvements in methods, in layout and in equipment of operations rooms, are constantly being introduced. However, the existing arrangements today are, in their essentials, the same as they were in the days of the Battle of Britain.

A.A. Guns

The anti-aircraft guns, under the Command of General Sir Frederick Pile, took no small toll of enemy aircraft, and during the heavy attacks on London rendered great service in turning them back, both by day and night, through the weight of their barrage. On some nights as many as 60 per cent, of the enemy aircraft approaching London from the South, dropped their bombs in open country or on the fringe of the barrage, and then went home. They also rendered direct service to our fighter aircraft, first by breaking up enemy formations, thus rendering them more vulnerable to fighter attacks, and secondly by indicating to our pilots in the air the position of enemy aircraft by shell bursts. On the dais are the tellers, passing on plots as they appear on the centre table to fighter group and sector operations rooms and adjacent observer centres.

Where conditions permit, posts are spaced so that all aircraft flying over the country are within sight or sound of at least one post and continuous tracks are therefore obtained at the centres.

Each track is given a separate symbol to maintain its identity, and when 'seen' the height and number of aircraft are reported and 'told' forward. The Observer Corps organization was the sole method of tracking enemy aircraft overland during the battle, and its efficiency enabled many successful interceptions to be made and this contributed in no small degree to the result. It was also essential for the air raid warning systems.

In addition to the work in connection with Air Defence the organization was of great value in enabling our own aircraft, lost in thick weather or at night, to be grounded. Any aircraft thought to be in difficulty owing to its erratic course, the sound of its engines or distress signals was specially tracked and told forward. In some cases R.A.F. airfields were asked by centres to light their landing lights and fire pyrotechnics to help the aircraft down.

The organization was a very democratic one, members being drawn from all classes of society, but all were animated by the knowledge that their work was of vital importance to the country and to the Royal Air Force. Their skill at recognition reached an astonishingly high standard. During the severest winter known for half a century, every post and every centre was continuously manned day and night by these civilian volunteers, many of them over sixty years of age. Their motto is 'Forewarned is Fore-armed'.[9]

This, then, was the defensive system that would hopefully save Britain from a 'knock-out blow'. It is staggering, however, that irrefutable evidence exists from as early as 1938 confirming that the AOC of 12 Group, Leigh-Mallory, the army co-operation expert, failed to understand it. In October 1938, Leigh-Mallory reported on his air defences. At that time, Hurricanes and Spitfires had begun replacing biplanes – but Leigh-Mallory's memorandum made no mention of them whatsoever, concentrating his thoughts only on two-gun biplanes. Significantly it was parochial, considering local as opposed to overall defence, not to mention showing no appreciation of the newly expanded searchlight areas or communications. Fighter Command possessed but forty-one squadrons, twenty-nine of which Leigh-Mallory demanded for 12 Group. This was absurd, leaving only twelve squadrons to defend London and the South! Dowding told his SASO that Leigh-Mallory's report 'shows a misconception of the basic ideas of fighter defence'. The AOC-in-C spoke personally to the commander of 12 Group – but 'unfortunately, Dowding did not seek his replacement'.[10] This took place a month after Munich, at a point in time when, in spite of the British Prime Minister Neville Chamberlain's triumphant return to Heston, clutching his piece of paper supposedly guaranteeing peace, it was obvious that war with Germany was ultimately inevitable. That the commander of 12 Group demonstrated such clear incompetence at such a juncture was bad enough, but for his superior not to replace him with a more suitable commander is equally astonishing. The following year, in response to Dowding's inquiry as to whether Duxford should remain in 12 Group or be transferred to 11, Park's view was that it should remain with Leigh-Mallory. In so deciding, Dowding's SASO set in train a course of events in which Squadron Leader Douglas Bader would soon feature prominently.

Without precedent and given that monoplane fighters were new, the size of intercepting formations was mooted. On 9 August 1939, the Air Ministry wrote to Dowding on the subject of 'Tactics *v.* Massed Bomber Formations', concluding with the Air Fighting Development Establishment's (AFDE) view that a tactical unit bigger than one squadron was impractical and that formations of up to squadron strength were required for interceptions. Ten days later, Dowding replied. The training required for mass fighter formation deployment, he pointed out, was extensive and impractical, confirming that 'we are working towards the habitual deployment of complete squadrons'. Nonetheless – and this is crucially important – he added that he did not 'discount the possibility of mass deployment at some future time', emphasising that to do so now, however, would be 'premature'. Dowding's personal opinion, though, which he did not want to over-stress, was 'that the squadron will always be the largest tactical unit which it will be practically expedient to deploy'. Speed in delivering an attack, he stated, should not be sacrificed 'for theoretical advantages which are likely to be illusory in practice'. The important thing to note is that the size of intercepting formations had been very carefully considered before the war.

In September 1939, Leigh-Mallory caused further concern at Bentley Priory. Dowding had expressly told his group commanders not to issue their own local instructions in addition to Fighter Command Battle Orders. These included the movement of squadrons, Dowding having fully appreciated that reacting quickly to developing military situations would require his squadrons the ability to move freely throughout his command. Local orders, therefore, only confused the issue. In spite of having been told to cancel his local orders of 5 September, Leigh-Mallory wrote further to his sectors and Dowding, concerning the disposition of squadrons: 'In view of the small number of squadrons in any one sector, and taking into consideration the fact that the Germans may deliver large-scale raids on such important places as Birmingham, Derby and Sheffield, it is highly desirable that it should be possible to concentrate aircraft from as many other sectors as possible onto the front of the threatened target.' On 1 October 1939, Dowding replied, indicating that under the circumstances he had found much of Leigh-Mallory's communication 'difficult to understand'. Tellingly, Dowding's fourth and final paragraphs read thus:

> Now I have delegated tactical control almost completely to groups and sectors, but I have not delegated strategic control, and the threat to the line must be regarded as a whole and not parochially. The units at Debden and Duxford may be urgently required at short notice for the defence of London and, although they have been put under you in order to balance the number of stations in groups, this function of theirs must not be overlooked.
>
> Please do not think that I am criticising you in this letter. I admire the energy and foresight which you are bringing to your task. I would only ask you to remember that Fighter Command has to operate as a whole, and reinforcements and readjustments may have to be made between groups and not within them. We require a simple, flexible, system which can be put into effect at short notice and with the minimum of preliminary arrangement.

Dowding had clearly laid out to Leigh-Mallory what he, the Commander-in-Chief, required. Nonetheless, as Orange wrote, 'keeping Leigh-Mallory in line with the rest of the command proved an endless task'.[11] The matter of how many fighter squadrons were at his disposal, however, was a far more pressing concern than corresponding with Leigh-Mallory, and regarding this critical issue Dowding was engaged in protracted communication with the Under-Secretary of State for Air. Further correspondence from Leigh-Mallory, coupled with his failure in at least two air exercises, however, led to the commander of 12 Group being summoned to Bentley Priory for an interview with his boss. Afterwards, Park remembered how Leigh-Mallory had strode into his office: 'He was very angry and made a rude comment about what he called Dowding's obstinacy. He said that he would move heaven and earth to get Dowding sacked from his job. I was very annoyed at this and told Leigh-Mallory so. Although at the time I was an Air Commodore and he an Air Vice-Marshal, I told him just what I thought of his remark and his obvious disloyalty.'[12]

Although 12 Group was considered the front line, 11 Group, because it included London, was looked upon as the most senior appointment. Having been promoted to Air Vice-Marshal and given command of 12 Group in December 1937, Leigh-Mallory could arguably have expected to take over 11 Group. On 13 April 1940, Leigh-Mallory was rightly passed over when Park was promoted to Air Vice-Marshal and entrusted with the London's defence. This was undoubtedly the perfect choice. In addition to his personal fighter experience, Park had been Dowding's SASO for two years and fully understood both the system and what the Commander-in-Chief required from his subordinates – his loyalty and integrity were unquestionable. Dowding had laid down the strategy – the tactics of the battle ahead would be for Air Vice-Marshal Park to decide.

10

BATTLE OF BRITAIN

Since the Fall of France, the Luftwaffe had amassed its units in France in preparation for a determined aerial assault upon England. Wresting aerial supremacy from the RAF had but one purpose: to facilitate the seaborne invasion of England. Although the Air Ministry decided that Churchill's anticipated 'Battle of Britain' began on 10 July 1940, the two fighter forces had clashed over Channel convoys frequently during the previous fortnight. With convoys frequently chugging around the Wash, Coltishall's squadrons found themselves flying numerous patrols over the supply ships.

Naturally enemy reconnaissance aircraft were very active. Throughout the morning of 11 July, these intruders constantly monitored British coastal waters – over eighty such sorties were plotted by RDF stations from the north of Scotland to Land's End. On one such flight a Do 17 of *Wetterkingsdungsstaffel* 261 snooped around off Yarmouth, reporting on weather conditions off the east coast. At 0600 hours, Squadron Leader Rupert Leigh and Sergeant Reg Hyde of 66 Squadron intercepted the Dornier – return fire from which holed Leigh's oil tank. As the CO of 66 Squadron nursed his damaged Spitfire, the enemy aircraft slid into low cloud and made off.[1] The Controller, according to Brickhill, had asked Douglas if, in view of the bad weather, it was possible to get a section of 242 Squadron Hurricanes up and search for a 'bandit' off Cromer. The CO declined but agreed to go himself.[2] Given the weather, with thick cloud between 1,000 and 2,500 feet,[3] his take off, at 0600, was virtually on instruments. According to Burns, who incorrectly cites the Controller's call as having taken place at 0700, 'the cloud lifted to 1,000 feet over the coast ... Then, surprised, he saw it, barely 400 yards in front of him;'[4] Lucas wrote the same.[5] Turner described Douglas sighting the Do 17 'a couple of miles off the Norfolk coast from Cromer',[6] Brickhill that the raider was 'far ahead'.[7] Regardless, Douglas opened fire from 200 yards, chasing the enemy aircraft back into cloud. Back at Coltishall the 242 Squadron CO reported the Dornier's escape – but the Observer Corps confirmed having seen a Do 17 plunge into the sea off Cromer at 0610 hours. Brickhill trumpeted that 'he had got the Squadron's first enemy bomber in weather which was too bad for him to let the other pilots fly'.[8] A brave act though Douglas performed that day, Brickhill made no mention that Leigh and Hyde had previously engaged what was probably the same Do 17 – confirming that Douglas Bader was not, in fact, the only pilot sufficiently competent or courageous to operate in such bad weather. Moreover this was *not* 242 Squadron's 'first enemy bomber': the previous day Sub-Lieutenant R. E. 'Jimmy' Gardner, a Fleet Air Arm (FAA) pilot seconded to 242 Squadron, had destroyed an He 111 of III/KG 53 off Cromer. It was Gardner, therefore – *not* Squadron Leader Bader – who opened 242 Squadron's account. Unfortunately, this is yet another example of Brickhill twisting the tale – which has since become acknowledged 'fact'.

The media made much of this victory by the anonymous legless squadron commander. Already, though, the facts were becoming mythicized. An example of this appeared in Worcestershire's *Malvern Gazette* in July 1940, aimed at encouraging donations to the town's Spitfire Fund:

> Remember the story of the young pilot who lost his legs in a crash? Fitted with artificial legs he argued his way back into the RAF; argued his way through the medical boards; argued his way into a squadron, and one day, quite recently, he went up alone and shot a Dornier down into the sea. Did he say 'I've given the country my legs; why should I now be expected to give them my neck?' Not a bit! Like all those gallant lads he was ready to give the extra. God bless them for it.[9]

Now Douglas's tenacity and bravery are beyond dispute – but he had certainly not 'given the country my legs'. The circumstances of his crash during peacetime are well documented and by Douglas's own admission was his own fault. This, then, is a prime example of how Douglas was beginning to be used by the press to raise morale. A legless fighter pilot was inspirational stuff, at a time when the nation needed heroes. This was manna indeed for the British media – and the beginning of a legend. The fact was that Douglas Bader's usefulness and contribution to the war effort actually far exceeded fighting the hot war from a Hurricane cockpit – he was, in short, a propagandist's dream and would increasingly find himself used in that direction.

Two days later Douglas was sent off again to search for an He 111, but failed to make contact. Interestingly, on 20–24 July, 66 and 242 Squadrons practised 'wing exercises'. Burns described the two-squadron wing as 'one of the standard formations of Fighter

Command'.[10] It was not. Indeed, Dowding had already stated that a single squadron would be the largest tactical formation. It is difficult to understand, therefore, why 12 Group squadrons were practising in this way – but indicates an early leaning towards large formations, even if contrary to the AOC-in-C's view. Throughout this period, however, the principal flying activity for Coltishall's squadrons remained convoy protection patrols and interceptions.

On 27 July, a flight of 19 Squadron's Spitfires began daily flights to Coltishall, from which it operated to both support 66 Squadron and provide an opportunity for pilots to engage the enemy with their experimental cannon-armed Mk IBs. In response to news that the RAF's new fighters were being armed with eight machine-guns, Professor Willy Messerschmitt's response was to add a pair of 20 mm Oerlikon cannons to his 109 – the original armament of which was but two 7.62 nose-mounted machine-guns. Due to the 109's thin wing section the only means of installing an Oerlikon in each wing was to add a blister to both upper and under surfaces to accommodate he bulbous ammunition drum. Early experience fighting the 109 on the Continent indicated that Messerschmitt's unanticipated expedient had given his fighter a distinct edge. Although the cannon had a slower rate of fire, requiring greater accuracy, the destructive power of cannon shells was significantly greater than the RAF fighters' rifle-calibre bullets. Indeed, both fighters and bombers were being fitted with an increasing amount of armour plate – making them much more difficult to destroy with .303 rounds. The RAF needed to act fast, so hastily created the Spitfire Mk IB, armed with two Hispano-Suiza 20 mm cannons but no machine-guns. Like the 109, the Spitfire's wing was also too thin to accommodate the cannon's ammunition drum – so the Hispano cannon was side-mounted and fed by an ammunition tray. The problem with this arrangement was that the stresses of combat frequently led to stoppages because the weapon was not designed to lie on its side. Without back-up machine-guns, 19 Squadron's pilots often found themselves greatly disadvantaged and in mortal danger – but when the cannon worked the benefit of it was plain to see. Difficult though it was, the RAF had to find the answer to the cannon problem, which eventually it did by likewise adding blisters in addition to four machine-guns. This would prove a winning combination – but that day remained far off.

On 29 July, 19 Squadron's 'B' Flight was scrambled, according to the Squadron's Operations Record Book (ORB), 'in a big alarm at Coltishall, when all available squadrons left the ground'. Interestingly, the Spitfires flew in three sections of two – not the stipulated vic of three; some squadrons were clearly learning fast. The 12 Group Controller was responding to an attack on a convoy off Harwich. 66 Squadron engaged and destroyed two raiders, but 19 and 242 Squadrons made no contact. Incredibly, 12 Group had scrambled thirty fighters to meet this threat – leaving Coltishall defended by a single flight of fighters. The wisdom of such a deployment appears questionable – but is further evidence of the attitude in 12 Group towards large formations. Indeed, David Cox was a sergeant pilot with 19 Squadron at the time, and remembered that in June 1940, Leigh-Mallory visited the Squadron, 'who, stabbing his finger at a map on the wall, exclaimed "My fighters will be here, here and here!", from which I now deduce that he always had in mind to intercept the enemy in numbers, as opposed to what went on down south later on'.[11] Two days later, 19 Squadron had occasion to celebrate when Flight Lieutenant Brian Lane – the flight commander so untruthfully maligned by Brickhill regarding Douglas's *faux pas* in hitting Duxford's cricket pavilion – was awarded the DFC; Wallace 'Jock' Cunningham was a pilot officer in Lane's 'A' Flight:

> We were lying in the sun at Coltishall along with Douglas Bader and other 242 Squadron pilots. It was before our involvement in the Battle of Britain proper, but Brian Lane had already received a 'gong' for his good leadership of the Squadron and general activities at Dunkirk. There was some banter going on and Douglas asked Brian 'What's *that*?' in his usual cocky fashion, thrusting his pipe at Brian's DFC ribbon. '*I* must get one those!' said Bader. There was no antipathy between Brian Lane and Douglas Bader, however – they were good friends.[12]

Throughout the latter half of August, the tempo of battle increased over southern England. Extensive aerial reconnaissance was followed by heavy attacks on shipping, ports and installations, radar stations and, crucially, Fighter Command's airfields. The main difficulty for Park and his controllers was identifying diversionary attacks, so as to preserve sufficient reserves to meet the main raid when it came. To meet coastal attacks, virtually all squadrons at 'Readiness' were maintained at forward aerodromes, such as Lympne, Hawkinge, Rochford and Manston. The greatest vigilance was required to prevent these precious fighters being destroyed on the ground. Park's tactic was to despatch half his available fighters (including all his superior Spitfires) against enemy fighters, the remainder against the bombers. 11 Group clearly had a very difficult balancing act in maintaining a high state of preparedness and picking the moment to engage. For Douglas Bader, however, the constant hanging around and waiting up in 12 Group was unbearable. Constantly he berated his AOC, imploring him to send 242 Squadron to reinforce 11 Group; Denis Crowley-Milling: 'Naturally Douglas wanted to get we of 242 Squadron into the action. He used to say "Why don't they get us airborne when the Germans are building up over the Pas-de-Calais?" He felt that we could then proceed south and meet the enemy formation on the way in.'[13]

Douglas's idea, however, was impractical, for a variety of reasons. RDF, for example, was unable to identify when a raid was 'building up' due to the constantly high level of enemy air traffic over the Pas-de-Calais. The only real indication was when a raid began moving out from the French coast – by which time, given the distance involved, it was too late to commit 12 Group's squadrons as he suggested. In addition to having its own geographic area of responsibility, a crucial function of 12 Group's fighters was to protect 11 Group's airfields while Park's fighters were engaged further forward. Moreover, controllers could never be sure if or when a heavy attack would develop against the industrial Midlands and the North. The far-sighted merit of maintaining a strong fighter presence throughout the country – instead of simply in the South – was vividly confirmed on 15 August, when a large raiding force attacked northern England from bases in Norway. Seven Fighter Command squadrons, including several from 12 Group, mauled the enemy without loss. The action was the absolute vindication of Dowding's policy. Curiously, given his previous over-reaction to the Harwich threat, Leigh-Mallory only responded to this huge attack with eighteen fighters. Exasperatingly, 242 Squadron was situated too far south to be of assistance.

So heavy were the attacks on southern England too that day, though, that 11 Group requested assistance from 12 Group; David Cox:

19 Squadron was scrambled from the Duxford Sector to intercept a raid on Martlesham Heath airfield, near Ipswich. This raid was mounted by some twenty-five Me 110s of *Erprobungsgruppe* 210, led by their brilliant *Kommodore*, Erich Rubensdorfer. The enemy's approach went completely undetected until they were only a few minutes from their target. Only three Hurricanes of 17 Squadron managed to get from Martlesham before the 110s arrived. Our chances of intercepting the raid, however, were nil – taking into account that the distance from our airfield at Fowlmere to Martlesham was sixty air miles. Taking an optimistic speed for our Spitfires of 300 mph, it would take twelve minutes from take-off to reach Martlesham. I doubt that our altitude, 2,000 feet, our cannon-armed Spitfires were capable of that speed, as its maximum speed was not reached until 19,000 feet. I would suggest that 280 mph was the maximum possible speed for height, but even at 300 mph the Squadron could not achieve the impossible.[14]

Park, however, was incensed by 12 Group's failure to protect his airfields. This was unfair – no one was at fault, in fact. The following day, Flight Lieutenant Lane led his Spitfires of 19 Squadron's 'A' Flight into action against a formation of ZG 26 Me 110s off Harwich. In spite of the Spitfires' cannon stoppages, three 110s were claimed destroyed and one probable – a remarkably accurate assessment, in fact, given that the actual enemy losses were two destroyed and one damaged. That day, Douglas intercepted two 'X-Raids', but both transpired to be friendly aircraft. His mounting frustration can only be imagined!

Down south, the battle raged, 11 Group's airfields beginning to take a critical battering. Park gave his controllers very clear instructions regarding how he wanted the battle fought – emphasising that in order to preserve their fighters, only the minimum number of squadrons were to be engaged, and that if necessary, in order to protect the 11 Group airfields of Debden, North Weald and Hornchurch, reinforcements to patrol and protect them should be requested directly from 12 Group or via Fighter Command HQ. Previous accounts have often accused 11 Group of 'hogging' the Battle of Britain – but clear that was not the case. Park was simply adhering to Dowding's strategy – which included being reinforced, whenever necessary, by 12 Group.

On 21 August, poor weather over England prevented massed raids. Instead, the Luftwaffe maintained pressure on the beleaguered defenders by making numerous scattered raids across a broad front. A number of raiders were active over Norfolk. While returning with his section to Coltishall upon conclusion of another training flight, Douglas heard his friend, Squadron Leader Rupert Leigh of 66 Squadron, being vectored to intercept an 'X-Raid'. Without having been instructed by the Controller to do so, Squadron Leader Bader broke away and headed south-east – towards Yarmouth and the action. Arriving before the Spitfires, Douglas peered through a thin veil of cloud at 8,000 feet and saw the now familiar silhouette of a Do 17. Climbing through the 'clag', the raider's sharp-eyed rear gunner spotted and opened fire on the rapidly closing Hurricane. Taking aim and being careful not to overtake his target too quickly on this occasion, Douglas briefly returned fire. Nonetheless the 'Flying Pencil' disappeared again into thick cloud. Although believing that he hit the bomber, Douglas made no combat claim. At the same time that he engaged that lone intruder, 1215 hours, 242 Squadron's Blue Section was also in action close-by, Sub-Lieutenant Gardner, Flight Lieutenant Powell-Sheddon and Pilot Officer Latta sharing the destruction of a 2/KG 2 Do 17 which crashed at Conifer Hill, Starston. Five other Dorniers were also confirmed destroyed over eastern England or off its coastline that day by 56 and 611 Squadrons. Several days later, Douglas was informed by the Coltishall Intelligence Officer that the body of a Do 17 crewman had been recovered from the sea in the area of his inconclusive combat on 21 August; the dead enemy airman's watch had stopped at the time concerned. On that basis the CO of 242 Squadron was rightly credited with having destroyed this bomber, which, it would appear from German casualty records was another 2/KG 2 *Holzhammer* machine, based at Épinoy, 19 miles south-east of Arras.[15] The crewman recovered was *Leutnant* Ermecke; his three fellow crewmen remain missing.

On 26 August, 11 Group called upon Leigh-Mallory for assistance. 19 Squadron was scrambled from Fowlmere and ordered to patrol Debden at 10,000 feet; David Cox:

The actual raid came in at 1,000 feet. As 19 Squadron was at 10,000 feet and above 10/10ths cloud, we saw nothing of what was going on below. It appears that the Observer Corps had reported a raid coming in at 1,000 feet but the 11 Group Controller thought this was a mistake – so consequently asked 19 Squadron to patrol at 10,000 feet, which, of course, we did. The subsequent intelligence report stated that

'Spitfires from Fowlmere were slow in getting off the ground' – which was certainly *not* the case.[16]

Pilot Officer 'Teddy' Morten worked in the Operations Room at Duxford: 'The 11 Group Controllers definitely called for 12 Group too late. By the end of August there was a certain amount of hostility between the respective operations rooms. 11 Group accused us of always being too late; we said they always called for us too late. Whenever 12 Group squadrons arrived after the action we would have to suffer sarcastic remarks from the 11 Group Controller – so the situation was not good.'[17] The 12 Group Controller was Wing Commander 'Woody' Woodhall:

In those early days, the RDF information was not very accurate, particularly regarding height and numbers of aircraft, and of course there was a time lag of several minutes before the information reached the Sector Operations Room. The Sector Controller therefore had to use intelligent guesswork to direct his fighters on an intercepting course and also to position them up-sun of the enemy. To begin with, the operations table in 12 Group only extended to the north bank of the Thames, and enemy plots were only passed to us when they reached this point. In 11 Group, however, plots were received while the enemy was still over France. Command Operations Room had the whole picture, of course, but in my opinion there was never enough liaison between 11 and 12 Groups.

Luckily, Wing Commander Victor Beamish, the Sector Commander at North Weald, was a good friend of mine, so I extended our operations table to the south as far into

France as St Omer. As soon as North Weald was informed of enemy activity we kept the tie-line telephone open, and plots were passed from North Weald to us at Duxford. In that way we obtained earlier warning, but in spite of this we were frequently scrambled too late because we were not allowed to fly over 11 Group unless asked for by them. It was frustrating to see an enemy raid plotted on our board, obviously going for a target in 11 Group, then to wait on the ground, with the pilots in their cockpits, for fifteen or twenty minutes – and finally be scrambled too late to get into the fight.[18]

The following day, Park wrote to Dowding's SASO, Air Vice-Marshal Evill, complaining about the problems. The AOC 11 Group also issued damning instructions to his controllers. Unlike 10 Group, he argued, 12 Group had not shown the 'same desire to co-operate by despatching their squadrons to the places requested'. From that point on, Park ordered, requests for assistance from 12 Group should only be routed through Fighter Command. Although accepting that this would be slower in achieving reinforcement, the strategy was justified because it 'should ensure that the reinforcing squadrons from the north are in fact placed where they can be of the greatest assistance'.[19] Evill, however, did nothing. Had he placed the matter before Dowding, and had the AOC-in-C intervened decisively at this stage, subsequent sorry events would not have happened. It is safe to say, however, that it was on this date that relations between 11 and 12 Groups could be said to have broken down.

On 28 August, Leigh-Mallory began sending 611 Squadron from Digby to Duxford. There, Squadron Leader McComb's

Spitfires joined those of 19 Squadron and the Hurricanes of the new Czech 310 Squadron, remaining at readiness all day. Duxford was 12 Group's closest station to London and therefore offered the greatest chance of action. Nonetheless, 66 and 242 Squadrons remained relatively inactive further north at Coltishall. For Douglas, this situation was absolutely intolerable. His squadron had trained hard, drawn blood, and was bursting with high morale. Feeling like a caged tiger, he sulked and ranted to anyone who would listen regarding Fighter Command's apparent stupidity in not committing 242 Squadron to the battle raging further south. Orange, however, argued that Douglas and 242 Squadron should have been rotated into 11 Group, serving a turn in the front line, 'but Leigh-Mallory refused to permit him to go south and he did not ask to go'.[20]

Across the Channel, following heavy bomber losses, *Reichsmarschall* Göring had insisted that his fighters provide an inflexible close-escort service – and concentrated them in the Pas-de-Calais. For the renewed assault, this gave *Generalfeldmarschall* Kesselring an apparently overwhelming number of fighters for the great daylight battles over England that lay ahead. For Douglas Bader, the wait for the action he so craved was nearly over.

11

'TALLY HO!'

By 30 August 1940, Luftwaffe attacks on England had increased in ferocity. This effort was now concentrated on 11 Group's airfields – the Battle of Britain's most critical phase. It is necessary to deconstruct the air battle of that day in some detail.

That morning, Squadron Leader McComb once more led 611 Squadron to the Duxford Sector, joining 19 and 310 Squadrons on readiness there. At 1100 hours, the enemy made a *Freie Jagd* in strength, the Observer Corps reporting over 100 bandits incoming over the south-east coast. This formation split up, attacking the airfields of Biggin Hill and Eastchurch. The latter was not, however, a Fighter Command station and emphasised that enemy intelligence was, in fact, lacking. As these raiders withdrew, another wave of bombers came in, fighting their way northwards. 19 and 310 Squadrons were scrambled to patrol base but without incident. The scale of fighting, however, was such that Leigh-Mallory decided to send another of his squadrons to join those already at readiness down at Duxford: 242 Squadron. While en route, though, 242 was stood down and required to return to Coltishall. Douglas was fuming and 'harangued Ops over the phone'.[1] An hour later, 242 Squadron was ordered again to Duxford, this time arriving in due course. Douglas knew that this was his first chance of becoming embroiled in the battle raging over southern England.

At 1600 hours, 300-plus bandits were reported incoming over Kent and the Thames Estuary. Again the raiding force split, attacking the airfields at Kenley, North Weald, Hornchurch, Debden, Lympne, Detling and Biggin Hill. Twenty minutes later, sixty He 111s of I/KG 1 and II/KG 53, escorted by Me 110s, crossed the British coastline north of the Thames. Anticipating an attack on North Weald and Hornchurch, the 11 Group Controller requested assistance from 12 Group via Fighter Command. At 1623 hours, Wing Commander Woodhall consequently scrambled 242 Squadron. An absolutely delighted Squadron Leader Bader led fourteen Hurricanes off from Duxford with orders to patrol North Weald at 15,000 feet. Worthy of note is that on this occasion Leigh-Mallory did not commit all four squadrons on readiness at Duxford, just 242. It is likely that Fighter Command HQ had specified that just one squadron was required, and where. The other Duxford squadrons, in fact, sensibly patrolled base, although again without incident.

As 242 Squadron scrambled, the incoming threat separated and headed for two different targets: I/KG 1 heading for the Vauxhall Motor Works and aerodrome at Luton, while II/KG 53, the larger of the two formations, fought its way to the Handley Page aircraft factory at Radlett. As the Radlett-bound raiders forged ever-westwards, at 1625 hours the 11 Group Controller scrambled 56 Squadron from North Weald, by which time the enemy was approaching that Sector Station. Six minutes later, eleven Hurricanes of 1 Squadron scrambled from Northolt. At 1655 hours, two 222 Squadron Spitfires likewise scrambled from Hornchurch. Having taken off from Gravesend at 1600 hours, fifty minutes later Squadron Leader Harry Hogan's 501 Squadron was flying east over Chatham and espied a large force of He 111s, subdivided in *Staffeln*, each in an arrowhead formation:

> The bombers were at 15,000 feet and flying west, south of the Thames Estuary towards London. Stepped up behind them were formations of Me 109s and 110s. The enemy aircraft turned north over Southend and the Squadron circled round them before attacking the second vic head-on. This broke up and one He 111 jettisoned its bombs. Another was pursued by two of our fighters and landed on the water near the *Girdler* lightship; another crashed in Southend. Our aircraft were not attacked by fighters, which were some distance behind.[2]

Back at Gravesend, 501 Squadron claimed the destruction of two He 111s and three more damaged; certainly one Heinkel had crashed at Lifstan Way, Southend.

Shortly after taking off, 1 Squadron sighted six apparently enemy aircraft north of London, but these transpired to be Blenheims on an affiliation exercise. Upon breaking away, Squadron Leader Noel Pemberton's pilots saw 'thirty–forty bombers protected by a similar number of fighters in no standard formation from 12,000–25,000 feet'.[3] The Squadron attacked, each pilot doing so independently; Sergeant Marchand:

> I was Number Two of Red Section and upon sighting the enemy followed my Section Leader in line astern. After attacking a Do 17, which was in company with another E/A, an Me 110 dived on me from astern. Breaking away I shook him off, then saw a single He 111K. Climbing and

going ahead, I attacked from the beam. On the second attack the port engine stopped. At this moment a Hurricane from another squadron dived from the rear of the He 111 and got in a burst. Again attacking from the front I got in a long burst, and a man jumped by 'chute. A further two parachutists jumped after about one minute as I put in another burst. The aircraft dived down and crashed in the middle of a road near a cemetery east of Southend.[4]

In his identification of a 'Do 17', Marchand was mistaken, but the He 111 he claimed destroyed was also that credited to 501 Squadron. This particular He 111 was also attacked and claimed as a 'probable' by 1 Squadron's Pilot Officer Hancock, possibly by Sergeant Clowes of the same unit, and definitely by 222 Squadron Flying Officer Cutts and Sergeant Davies. Likewise the He 111 destroyed by 56 Squadron's Flight Lieutenant 'Jumbo' Gracie, which crashed at Colne Engaine, near Halstead, was attacked by many other RAF fighters, including 1 Squadron's Pilot Officer Matthews who reported having seen a 56 Squadron Hurricane during his intercept. This is a perfect example of how, due to the speed and confusion of aerial combat, a single enemy casualty could be unwittingly multiplied many times on the balance sheet – providing an inaccurate assessment of both enemy losses and the defenders' effectiveness. Indeed, Squadron Leader Pemberton, the experienced CO of 1 Squadron, reported having attacked an enemy aircraft 'in company with a Hurricane of "LE" Squadron; the rear gunner continued to fire until a few seconds off hitting the ground. This E/A, which fell near Epping, will be claimed by that Hurricane.'[5] This report is crucial to our understanding of this action: 'LE' were the code letters of 242 Squadron; the 'E/A' one of two Me 110s, of 5/ZG 2 and 4/ZG 76, both of which crashed at Ponders End, to the east of Enfield.

According to Brickhill, while en route to North Weald, Douglas decided that the Controller had got it wrong by ordering 242 Squadron to patrol over that airfield. Instead, Brickhill wrote, 'disregarding the Controller's words, he swung 30 degrees west'.[6] If this is true, Park's allegations that 12 Group's squadrons were not complying with 11 Group's instructions were correct. Lucas commented that 'he resolved ... to make the instructions he was receiving from the ground his ally, not his master. Working 15 or 20 miles round to the west of the raiders, he climbed another 3,000–4,000 feet above the given altitude.'[7] Primary evidence, however, contradicts this. The 242 Squadron combat report confirmed that having initially been despatched by the Controller to Angels Fifteen (15,000 feet) on a vector of 190°, this was soon changed to 340° – no doubt in response to the raiders' changing tack.[8] It was not Squadron Leader Bader, therefore, who decided to change course but the Controller, which is as it should be, and nor does any evidence to suggest that 242 was at anything other than the prescribed height.

Three aircraft were noticed to 242 Squadron's right, so Douglas despatched Blue Section to investigate. Again, these transpired to be the Blenheims wandering about in the combat area. Douglas reported that '242 Squadron was flying in line astern and at 15,000 feet when a large enemy formation was sighted on the left'.[9] The 242 Squadron report added that 'Green Leader then drew attention to a large enemy formation on their left, so the rest of the Squadron turned to see a vast number of aeroplanes flying in an easterly direction. These were recognised to be 70–100 E/A, twin-engined, in tight formation, stepped up at 12,000 feet, after which there was a gap of 1,000 feet, then another swarm of twin-engined machines stepped up from about 15,000–20,000 feet.'[10] Clearly, therefore, the bombers, 242 Squadron's intended target, were 3,000 feet below 242 Squadron – not because Squadron Leader Bader knew better than the Controller and disregarded his instructions, but because the Controller, fully aware of the enemy formation's height, speed and tack, and the sun's position, placed him there.

While many of the 11 Group pilots already engaged were no strangers to such so-called *Valhallas*, this was the first time that Squadron Leader Bader and his 242 Squadron pilots had ever seen anything like it. Douglas wrote that

> soon we spotted one large formation, and it was rather an awe-inspiring sight – particularly to anyone who hadn't previously been in action. I counted fourteen blocks of six aircraft – all bombers – with thirty Me 110 fighters behind and above. So that altogether there were more than 100 enemy aircraft to deal with ... I sent three Hurricanes up to keep the 110s busy, while the remaining six of us tackled the bombers ... When we first sighted them they looked just like a vast swarm of bees. With the sun at our backs and the advantage of greater height, conditions were ideal for a surprise attack and as soon as we were all in position we went straight down on to them.[11]

There was no time, even had Douglas been so minded, to orchestrate a set-piece squadron attack: 'We didn't adopt any set rule in attacking them – we just worked on the axiom that the shortest distance between two points is a straight line.'[12]

242 Squadron's combat report continued:

The Squadron Leader dived straight into the middle of the formation, closely followed by Red Two and Three; the packed formation broke up and a dogfight ensued. Squadron Leader Bader saw three Me 110s do climbing turns to the left and three to the right. Their tactics appeared to be to climb in turns until they were nearly stalling above the tail of Squadron Leader Bader's aircraft. Squadron Leader Bader fired a short burst into the Me 110 at practically point blank range and the E/A burst into flames and disintegrated almost immediately. Squadron Leader Bader continued his zoom and saw another Me 110 below and so turned in behind it and got a very easy shot at about 100–150 yards range. After the E/A had received Squadron Leader Bader's first burst of between two–four seconds, the enemy pilot avoided further action by putting the stick violently forwards and backwards. Squadron Leader Bader got another burst in and saw pieces of the enemy's starboard wing fly off; then the whole starboard wing went on fire and E/A went down burning in a spiral dive. Squadron Leader Bader then saw in his mirror another Me 110; he did a quick turn and noticed five or six white streams coming out of forward-firing guns; the E/A immediately put his nose down and was lost, but subsequently seen far below. Squadron Leader Bader saw nothing else around him so called Duxford and was told to land.[13]

Of this phenomenon, Douglas said, 'Now there's one curious thing about this air fighting. One minute you see hundreds of aeroplanes in the sky, and the next minute there's nothing. All you can do is to look through your sights at your particular target – and look in your mirror too, if you are sensible, for any Messerschmitts trying to get on your tail. Well, that particular battle had lasted about five or ten minutes. We hadn't shot them all down, of course; they hadn't waited for that, but had made off home in all directions at high speed.'[14] Back at Duxford, Squadron Leader Bader claimed two Me 110s destroyed. Interestingly, of the six Me 110s to crash in England during this action, or those which limped back to France damaged, however, none can be attributed to him.

The 242 Squadron report continued, describing kills by another 242 Squadron pilot and regarding which there is no doubt:

Red Two, Pilot Officer WC McKnight, went into attack with Squadron Leader Bader; he got behind an Me 110 and opened fire at 100 yards. The E/A burst into flames and crashed to the ground. Next he attacked an He 111 formation, carrying out a beam attack on the nearest one; E/A rolled over on back, port engine caught fire and it finally crashed to the ground. P/O McKnight was then being attacked by an Me 110 but succeeded in getting behind and followed E/A from 10,000 feet to 1,000 feet. P/O McKnight opened fire at about 30 yards; E/A's starboard engine stopped; the port engine caught fire and E/A crashed in flames alongside a large reservoir.[15]

The only German loss apparently attributable to McKnight, however, was the latter, of 4/ZG 76, which crashed upon the Enfield Sewage Farm.

Flight Lieutenant Ball and Pilot Officer Stansfeld attacked an He 111 which they saw crash on 'an aerodrome full of cars'.[16]

This was a 6/KG 53 machine which crashed at Goodman's Farm, near Manston. Flying Officer Christie attacked an Me 110 head-on, harrying the German like a terrier until 'finally causing the E/A to dive from 2,000 feet, crashing into a greenhouse 500 yards west of Welsh Harp Lake'.[17] This kill can also be accounted for: a 5/ZG 2 *Zestörer* which crashed at Rochford's Nursery, Ponders End. Both this and the 110 destroyed by McKnight could have been that also engaged by Squadron Leader Pemberton. In total, an absolutely elated 242 Squadron returned to Duxford and claimed eight Me 110s destroyed, one probably destroyed and another damaged, and five He 111s destroyed.

Although confirmed, these claims were wildly exaggerated. Indeed, it is only possible to definitely confirm two Me 110s destroyed and one He 111. Pilot Officer Crowley-Milling's contribution to the fight perfectly illustrated the difficulties involved: 'Seeing an He 111 break away from the formation he made an astern attack, giving a five-second burst. The enemy did not avoid action, but rear-gun fire was experienced. Starboard engine of E/A started to smoke, then E/A made dive to the ground. At this particular moment an Me 110 was commencing an attack so did not observe He 111 crash, though Pilot Officer Hart confirms seeing this aircraft go down in flames.'[18] By his own admission, 'Crow' 'did not observe He 111 crash' – and neither did Hart, who simply saw it diving and on fire. Any damaged aircraft was often best advised to make for ground-level and hedge-hop home – RAF fighter pilots would learn that diving aircraft, even though trailing smoke, did not necessarily mean their fate was sealed. Crowley-Milling, though, was credited with one He 111 destroyed. More recently, Sebastian Cox, head of the Ministry of Defence's Air Historical Branch, confirmed that

'Air Intelligence, perhaps because of its relative inexperience in the field, was certainly too ready to accept RAF claims at face value. In the period 8 August to 16 August the defences claimed 501 enemy aircraft confirmed as destroyed, and a further 231 probably destroyed, when the actual scale of loss was only 283.'[19] Over-claiming was nothing new, and a common feature of air fighting, especially when large numbers of fighters are engaged or the pilots involved inexperienced – and 242 Squadron was, in terms of combat experience, the most inexperienced squadron engaged that afternoon. It was perhaps that fact which led Douglas to later write that 'they broke up all over the sky'.[20] The enemy formation did not: short of fuel and ammunition, 10 miles short of the enemy's target, the RAF fighters were forced to break off the engagement; hampered only by anti-aircraft fire, the He 111s reached the Handley Page factory. Fortunately only slight damage was caused, not affecting production of the new four-engined Halifax bomber – but fifty-three people were killed at the Vauxhall Works, which was hard-hit. In all my researches I have never, ever, verified any claim that enemy formations were turned about. They were not. Slow bomber formations rely upon mutual fire support, so to break up would be suicidal – such was the case on 30 August 1940. Bomber formations being broken up, however, made good copy for the propagandists.

Whatever the true and accurate figure of enemy aircraft destroyed or damaged that afternoon, however, 242 Squadron had seen its first major action – and inflicted damage upon the enemy without loss. Squadron Leader Bader and his pilots were cock-a-hoop, even more so when congratulatory signals arrived; Leigh-Mallory: 'Heartiest congratulations on a first class show. Well done 242.' Even the Chief of the Air Staff (CAS), Air Marshal Sir

Cyril Newall, added his voice in what, so far as can be ascertained, was an unprecedented signal: 'Magnificent fighting. You are well on top of the game and obviously the fine Canadian traditions of the last war are safe in your hands'; a similar message was received from the Under-Secretary of State for Air. There was clearly more afoot here. 242 Squadron was Canadian; although loyal to the Crown, Canada had not rushed to join Britain in declaring war on Nazi Germany, debating the issue for a further week, the country's mood differing markedly to that of 1914.[21] Just as their legless commander was newsworthy, so too was his squadron important to the propagandists – especially considering how poor its morale had previously been. Demoralised during the Battle of France, and only now engaged in the heavy fighting over southern England, this was the propagandists' first opportunity to trumpet the contribution of Canadian fighter pilots. Leigh-Mallory, of course, had other reasons.

From Douglas's perspective the world must have been aglow. So far as he and his pilots were concerned they alone had broken up a determined enemy attack and inflicted numerous losses upon the raiders without loss. 11 Group squadrons did not make claims like this, leading Douglas to conclude that he, above all others, including both Air Chief Marshal Dowding and Air Vice-Marshal Park, had got the right idea. Feverishly, he set pen to paper, scribbling a report on the action entitled 'Fighter Tactics *v.* Escort and Bomber Formations'. Given that 11 Group's squadrons had been in action daily, sometimes several times a day and often against even bigger enemy formations, this is astonishing. Douglas wrote that

at the suggestion of the Intelligence Officer I am writing a report on the tactics employed on 30 August against a large formation of enemy bombers and twin-engined escort fighters. It has been suggested this report may be of interest in view of the warning signal from 11 Group of increased casualties suffered in that Group due to enemy tactics of tight formation with bombers and escort fighters intermingled, and the good fortune enjoyed by 242 Squadron of complete immunity from damage to aeroplanes or personnel. In regard to the second point it must be appreciated that luck definitely played a part since any squadron leaving an engagement without any damage cannot claim all credit for cleverness in flying etc.

It appears that bombers escorted by twin-engined fighters can be dispersed by shock tactics of the sudden arrival of a Hurricane or Spitfire in their midst, preferably out of the sun … It was anticipated (and the fight in question proved it) that if a squadron of Hurricanes or Spitfires met a large enemy bomber formation (provided there were no single-engined fighter escorts) the Hurricanes or Spitfires would have the advantage (in spite of numerical inferiority) if the enemy formation could be broken up, and provided the squadron started with the height advantage. In any case, the primary object is achieved if the formation is broken because it ruins the enemy's chance of accurate bombing, and even if one's own squadron's successes in E/A shot down is slight, the E/A are scattered in small groups or singly and other fighters which are certain to be at hand can pounce of them.

Douglas concluded that 'as far as 242 Squadron is concerned the attacking and fighting conditions were very favourable'.[22] They were indeed. Not only had the Controller perfectly positioned the Hurricanes to strike from the sun, but, perhaps even more importantly, there were no Me 109s engaged. Flying very high, the 109s would undoubtedly have bounced the Hurricanes lower down – possibly with disastrous consequences.

Douglas later described subsequent events:

When we were writing up our combat reports afterwards, Leigh-Mallory rang me up and said, 'Congratulations, Bader, on the Squadron's performance today.'

I said, 'Thank you very much, Sir, but if we'd had more aeroplanes then we would have shot down a whole lot more.' He asked what I meant and I explained that with more fighters our results would have been even better. He said, 'Look, I'd like to talk to you about this,' so I flew over to 12 Group HQ at Hucknall and told the AOC what I thought. He agreed and created the 'Duxford Wing', under my leadership and comprising 19, 242 and 310 Squadrons. Leigh-Mallory said to try the idea and see what we could do.[23]

Leigh-Mallory, of course, had been told by Dowding on a number of occasions regarding how he expected squadrons to be deployed. That Leigh-Mallory had a penchant for large formations had already been demonstrated. Given 242 Squadron's apparently all-conquering victory of 30 August, and Squadron Leader Bader's huge enthusiasm for his idea, Leigh-Mallory clearly saw the prospect of a 12 Group wing as a means of getting his squadrons into the battle proper – even if such tactics were contrary to the System and the requirements of his AOC-in-C. There was much more to this decision than Douglas's simple explanation to Lucas: 'We were learning … We were all learning. That was the point.'[24]

The truth was, however, that it was Squadron Leader Bader who had missed 'the point'. That 242 Squadron wildly over-claimed on 30 August 1940 is a demonstrable fact, possibly in the ratio of 4:1. The attack was not, therefore, as successful as believed. Moreover, not one 242 Squadron report on the action mentions the presence of fighters from other RAF squadrons. This could well be because in their high state of excitement in what was their first major action, 242 Squadron's pilots simply failed to register them. We know, however, from official records – and in particular personal combat reports from various experienced 11 Group pilots, that other Hurricanes and Spitfires successfully engaged. In fact, over fifty RAF fighters were actually engaged, destroying a total of nine enemy aircraft – a somewhat different scenario to 242 Squadron single-handedly destroying thirteen! Given that fifty fighters were actually committed to that battle, Squadron Leader Bader's theory that more fighters (than just 242 Squadron) would have executed greater damage was simply incorrect. This action and Douglas's theory, however, underpinned the remainder of his own personal 'hot' war – and had far-reaching consequences for Fighter Command as a whole.

Above: 1. Pilot Officers Douglas Bader (left) and Geoffrey Stephenson (right) with Flight Lieutenant Harry Day – the RAF aerobatics team for the 1931 Hendon Air Pageant. All would later become prisoners of war.

Below left: 2. The aftermath of Douglas's crash at Woodley in 1931, as a result of which both legs were amputated. Somewhat poignantly, his shoes are in the foreground.

Below right: 3. The AOC of 12 Group: Air Vice-Marshal Leigh-Mallory – Douglas Bader's greatest wartime supporter.

Above: 4. With the backing of 'LM', Douglas was soon posted to fly Spitfires with 19 Squadron at Duxford. He found it difficult serving beneath his old friend, Stephenson, and looked down on the squadron's young pilots. Douglas is seen here, in civilian dress (sixth from right), with Stephenson (fourth from right) and other 19 Squadron pilots in the spring of 1940. *Centre right*: 5. 19 Squadron was the first to receive the Supermarine Spitfire, in August 1938. This was a very different machine to the biplanes Douglas had previously flown, with such features as retractable undercarriage, an enclosed cockpit and, by the time Douglas flew with 19 Squadron, a three-bladed variable-pitch airscrew. *Below right*: 6. Pilot Officer Frank Brinsden was a young New Zealander serving with 19 Squadron and detailed to go through a cockpit drill with Douglas before his first flight. Douglas subsequently forgot to raise the undercarriage and charged that Brinsden had omitted this detail from the briefing. This was completely untrue and Brinsden strongly objected to the allegation, which was concocted the conceal what was entirely Douglas's error.

Top left: 7. Douglas had a hard time getting to grips with the new Spitfire. While flying in formation with his twenty-three-year-old Flight Commander, Flight Lieutenant Brian Lane, Douglas collided with and removed the roof of Duxford's cricket pavilion. The impression in *Reach for the Sky* is that Lane was irresponsible, reckless and flippant. Nothing could be further from the truth. Lane was officially rated as an 'Exceptional' pilot; this quiet intellectual was nonetheless a compelling leader who won a DFC over Dunkirk and became an ace. Sadly Lane was reported missing on 13 December 1942.

Top right: 8. Squadron Leader H. W. 'Tubby' Mermagen – another Cranwellian – commanded 222 Squadron at Duxford. According to myth, Mermagen approached Douglas and invited him to become a flight commander in his unit. Again, this is untrue. So unbearable did Douglas find serving under his old friend, Stephenson – and being the most junior in rank, but not age – on 19 Squadron that he pressured Mermagen to take him on.

Below: 9. Flight Lieutenant Douglas Bader (centre), while commanding a flight in 222 Squadron and pictured at Hornchurch during the air operation covering the Dunkirk evacuation. Also pictured is another future fighter ace – Flight Lieutenant Robert Stanford Tuck of 92 Squadron. Like Stephenson and Day, Douglas and Tuck would meet again as prisoners of war.

Above: 10. 242 (Canadian) Squadron returned from the French campaign having suffered heavy losses and in poor shape. 'LM' promoted Douglas, in spite of further Spitfire flying accidents, to command in the hope that his dynamic personality and example would restore morale. Squadron Leader Bader is pictured here (seated, centre) with his Hurricane pilots at Coltishall.

Above left: 11. Douglas, with inevitable pipe, pictured at Coltishall with two of his Canadians.

Above right: 12. Morale was rapidly restored – as indicated by this snapshot of Bader aping Admiral Nelson and from the personal album of Air Marshal Sir Denis Crowley-Milling – then a young pilot officer in 242 and captivated by Bader's charisma.

13. Douglas and Canadians – indicating another side to his incredibly determined personality.

14. A famous publicity photograph of Squadron Leader Bader and 242 Squadron, taken at Coltishall during the Battle of Britain. At extreme left is Pilot Officer Crowley-Milling and at third left the tough, no-nonsense Flight Lieutenant Stan Turner.

15. More morale-boosting: Flight Lieutenant Eric Ball (left), Squadron Leader Bader and Pilot Officer Willie McKnight pose with the CO's Hurricane.

16. A famous photograph of Squadron Leader Bader and his 242 Squadron Hurricane.

17. A snapshot that says it all: Douglas found it intolerable to have a secondary role in the Battle of Britain, up in 12 Group, while 11 Group was in constant action. He is pictured here, with other 242 Squadron pilots, at Coltishall, dejectedly awaiting a call to scramble – which rarely came.

18. Duxford's Station Commander and Sector Controller, Wing Commander A. B. 'Woody' Woodhall, was another big Bader supporter – and agreed with his subordinate's theory that 12 Group should operate in mass-fighter formations and sally forth over South East England. 'LM' also supported this flawed concept.

Above left: 19. In March 1941, in readiness for the 'Non-Stop Offensive', a Wing Commander (Flying) was appointed to every Sector Station, to command a three-squadron wing. Douglas was among the first appointments – and got the Tangmere Wing in 'LM's' 11 Group. He is pictured here returning from a sweep over France in April 1941 – note the black pre-war flying overalls and Wing Commander's rank pennant.

Above right: 20. Wing Commander Douglas Bader DSO DFC pictured at 616 Squadron's dispersal, Westhampnett, in the spring of 1941.

21. Douglas – the fighter ace without legs – exits his Spitfire after a sweep over France, April 1941. Wing Commander Bader was not entirely popular with the Wing's ground staff – men of a lower socio-educational status to himself.

Above left: 22. Douglas showing to good effect the fighter pilot's helmet, goggles and oxygen mask. *Above right*: 23. Wing Commander Bader at Westhampnett, during the 'season' of 1941.

24. 616 Squadron was also commanded by a Cranwellian – Squadron Leader H. F. 'Billy' Burton DFC, pictured here walking in at Westhampnett after a sweep. Douglas always led the Wing with his 'Dogsbody Section' of four, meaning that Burton – an extremely capable officer destined for high rank – rarely got to lead his squadron in the air. By exclusively basing himself with 616 and 610 Squadrons, Douglas created an elite – which was unpopular with first 145, then 41, Squadron, based at Merston.

25. Douglas also created an elite within an elite with his inner sanctum, at the heart of which were the pilots of his 'Dogsbody Section'. Among them was Pilot Officer Johnnie Johnson – destined to become the top-scoring RAF fighter pilot of the Second World War, and the service's Wing Leader *par excellence*. When his turn came to lead, Johnson actually did things entirely differently to Wing Commander Bader.

Above left: 26. Sergeant Alan Smith – the Tangmere Wing Leader's regular wingman.
Above right: 27. Sergeant Geoff West – another 'Dogsbody Two'.

28. The Wing Leader's Spitfire Mk IIA, P7666, 'DB', being fitted with a colour Kodak cine-gun camera, Westhampnett, summer 1941. The combat claims of the Big Wing during the Battle of Britain were wildly exaggerated, as were those over France in 1941 – providing a false impression of the actual benefit of mass-fighter formations.

29. The enemy; centre: *Oberst* Adolf Galland, *Kommodore* of JG 26; left: *Hautpmann* Gerhard Schöpfel, *Kommandeur* III/JG 26; right: *Oberleutnant* Joachim Müncheberg, *Staffelkapitän* 7/JG 26. All were *Experten*. JG 26, based around St Omer, and the Tangmere Wing clashed over France on a daily basis throughout the summer of 1941.

30. Squadron Leader Burton and Wing Commander Bader, Westhampnett, 1941. By continually leading his Wing at the head of 616 Squadron, Burton was prevented from leading his own squadron in the air and this also generated resentment from Merston-based squadrons.

31. *Oberst* Galland's Me 109F. The curvaceous lines and similarity to the Spitfire should be noted.

32. Wing Commander Bader's Spitfire Mk IIA, P7666, at Westhampnett, high summer 1941. Douglas preferred the machine-gun-armed variants and ultimately changed this aircraft to a new Mk VA, W3185, shortly before baling out over France on 9 August 1941.

33. On 9 August 1941, it is believed that Wing Commander Bader was actually accidentally shot down over France during a chaotic engagement involving many fighters by Flight Lieutenant 'Buck' Casson of 616 Squadron. Casson was shot down that day en route back to the French coast and also captured. The author first realised this in 1995 but maintained silence so as to protect the elderly Casson from unwanted media attention; he died in 2003, aged eighty-eight.

34. After Wing Commander Bader was captured, a defiant mood prevailed at Tangmere: Pilot Officer Johnson: 'Bader's Bus Company – Still Running.'

35. Galland and his staff chivalrously received their famous captive at Audembert. Among the enemy officers present were, from left: *Hauptmann* Gerhard Schöpfel, *Oberst* Galland, and the one-legged *Oberst* Joachim Huth (extreme right). (Via Don Caldwell)

36. Wing Commander Bader tours the enemy airfield, accompanied by his host, *Oberst* Galland and officers. (Via Don Caldwell)

37. A Luftwaffe man poses with the crate containing Wing Commander Bader's new legs. The Tangmere Wing was among the bombers' escorting fighters that day. (Via Don Caldwell)

38. On 15 September 1945, Wing Commander Douglas Bader led a mass fly-past over London, celebrating the first post-war Battle of Britain anniversary. He is seen here climbing into his Spitfire Mk IX at North Weald for that spectacular sortie.

39. After retiring from the RAF as a group captain in 1946, Douglas returned to work for Shell – and is seen here at the controls of his company aircraft, a four-seater Miles Gemini.

Above left: 40. Thelma and Douglas Bader, and Labrador 'Shaun', at the time Paul Brickhill's best-seller *Reach for the Sky*, a romanticised version of Douglas's life story to date, was published.

Above right: 41. In the first few months of 1954, *Reach for the Sky* sold 172,000 copies and was destined to become a global best-seller.

Left: 42. Although Brickhill considered Douglas Bader to be a genius of aerial tactics and strategy, that was actually far from true. If any fighter pilot of the Second World War deserves such a mantle it was this man: *Oberst* Werner Mölders, who worked out the basics of modern fighter combat during the Spanish Civil War.

43. In 1956, *Reach for the Sky* was released as an epic film, starring Kenneth More as Douglas and Muriel Pavlow as Thelma. Here More is seen during filming discussing a point of detail with Johnnie Johnson. The film was a worldwide box-office success – cementing the Bader myth on an international and perennial basis.

44. In 1965, Douglas was made an honorary citizen of St Omer and was reunited with Madame Hiècque, the brave French matriarch who orchestrated his escape and hid 'Le Colonel' in her home. The old lady survived, spending the remainder of the Second World War in jail. (Courtesy Douglas Bader Foundation)

45. Ever a crowd-puller, Douglas is seen here at a 'Battle of Britain at Home' air show during the 1960s with former Supermarine Chief Test Pilot Jeffrey Quill, and Group Captain Johnnie Johnson.

46. Douglas on the set of *Battle of Britain*, at Duxford in 1968.

Left: 47. The publicity photograph accompanying Douglas's book *Fight for the Sky*, published in 1976.
Above: 48. Douglas revelled in the company of his wartime comrades and other airmen who had shared the wartime experience. Group Captain Sir Douglas Bader is pictured here with Air Vice-Marshal Johnnie Johnson at a Canadian Fighter Pilots' Association reunion in Winnipeg, 1980.

49. After the war, Douglas and former General Adolf Galland became firm friends, frequently attending aviation events together all over the world.

50. Shortly before his death in 1982, Douglas's story was featured in the popular television series *This Is Your Life*. Here presenter Eamon Andrews shares a joke with 'Dogsbody Section', from left: Douglas, Johnson, West, Smith and Dundas. (Courtesy Douglas Bader Foundation)

51. 'Alf' Galland was among the guests on Andrews's programme; 'We didn't know who shot Douglas down,' he said. This was because Wing Commander Bader was actually the victim of friendly fire – as the author first discovered in 1995. (Courtesy Douglas Bader Foundation)

Above left: 52. Group Captain Sir Douglas Bader dancing with the Queen Mother, patron of the Battle of Britain Fighter Association, at an annual reunion dinner. (Courtesy Douglas Bader Foundation) *Above right*: 53. Sadly, Thelma Bader died in 1971. In 1973, Douglas married Joan Murray, a regular golfing partner for many years and who was actively involved with providing riding for disabled children. (Courtesy Douglas Bader Foundation)

54. The only photograph ever taken showing Douglas wearing artificial legs, on the occasion of an inspirational personal visit to four-year-old Paul Ellis-Smith and Thys Nortje in South Africa, 1981. (Courtesy Douglas Bader Foundation)

55. Douglas sups the first pilot at 'The Douglas Bader' pub, near Martlesham Heath, which he opened. (Courtesy Douglas Bader Foundation)

56. Two years after Douglas's death, the Douglas Bader Foundation was launched as a living memorial at the RAF Museum. The 'DBF' exists to promote Douglas's example as an inspiration and provide assistance to amputees in his name. The driving force behind this new charity was his old, close friends, pictured here on that day in 1984 with a young amputee; from left: Group Captain Sir Hugh Dundas, Air Marshal Sir Denis Crowley-Milling, and Air Vice-Marshal Johnnie Johnson. (Courtesy Douglas Bader Foundation)

57. On 11 August 1984, Lady Bader opened Bader Close in Stevenage, Hertfordshire. Permanent memorials such as this do much to keep the memory and myth evergreen. (Courtesy Douglas Bader Foundation)

Right: 58. On 9 August 2001, Lady Bader unveiled a statue of her late husband outside Goodwood Flying Club – formerly known as Westhampnett – and from where, on 9 August 1941, Douglas had taken off for what became his last operational flight. The life-and-a-quarter bronze was created by sculptor Kenneth Potts. The unveiling received international media attention, indicating just how alive and well Sir Douglas's memory remains.

Above: 59. Model kits of Douglas's Spitfires abound. Appropriately, sales of this Airfix kit also benefit the RAF Benevolent Fund and 'Help for Heroes'. Schoolboys forevermore, it seems, will have no shortage of material inspiring them with the story of Britain's legless fighter ace.

Above left: 60. Keith Delderfield (left), operations director of the Douglas Bader Foundation, applauds while the chairman, David Bickers, and Sir Richard Branson unveil the English Heritage Blue Plaque commemorating Sir Douglas Bader at Petersham Mews. *Above right*: 61. The English Heritage Blue Plaque at Petersham Mews, erected in 2009. It is noteworthy that yet again, Sir Douglas is remembered as 'RAF Fighter Pilot'. His greatest achievement, however, was as an inspiration and an ambassador for the global amputee community. Nonetheless, the Foundation's work, coupled with recent commemorations like the Goodwood statue and this plaque, are clear indicators that the story – and myth – of Britain's legless air ace remain alive and well, thirty years after his untimely death.

12

DUXFORD WING

During the first week of September, the Luftwaffe continued pounding 11 Group's airfields. Throughout this time, Park frequently called for and received co-operation from Air Vice-Marshal Brand's 10 Group – whose squadrons at Middle Wallop were well positioned to patrol aerodromes and aircraft factories south of London. Further west, the Spitfires of 609 Squadron frequently patrolled the area west of London. Although the enemy were not met, had a raid developed against Northolt, Kenley, Croydon or Biggin Hill, the 10 Group fighters would have been in a position to intercept. The relationship between 11 and 12 Groups, however, remained unchanged.

On 1 and 2 September, 242 Squadron patrolled from Duxford but without incident. The following day, 242 remained at Coltishall, flying further fruitless patrols. Such was the case over the next few days. On 6 September, Leigh-Mallory, following consultation with Squadron Leader Bader, ordered that in future 19, 242 and 310 Squadrons would operate from Duxford as a wing. On the morning of 7 September, codename CROMWELL was broadcast: invasion imminent. Pilot Officer Johnnie Johnson, a new replacement pilot flying Spitfires with 616 Squadron, was at Coltishall that morning and espied a squadron leader bearing down upon him:

His vital eyes gave me a swift scrutiny, at my pilot's brevet and one thin ring of a pilot officer. 'I say old boy, what's all the flap about?' he exclaimed, legs apart and putting a match to his pipe.

'I don't really know, Sir,' I replied. 'But there are reports of enemy landings.'

The Squadron Leader pushed open the swing doors and stalked into the noisy, confused atmosphere of the ante-room. Fascinated, I followed in close line-astern because I thought I knew who this was. He took in the scene and then demanded in a loud voice, and in choice, fruity language, what all the panic was about. Half a dozen voices started to explain, and eventually he had some idea of the form. As he listened, his eyes swept round the room, lingered for a moment on us pilots and established a private bond of fellowship between us.

There was a moment's silence while he digested the news. 'So the bastards are coming. Bloody good show! Think of all those targets on those nice flat beaches. What shooting!' And he made a rude sound with his lips which was meant to resemble a ripple of machine-gun fire.

The effect was immediate and extraordinary. Officers went about their various tasks and the complicated machinery of the airfield began to function smoothly again. Later we were told that the reports of enemy landings were false and that we could revert to our normal readiness states. But the incident left me with a profound impression of the qualities of leadership displayed in a moment of tension by the assertive Squadron Leader. It was my first encounter with the already legendary Douglas Bader.[1]

It would later become a meeting of significance – and was a perfect example of how Douglas could take instant command of any situation.

That morning, Douglas led 242 Squadron to Duxford, in readiness for the initial operation of what became variously known as the 'Big Wing', the 'Duxford Wing' or the '12 Group Wing'. Douglas himself once explained the thinking behind this idea:

'Woody' would ring me up and say that the Germans were building up over the Pas-de-Calais, and I remember saying 'Well why the hell don't we go off now and get the buggers while they're forming up?' You see the bombers would come from their bases in France and orbit the Pas-de-Calais, that area around Calais and Boulogne, and the fighters would then take off from their airfields within that area, such as Wissant and St Omer. Of course the fighters have very short range, not more than forty-five minutes. They would climb up and join the bombers and then the whole armada would set course over the Channel. If our Duxford Wing had got off when they were building up, we'd have got about seventy miles south of base, probably down to the Canterbury area, and we had got them there, on the way in. We would have been at the right height and therefore have controlled the battle.[2]

The new formation's first patrol was an uneventful sortie over the 11 Group airfields of Hornchurch and North Weald. Douglas led with 242 Squadron in the van, followed by the Czech Hurricanes of 310, while 19 Squadron's Spitfires, with their superior performance, provided top cover.[3] 19 Squadron, in fact, concluded that flying in such strength of numbers was a 'most comforting feeling indeed'.[4]

It must be understood, though, that this somewhat ad hoc formation was not a wing in the same way as those operated by every sector station in 1941. Gordon Sinclair was a flight commander in 1940 with 310 Squadron, and explained that

> there was never any possibility of three or more squadrons taking off from Duxford together and receiving battle orders from a Wing Leader while airborne. Our R/T sets, TR9s, were not up to it, but in any case such a situation never arose or was even contemplated. Each squadron acted on its own, down to flight or section level, and we received information regarding the whereabouts of enemy aircraft from the Duxford Operations Room, based upon advice they had received from the relevant RDF station. Douglas Bader was a natural leader of men, but I never heard of the other squadrons' COs operating in the Duxford Sector agreeing to his leadership in the air.[5]

Emphasising the difficulties faced by the oral historian, however, Douglas Blackwood – the CO of 310 Squadron – had a contradictory recollection:

> The Big Wing thing was all started by Douglas Bader, who of course had a Cranwell background so naturally became leader. At the time, I was younger than he and had received command of 310 Squadron only shortly before Douglas received 242. Certainly among the three squadrons initially involved,

Douglas was the senior squadron commander; Brian Lane had only just received command of 19 Squadron, so although he had the most combat experience he was the Sector's most junior squadron leader. When Douglas suggested the Wing, as he was senior we just automatically assumed that he would lead. He was a *very* forceful character, of course, so even if we had wanted to it would have been *impossible* to argue with him! An example of this occurred when we were all together at Duxford many years later during the making of *Battle of Britain*. Douglas was there as a consultant but would not stop interfering with the shoot. In the end the director said, 'I'm making this film, not you' – and ordered him off the set. That was Douglas to a T.

In 1940, his ideas regarding the Big Wing had the support of Duxford's Station Commander, Wing Commander Woodhall, but even he could not have stood up to Douglas if ever it had come to that. Douglas just said 'I'm doing this' – and that was that. There was no doubt, however, that Douglas Bader was a very brave man and it was because of the way he had conquered his disabilities caused by the crash in 1931 that he became popular with his acquaintances. His 242 Squadron pilots would have followed him anywhere. We are talking, after all, about a man who played squash well and had a low golf handicap despite having no legs! We never did any practice sorties as a wing, we just went off on an operational patrol together one day with Douglas leading.[6]

The Battle of Britain had now been raging for nearly two months. There was still no sign of the Hurricanes and Spitfires being beaten. Having concentrated his fighters in the Pas-de-Calais,

Reichsmarschall Göring was continually thwarted in his desire to destroy Fighter Command *en masse* by Park's careful preservation of his force. Instead of committing large numbers of fighters to battle – as Leigh-Mallory now intended – Park attacked in penny-packet formations and kept his aircraft well dispersed. The Luftwaffe, however, due to 'over-confidence and poor intelligence', were fighting, argued Cox, 'an ill-directed campaign, which breached a fundamental principle of war – maintenance of the aim'.[7] Already the aim had changed several times and, at what was a vital moment, considering the battering 11 Group's airfields had received, was about to change again. On the night of 24 August, Bomber Command had attacked Berlin – Hitler immediately seizing upon this as justification for changing tack once more and ordering an all-out assault upon London.[8] In previous campaigns the Poles and Dutch had surrendered after the bombing of their main centres of population, and the Danes had done so simply at the threat of it. Hitler hoped, therefore, that the same would be true of Britain. Göring believed that round-the-clock bombing of London would exhaust Fighter Command and considered London to be the only target capable of forcing Dowding to commit his entire force to defend.[9] Göring now personally assumed command of the campaign. The first major attack of this latest phase began at 1635 hours on Saturday, 7 September 1940. Standing on the French cliffs at Cap Gris-Nez, Göring and his entourage marvelled at Germany's aerial might as 350 black-crossed warplanes roared overhead towards London. The approach of this aerial armada – the largest unleashed against England thus far – was anxiously monitored by 11 Group, which naturally assumed that sector stations were again the target. At 1617 hours, eleven squadrons were scrambled, and by 1630 hours all of Park's twenty-one squadrons were airborne.

At 1645 hours the Duxford Wing was scrambled to patrol North Weald at 10,000 feet. Douglas, however, climbed the Wing 5,000 feet higher – arriving over the allocated patrol line at 15,000 feet. To the east, anti-aircraft fire alerted the 12 Group pilots to an enemy formation at 20,000 feet–5,000 feet higher than themselves. Orange charged that 'as usual' Douglas interpreted his orders 'broadly and went in search of action. By the time he found it, his wing had lost all cohesion' and failed 'to guard North Weald'.[10] This, however, is not entirely the case. Douglas certainly disregarded instructions by climbing an extra 5,000 feet, but, as it happened, even that was insufficient. The enemy climbed over their rendezvous points and throughout the outward bound journey across the Channel – the escorting Me 109s frequently incoming very high indeed, often, in fact, just beneath the stratosphere. He who has the advantage of height – and sun – controlled the battle, so, knowing this, it is difficult to understand why the Duxford Wing was instructed to patrol at the suicidal height of 10,000 feet. Moreover, Douglas did not 'go in search of action'. Upon sighting the enemy from his allocated patrol line he requested permission from Duxford Control to engage – which was granted.[11] Immediately, this highlights the problem of communication, and why the System simply did not provide for tactical control of 12 Group's Wing by 11 Group – over whose area the Duxford Wing now operated. The 11 Group Controller had no means of communicating directly with the 12 Group formation leader – and it is unlikely that Duxford referred to 11 Group before giving Douglas permission leave his allocated patrol line and engage. Any failure to 'guard North Weald', therefore, was not down to Douglas but to the 12 Group Controller. Moreover, the main German formation was at 20,000 feet – but typically the Me 109s were another 5,000 feet higher – giving the enemy escorts a 10,000 feet height advantage on the Duxford Wing. Douglas later wrote that his Wing had been 'alerted late'[12] – hence why the Wing was now in an extremely tactically disadvantaged position. More accurately, the Wing had been poorly positioned height-wise – and had Douglas not used his own initiative and climbed that extra 5,000 feet, that disadvantage would have been greater still. These two immediate problems of height and control emphasise from the outset the difficulties involved for both 11 and 12 Groups where operating the Duxford Wing was concerned. The System had simply not provided for this unexpected scenario.

Climbing at full throttle to at least get level with the Germans, the element of surprise was lost. Hardly surprisingly, given the difference in performance between the Spitfires and slower Hurricanes, and individual aircraft, the Wing became 'straggled out so that full weight could not be pressed home'.[13] The Wing had certainly lost 'cohesion' – but the reason for that was not the fault of either Duxford's Controller or Squadron Leader Bader. Inevitably, the German fighter escort fell on the thirty-six Duxford fighters; Douglas: 'To be attacked by an enemy fighter when you are climbing is fatal if your opponent is experienced. You are flying slowly and are thus virtually unmanoeuvrable as well as being a sitting target for an opponent flying above you and flying faster.'[14] Douglas climbed flat-out and turned left to cut off the enemy. Confirming how 'straggled out' his formation was, the only other fighter to arrive with him was Douglas's Red Two, Sub-Lieutenant Cork:

Squadron Leader Bader gave a very short beam burst at about 100 yards at E/A which were then flying section of three line astern in a large rectangle. Then, accompanied by Red Two, gave short bursts at the middle E/A of back section. The E/A started smoking preparatory to catching fire. Squadron Leader Bader did not notice result which was later confirmed by Pilot Officer Turner as diving down in flames from the back of the bomber formation. At the time of Squadron Leader Bader's attack on the Me 110, a yellow-nosed Me 109 was noticed reflected in his mirror, and he turn to avoid the E/A. Big bang was heard by him in the cockpit of his Hurricane. An explosive bullet came through the right-hand side of the fuselage, touching map case and knocking off corner of the undercarriage selector quadrant and finished up against the petrol priming pump. Squadron Leader Bader executed a steep diving turn and found a lone Me 110 below him, which he attacked from straight astern and above him, and saw E/A go into a steepish straight dive finishing up in flames in a field just north of railway line turning approximately East (West of Wickford, due North of Thamsehaven).

Red Two, sighted E/A to East and above. He climbed to meet E/A and carried out beam attack on the leading section of bombers, firing at a Do 215 on the tail-end of the formation. Port engine burst into flames after two short bursts and crashed vertically. Red Two was then attacked by E/A from rear and hit in starboard mainplane. He broke away downwards and backwards, nearly colliding head-on with an Me 110. Red Two gave short burst before pulling away and saw front cabin of 110 break up and machine go into vertical dive. Two of the crew baled out. While Red Two was following E/A down, E/A was stalling and diving. An Me 109 attacked Red Two from the rear, one shot from the E/A going through the side of Red Two's hood, hitting bottom of reflector sight and bullet-proof windscreen. Red Two received a number of glass splinters in his eyes so broke away downwards with half roll and lost sight of E/A.[15]

Red Three, Pilot Officer Crowley-Milling, attacked an Me 110, setting its port engine ablaze before being attacked by an Me 109. One cannon shell smashed into the Hurricane's radiator, and others hit the aileron and pilot's seat; David Evans: 'He was lucky: there was a spent 7.9 mm bullet jammed in the space between the laminated glass of the armoured windscreen.'[16] 310 Squadron's Sergeant Furst hit an Me 109 over Canterbury which exploded after its pilot baled out. The Czech then attacked an Me 110 which ditched in the Channel, off Birchington. The exchange was far from one-sided, however. One of 310 Squadron's Czechs was badly burned, his Hurricane a write-off while another was damaged; in addition to Douglas's Hurricane having been damaged, 242 Squadron lost Pilot Officer John Benzie, who was killed. Douglas: 'It was windy work, let there be no mistake. On landing I rang the Operations Room in a fury, to be told that we had been sent off as soon as 11 Group had called for us at Duxford.'[17] As explained, the question of height was the critical factor in this engagement, and 11 Group's order for the Duxford Wing to patrol at 10,000 feet was questionable indeed. The intention, however, had not been for the Wing to attack the incoming enemy, so the 11 Group Controller was not, in fact, instructing 12 Group to intercept these. Nonetheless, had the Wing stayed put and patrolled nearby North Weald at 10,000 feet, not only would it have invited attack from above but what that would have achieved on this occasion, given the size of the enemy attack and that its objectives had already become obvious, is also questionable.

The allegation that the Duxford Wing were always called for late would become a constant bug-bear; 'Teddy' Morten: 'Squadron

Leader Bader would frequently telephone Ops "B" at Duxford to get the form. At mess parties he would discuss tactics, the "Hun in the sun" and all that, demanding to know why the Wing wasn't scrambled sooner by 11 Group. Alternatively he would insist on speaking to "Woody" to get scrambles effected. It did seem that 11 Group were a law unto themselves.'[18] The limitations of RDF and the System, however, meant that it was not just squadrons in 12 Group which complained about being scrambled late; Peter Brothers was an experienced flight commander serving in 11 Group: 'Until 9 September 1940 I flew with 32 Squadron. During our time at coastal aerodromes at Hawkinge and Manston, or even Biggin Hill, which was further inland, we were often scrambled late. The Controller obviously had to ensure that it was the real thing and not a "spoof" to get us airborne and catch us while refuelling. This was frustrating as at such forward bases there was so little time anyway.'[19] For reasons beyond the control of those directing the battle, this would remain an irresolvable difficulty. Douglas himself once expressed his own thoughts on the time factor:

Some ignorant people have stated in print that the Wing took a long time to get off the ground. Not so. As the two Hurricane squadrons got off the ground from Duxford, the Spitfires did so from Fowlmere. There was no time wasted in forming up. I just set course and kept going, and everyone else just formated on my lead. We took off in sections of three, in line abreast, and as soon as the first three were getting towards the far hedge then the next three would be taxiing into position and so on. There was no orbit. I used to get off the ground and get absolutely right on course. The chaps then joined me, the Spitfires staying 5,000 feet above us. I usually set the pace to climb at 140 mph.

We reckoned to be at the Thames Estuary at about 20,000 feet, which was 48 miles away. There was no time lost through us getting off. Once we were off, we were off, there was no milling about, all this was done on the climb and en route. No time lost. The leader is the fellow who sets the pace, to give the blokes at the back time to settle down and so on. Obviously a squadron in a hurry was faster than a wing because the leader has less blokes to worry about. I used to go on at Leigh-Mallory about why we couldn't get off early and be down there, but he said 'Look, we can't go until Air Vice-Marshal Park requests us. Do please remember, Bader, that they've got plenty of problems down there without us adding to them.'[20]

Although the Duxford Wing's first action on 7 September had been 'windy work', provoking Douglas's 'fury', for the loss of one pilot the Wing claimed a total of twenty enemy aircraft destroyed, five probables and six damaged. The Luftwaffe lost a total of forty aircraft on operations this date – seventeen of which either crashed in England or close enough to the coast for their crews to be captured or bodies recovered. From the evidence available it is difficult to confirm more than six kills by 242 Squadron, suggesting an over-claiming ratio of 3:1. Once more, though, the claims of Douglas and his pilots appear to have been accepted without question. The question of verifying combat claims would, in fact, vex both sides throughout the Battle of Britain. Accurate intelligence regarding losses and claims was, of course, crucial to both evaluating enemy strength and the success of one's own tactics. Cox argued that 'Air Intelligence ... was certainly too ready to accept RAF claims at face value'; between 8 and 16 August the defences claimed 501 enemy aircraft destroyed and 231 probables – when the actual German loss was 283.[21] Inevitably, however, the Duxford Wing's tally attracted further congratulatory signals from both Leigh-Mallory and the Secretary of State for Air, Sir Archibald Sinclair. Woodhall was certainly convinced that the Wing's claims were accurate: 'Bader and the intelligence officers checked these figures very carefully – with me.'[22]

Woodhall also supported Douglas's view that information from the Controller should be provided to assist – not restrict – the leader in the air:

> Douglas had made an intimate study of the fighter tactics developed by famous pilots like McCudden, Ball and Bishop in the First World War and was a great believer in the advantages of making the correct use of the sun, and first gaining superior height. As I saw it my job as Sector Controller was to vector the fighter leader on a course and to a height which would place him above and up-sun of the enemy, and keep him informed of the enemy's position, course and speed as accurately as possible from the information we had on the operations table. As soon as our fighter leader sighted the enemy, it was over to him.[23]

The problem of immediate communication between the Wing and 11 Group, which controlled the battle, has previously been mentioned; Douglas elaborated on the impossibility of communicating with the Wing himself:

> Only the squadron commanders were on the same frequency. We had four buttons on the VHF in those days, which we had received just before the Battle of Britain. It was ridiculous, anyway, trying to tune this thing with someone shooting up

your backside! Anyway, the other pilots each had their own squadron frequency. The Controller would talk to me on my frequency, but to talk to the chaps I would have to keep changing frequency from squadron to squadron. Later, of course, we got it so that we were all on the same frequency. When we were above the enemy I would say 'Diving, diving now, attacking now', and my Section of three would go down – followed by everyone else. As soon as we had made once pass, though, our formation was broken up. My objective was to get the Wing into the right position, then say 'Attacking now', after which it was up to them. They awaited my order, every man knew what he had to do, but the Wing was impossible for me to control after that point.[24]

After this apparently successful action, both Leigh-Mallory and Douglas were convinced that, with some fine-tuning, the Wing would positively contribute to the battle being fought over 11 Group. The following day, 242 Squadron despatched a servicing party from Coltishall by road to remain at Duxford. No action was forthcoming for the Duxford Wing that day, however. At 1635 hours on 9 September, it was clear that a major attack was incoming when some 300 German aircraft were incoming between North Foreland and Dover – heading for London. At 1650 hours, Squadron Leader McComb's 611 Squadron was scrambled from Duxford to patrol North Weald, firstly below cloud-base, then at 27,000 feet. Although a distant enemy formation was sighted, wisely McComb remained on his allotted patrol line. The Duxford Wing was not scrambled until 1700 hours – the time-lapse of twenty-five minutes adds weight to arguments that on occasions 11 Group called for help too late.

When the call for reinforcement came, it was for the Duxford Wing to patrol North Weald at 20,000 feet. According to Brickhill, the instruction Douglas received from Woodhall, however, was '*Will you patrol between North Weald and Hornchurch, angels twenty?*'[25] This 'order', if true, was open to personal interpretation by the Duxford formation leader. Douglas disagreed that the way to protect airfields was to patrol above them. He believed that the bombers should be intercepted while approaching their target. Consequently he ignored the given height by climbing to 22,000 feet, and led the Wing south-west, over London. According to 310 Squadron, a large enemy formation was sighted 'south of the Thames Estuary, heading north-west ... the attack was delivered south of London'.[26] This was, of course, exactly the scenario Dowding had sought to avoid. The sector stations north of the Thames were now unprotected – and yet the possibility of a threat against them could not be discounted. If evidence exists confirming that 12 Group was on occasion called for too late, this demonstrated that 12 Group's contribution was self-serving; it was hardly likely to improve relations between the two groups.

The usual confused fight developed. Although 310 Squadron reported attacking 'Do 215s',[27] it actually became embroiled with Me 110s and He 111s, the latter of KG 1 and Farnborough-bound. During the initial charge, Flight Lieutenant Gordon Sinclair collided with Flying Officer Johnnie Boulton; the former safely took to his parachute but the twenty-year-old Boulton was killed. His Hurricane, in fact, collided in turn with an Me 110 of 9/ZG 76 which crashed at Woodmanstone – some 30 miles south-west of North Weald. The Me 110 attacked by Flying Officer Bergman and Pilot Officer Fejfar exploded over Worcester Park; Pilot Officer Zimprich fired at a 3/KG 1 He 111 already engaged by 607

Squadron's Sergeant Burnell-Phillips, the bomber forced-landing near Sundridge.

Given their Spitfires' superior performance at high altitude (see *How the Spitfire Won the Battle of Britain*, Dilip Sarkar, Amberley Publishing, 2010), 19 Squadron had been detailed to protect 242 and 310 Squadrons from high-flying German fighters. Having climbed to 23,000 feet, the Spitfires were soon in action, subsequently making various claims. Pilot Officer Wallace Cunningham left an Me 109 'enveloped in flames';[28] the German crashed at Ditcham. Sergeant David Cox left another diving in flames. Sub-Lieutenant Giles 'Admiral' Blake, however, pursued the raiders across the Channel, leaving an He 111 with both engines stopped and descending seawards.

When the Wing attacked, Douglas himself fired a long burst at the leading He 111, which he left 'turning on its back',[29] later writing in his logbook that he had 'got the leader in flames'.[30] Pilot Officer Willie McKnight claimed a 'Dornier' in flames and the destruction of an escorting fighter.[31] Flight Lieutenant Ball also claimed an Me 109 flamer. Other claims brought 242 Squadron's claims in this engagement to ten destroyed; two Hurricanes were lost, with one pilot killed. 19 Squadron claimed five destroyed, two shared destroyed, three probables and one damaged; 310 Squadron: three destroyed, three probables and one damaged. It is noteworthy that 242 Squadron's tally is significantly greater than the other two squadrons – even though 19 Squadron was not only Spitfire-equipped but far more combat-experienced. The available evidence suggests that the Wing's claims on this occasion represented an over-claiming factor of some 5:1. Nonetheless, on the day a combined Wing score of twenty destroyed and two shared, along with six probables and two damaged, made impressive reading.

Soon, 242 Squadron received further congratulatory signals from Leigh-Mallory and the CAS. Those in high places were becoming increasingly convinced that 12 Group had got it right. The reality, however, was that the enemy lost but twenty-seven aircraft in action that day – only four of them having definitely been destroyed by the Duxford Wing.

On 10 September, Douglas flew to 12 Group HQ for an hour-long interview with Leigh-Mallory. The AOC listened while the legless squadron commander explained his belief that it was the formation leader who should decide when and where to attack – not the Controller – on the grounds that height information received from RDF was frequently inaccurate and that, in any case, the Controller could not see the enemy personally. This, however, was absolutely and completely contrary to Fighter Command's System. According to Brickhill, Leigh-Mallory agreed with Douglas and said, 'I'll put this to the right people and in the meantime you might as well carry on with your theory. It seems to work.'[32] So convinced, in fact, was Leigh-Mallory that 12 Group knew better than both Air Chief Marshal Dowding and Air Vice-Marshal Park, that he added two more squadrons to the Duxford Wing. This was now not just a wing, but a *big* wing of five squadrons – a 12 Group *Corps d'élite* indeed. Nothing could have been more contrary to how Dowding had expressly ordered the battle to be fought. Even Douglas was 'startled'.[33]

13

BIG WING

How Squadron Leader Douglas Bader felt regarding the prospect of leading fifty fighters into action we can only imagine – especially given Air Vice-Marshal Leigh-Mallory's consent to undertake sweeps of the 11 Group area – looking for trouble, rather than simply patrolling where 11 Group requested. This was exciting stuff indeed – and far removed from those depressing days whiling away the hours at Coltishall while 11 Group's squadrons virtually exclusively fought the Battle of Britain.

On 11 September, 242 Squadron remained at Coltishall. 611 Squadron was now operating from Fowlmere with 19, and the Polish 302 Squadron's Hurricanes joined those of 310 at Duxford. Interestingly, however, it was only Fowlmere's Spitfires that were scrambled that day. This formation, in fact, led by Squadron Leader Brian Lane, comprised, in addition to the usual 19 and 611 Squadrons, Squadron Leader A. G. 'Sailor' Malan's 74 Squadron and six aircraft of 266 Squadron. Following action over London, the Spitfire pilots claimed thirteen enemy aircraft destroyed and five damaged – two Spitfires were lost, one pilot being killed, and four damaged. It is noteworthy that without 242 Squadron's involvement, the Wing's claims were significantly less than previously – and no congratulatory signals were received.

12 September saw poor weather, cold and rain. 19 and 611 Squadrons stood by at Fowlmere, while 242 Squadron joined 302 and 310 Squadrons on readiness at Duxford. The following day was similar, with little flying. The weather improved slightly on 14 September; at 1550 hours Douglas led a four-squadron wing over London, at 23,000 feet, but without event. The same squadrons, 19, 302 and 310, followed 242 on another patrol that evening. The Wing's instructions were to patrol north of the Thames Estuary – but the evidence confirmed that the Big Wing was already acting as an independent entity: Douglas led the 12 Group 'Balbo' over 'Kent and almost France'.[1] 'Teddy' Morten:

On one of the many occasions on which Bader tackled me in the Mess regarding the 'Hun in the sun' etc. he said, 'Morty, you know that yesterday you told the Wing to patrol North Weald at Angels Twenty?'

'Yes,' I said.

'Well, d'ya know where we were upon reaching required height?'

'No,' I said.

'Over *Reading*! We were looking down on the patrol area, up sun and all eyes skinned!'

I found this astonishing. How could the battle be fought if controllers didn't know where their aircraft were?[2]

14 September was, however, a most significant date: Douglas was awarded the Distinguished Service Order (DSO). The citation read, 'This officer has displayed gallantry and leadership of the highest order. During three recent engagements he has led his Squadron with such skill and ability that thirty-three enemy aircraft have

been destroyed. In the course of these engagements Squadron Leader Bader has added to previous successes by destroying six enemy aircraft.'[3] While no one could deny that Douglas had 'displayed gallantry and leadership of the highest order', 242 Squadron's victory tally, we now know, was highly questionable. That said, every time Douglas Bader took off – a man without legs – was an unprecedented achievement and, at that time, without parallel. Given that Flight Lieutenant Eric Ball, commander of 242 Squadron's 'A' Flight, received the DFC that day, there was nonetheless just cause for celebration that night. For many aircrew on both sides of the Channel – considering the scale of the morrow's fighting – it would be their last alive.

By 1100 hours on 15 September it was obvious, given enemy air traffic over the Pas-de-Calais, that a very big attack was imminent. Surprisingly, however, the enemy formation took thirty minutes to form up and sally forth across the Channel. This delay provided 11 Group time to scramble ten squadrons – which were now being deployed in pairs, with Spitfires providing Hurricanes protection against the high-flying Me 109s – and request reinforcements from both 10 and 12 Groups. At 1125 hours, 19, 242, 302 and 310 Squadrons were scrambled from Duxford, being joined while en route to North Weald, by 611 Squadron. At 1133 hours, the first German formation crossed the coast between Dover and North Folkestone, followed three minutes later by two more incoming over Dover and South Foreland. The enemy proceeded on a dog-leg course, flying first towards the Thames Estuary, then south or south-west to Kent's north coast, and finally west to Maidstone before approaching the capital. The raiders' targets were gasworks, industrial targets and docks in the London area. Ready to meet this new assault were 312 Spitfires and Hurricanes.

310 Squadron's diary confirmed the Big Wing's deployment: 'The Squadron, with the CO leading, took off at 1130 hours to patrol North Weald. The Squadron ... was flying in a Wing formation by sections in line astern, with 242 Squadron in the van. It had been arranged that the Spitfires (19 and 611 Squadrons) would attack the fighter escort, the Hurricanes (242, 302 and 310 Squadrons) tackling the bombers.'⁴ Needless to say, this five squadron 12 Group force did not patrol North Weald as instructed. Douglas led the Wing towards London, from the north. At 1209 hours anti-aircraft fire alerted the Wing to twenty-four incoming Do 17s of KG 76 – to the south, over Brixton. Two 11 Group Hurricane squadrons, 257 and 504, were already attacking the bombers head-on at 16,000 feet. The Big Wing was at 20,000 feet and up-sun; Douglas later said that the bombers were 'without a single fighter to escort them. This time, for a change, we outnumbered the Hun.'⁵ His combat report read,

Saw two squadrons pass underneath us in formation, travelling NW in purposeful manner, then saw AA bursts so turned 12 Group Wing and saw E/A 3,000 feet below to the NW. Managed perfect approach with 19 and 611 between our Hurricanes and sun, and E/A below and down-sun. Arrived over E/A formation of 20–40 Do 17. Noticed Me 109 dive out of sun and warned our Spitfires to look out. Me 109 broke away and climbed SE.

About to attack E/A which were turning left-handed, i.e. to West and South, when I noticed Spitfires and Hurricanes (11 Group?) chasing them. Was compelled to wait for friendly fighters and dived down with leading Section in formation onto last section of three E/A. Pilot Officer Campbell took left-handed Do 17, I took middle one, Sub-Lieutenant Cork the right-hand one, which had lost ground on outside of turn. Opened fire at 100 yards in steep dive and saw a large flash behind starboard motor of Dornier as wing caught fire. Must have hit petrol pipe or tank. Pulled up, overshot and pulled up steeply. Then carried on and attacked another Do 17 but had to break away to avoid Spitfire. The sky was then full of Spitfires and Hurricanes, queuing up and pushing each other out of the way to get at the Dorniers, which for once were outnumbered.

I squirted at odd Dorniers at close-range as they came into my sights but could not hold them in my sights for fear of collision with other Spitfires and Hurricanes.

Saw collision between Spitfire and Do 17, which wrecked both aeroplanes. Finally ran out of ammunition chasing crippled and smoking Do 17 into cloud.[6]

Interestingly, of his attack on the bombers, Squadron Leader Brian Lane wrote that 'far from breaking up the formation, my efforts seemed to have the opposite effect as the Dorniers closed up until they were flying with their wings almost overlapping'.[7] This was the classic German defensive tactic of bombers relying upon mutual fire support – and evidence contradicting the various morale-boosting accounts of bomber formations simply breaking up and turning about. A lone bomber was vulnerable indeed – but a tight formation, hosing the surrounding sky with lead, at least had a chance.

From the start of this engagement, RAF fighters had continually arrived and joined in the execution. The number of fighters engaged, however, dictated much confusion – as 310 Squadron rightly commented: 'This fact also had its disadvantage because no individual pilot could claim one bird as his own.'[8] High over Brixton, for example, *Feldwebel* Wilhelm Raab's Dornier was attacked by numerous RAF fighter pilots: first Sergeant Tyrer of 46 Squadron, then Flight Lieutenant Rimmer of 229, Flight Lieutenant Brothers and Pilot Officer Mortimer of 257; as the German dived for cloud, Flight Lieutenant Powell-Sheddon and Pilot Officer Tamblyn joined the party. Squadron Leader Brian Lane, 19 Squadron's CO, sighted and made after Raab, at first unaware of the attacking Hurricanes. Realising that he had jumped the queue, Lane awaited his turn to fire.[9] After attracting the attention of even more RAF fighters, the Germans abandoned their bomber over Sevenoaks – just how many combat reports this aircraft featured in cannot be said – or how often its destruction was multiplied on the balance sheet. According to Douglas, 'believe me, no more than eight got home from that party'.[10] In fact, eighteen bombers got home. Among KG 76's six casualties was the Battle of Britain's most famous enemy loss: the Do 17 which crashed on Victoria Station. That raider was attacked by innumerable fighters – including at least four 310 Squadron pilots.

Back at Duxford the Big Wing's pilots claimed a total of twenty-eight enemy aircraft destroyed, four probables and three damaged. Clearly German losses were nowhere near this figure. Nonetheless, the Big Wing's only casualty was Flight Lieutenant Eric Ball, who had been shot up, forced-landed and was unhurt. Douglas concluded that 'it was the finest shambles I have been in, since for once we had position, height and numbers. E/A were a dirty looking collection.'[11] This doubtless convinced him further still that it was the leader in the air, not the ground controller, who should have tactical control.

Soon after 1345 hours it became evident that the enemy was concentrating over the Pas-de-Calais before another major assault. By the time this formation struck out over the Channel, twelve 11 Group squadrons had been scrambled. Between 1415 and 1420 hours, three enemy formations, comprising some 150 aircraft, crossed the coast between Dungeness and Dover, advancing on parallel lines towards Tenterden and Maidstone. Between 1420 and 1435 hours five groups of fighters followed the leaders. Although the defenders had less time to react than during the morning, the majority of squadrons were able to intercept before the raiders reached London. The Big Wing had been scrambled at 1415 hours with orders to patrol Hornchurch. Over south-east London, however, as Squadron Leader Brian Lane wrote, the Wing 'ran into the whole Luftwaffe ... Wave after wave of bombers covered by several hundred fighters.'[12] Again, however, the Wing was at a significant height disadvantage: the Germans were 4,000 feet higher. As the Me 109s fell on the Duxford fighters, the Big Wing immediately broke up. The Hurricanes, in fact, took the brunt of this attack, the Spitfires finding themselves in a better position to attack the German bombers. Breaking violently and momentarily blacking out, Douglas nearly collided with Pilot Officer Crowley-Milling. Levelling out at just 5,000 feet, the legless fighter leader climbed back into the fray, managing just a three-second burst at a bomber. Douglas was furious, and once more blamed 11 Group for scrambling the Big Wing too late. Even so, the Wing actually claimed the destruction of even more enemy aircraft than in the morning's action: thirty destroyed, nine probables and two damaged.

In total, on 15 September, Fighter Command claimed the destruction of 185 German aircraft (178 by fighters, seven by anti-aircraft guns). The actual enemy loss was fifty-six machines – representing an over-claim of 3:1. The day was undoubtedly a turning point, however, now celebrated annually as 'Battle of Britain Day', because the German bomber units could no longer continue to sustain such heavy losses – which were greater than the worst casualties suffered by Allied bombers over Germany and in due course.[13] David Cox was a young Spitfire pilot who flew with 19 Squadron on the great day, and commented on this, the Big Wing's 'best effort': 'I remember the words of Bobby Oxspring, a flight commander in 66 Squadron, saying what a wonderful sight it was to see sixty friendly fighters suddenly appear. No doubt it was a bit of a shock to the Luftwaffe!'[14] Another 19 Squadron pilot, Richard Jones, had previously flown Spitfires with 64 Squadron in 11 Group:

Flying with a wing of five squadrons of both Spitfires and Hurricanes, instead of between five to ten aircraft taking off from Kenley to intercept large numbers of enemy aircraft, gave enormous confidence – looking around and seeing anything from upwards of fifty fighters keeping me company! The Big Wing must have had a great effect on the lowering of enemy morale, who, for the first time encountered a formidable opponent.[15]

Douglas may well have been, according to 11 Group Spitfire pilot Brian Kingcombe, an 'egotist' who had 'felt out of things'[16] based in 12 Group, but he was certainly in it now – and the effect on enemy morale on 15 September may well have been his Big Wing's most important contribution.

Given the huge effort of 15 September, neither side was disappointed when the following day dawned overcast and stormy. The Luftwaffe flew few sorties and there was consequently no request for assistance by 11 Group. Nonetheless, Douglas's logbook records that on that day he led his Big Wing on a patrol of 'North Weald'.[17] Poor weather continued into 17 September, the enemy's main effort that day being a fighter sweep in *gruppen* strength. Sensibly, Park did not respond, preserving his precious fighters. That being so, and given that again there was no request for assistance from 11 Group, it is surprising that the Big Wing was scrambled at 1515 hours. 310 Squadron described this sortie as 'an offensive patrol in Wing formation'.[18] The word 'offensive' is significant, providing clear evidence that 12 Group was now acting independently and flying what amounted to fighter sweeps over 11 Group. On this day, Leigh-Mallory, however, reported to Dowding, trumpeting the Big Wing's supposed score, which now amounted to an astonishing 105 enemy aircraft destroyed, forty probables and eighteen damaged – offset against six pilots killed or missing, five wounded and fourteen fighters destroyed. Fighter Command's SASO, Air Vice-Marshal Evill, was sceptical regarding the accuracy of the Big Wing's claims, but included in his covering minute to Dowding that he was 'of the opinion that the AOC 12 Group is thinking along the right lines in organising operations in strength'; indeed, Dowding responded that he too was 'sure that Leigh-Mallory is thinking along the right lines' – but added 'his figures do not support his theory'. Many of the Big Wing's claims, the Commander-in-Chief concluded were little more than 'thoughtful wishing'.[19] Leigh-Mallory's report was forwarded to the Air Ministry, where Air Vice-Marshal Douglas, the DCAS, accepted the Big Wing's claims without question – in spite of Dowding's note of caution. The DCAS, in fact, agreed with the AOC 12 Group – targets should be protected by ground defences, leaving fighter forces free to assemble and deliver a concentrated attack on the raiders – *after* they had bombed if necessary.

Hereafter, the Big Wing's sorties were invariably recorded as being 'Offensive Patrols'[20] – often in the absence of any request for assistance by 11 Group. On 18 September, the Wing patrolled twice uneventfully, until the day's final attack came in – an unescorted formation of III/KG 77's Ju 88s heading for Tilbury Docks. Squadron Leader Bader's Hurricane squadrons were scrambled from Duxford at 1616 hours; simultaneously, the two Spitfire squadrons were up from nearby Fowlmere.[21] In spite of instructions to patrol Hornchurch at 20,000 feet, the Big Wing patrolled 'centre of London to Thameshaven at 24,000 feet'.[22] Anti-aircraft fire bursting above cloud once more indicated the presence of enemy aircraft below. Leaving the Spitfires patrolling above cloud, Douglas led his Hurricanes down through it – in search of action:

12 Group Wing turned NW and sighted E/A flying in two formations close together about 20–30 E/A in each, unescorted, at 15–17,000 feet. They were approaching first bend of Thames West of Estuary, near Gravesend, and were South of Thames when attacked. Attack was launched in a dive from East to West, turning North into the enemy. Conditions were favourable to 12 Group Wing which was screened from above by cloud – while E/A presented excellent target against white cloud base.

Red One, Squadron Leader Bader, made a quarter attack turning astern at leading three Ju 88s, hitting the left-hand one of this section. This Ju 88 turned in left-hand dive with port engine afire and disappeared down towards North bank of Estuary West of Thameshaven.[23]

This Ju 88, of 8/KG 77, crashed at Sheerness. It is possible that this machine had previously been damaged by Spitfires of 92 Squadron and also featured in the combat reports of both Pilot Officers Pilch and Karwowski of 302 Squadron.

Red One lost about 3,000 feet, re-gained control and proceeded SE and found a lone Do 17. He closed to short range and fired short burst. E/A did not return fire; instead rear gunner baled out immediately, getting his parachute entangled in tailplane. The Dornier immediately fell in succession of steep dives and two other members of crew baled out. The E/A disappeared into vertical dive into cloud at 4–6,000 feet and Red One considers it crashed either in estuary or South of it, near Sheerness.[24]

Again, this raider was also attacked by various RAF fighter pilots, including Pilot Officer Hill of 92 Squadron, and Flying Officer Kowalski and Sergeant Paterek of 302. Later, Douglas recounted his impression of this combat during a Ministry of Information (MOI) broadcast:

At one time you could see planes going down on fire all over the place, and the sky seemed full of parachutes. It was sudden death that morning, because our fighters shot them to blazes. One unfortunate German rear-gunner baled out of the Do 17 I attacked, but his parachute caught on the tail. There he was, swinging helplessly, with the aircraft swooping and diving and staggering all over the sky, being pulled about by the man hanging by his parachute from the tail. That bomber went crashing into the Thames Estuary, with the swinging gunner still there.[25]

Without fighter escort the Ju 88s suffered accordingly, losing eight of their number of the defending fighters. The Big Wing, however, claimed twenty-for enemy aircraft destroyed, four shared, three probables and one damaged. Needless to say, the inevitable congratulatory signals were sent to 242 Squadron (but none of the Big Wing's other units) by both the Secretary of State for Air and the CAS. Many of influence were now convinced of the Big Wing's value – among them 242 Squadron's adjutant, Flight Lieutenant Peter MacDonald MP. Without even reference to his CO, Station Commander or AOC, MacDonald exercised his right as an MP to seek an interview with the Prime Minister. Churchill listened to MacDonald's concern that the battle was not being properly managed by Dowding and Park, and considered his argument that attacking in strength was the way forward. Such disloyalty, however, would have profound and lasting consequences.

On 19 September, 611 Squadron's place in the line was taken by 616. The latter had been badly knocked about while flying from Kenley in August but had since received and trained replacements away from the front line at Kirton. Led by Cranwell Sword of Honour man Squadron Leader Billy Burton, 616 Squadron would soon become even more closely associated with Douglas Bader. 616 Squadron saw no action that first day on readiness at Duxford, and returned to Kirton that evening. The following day saw what would be the first 'tip 'n' run' raid by enemy fighter-bombers. Having found that Park steadfastly ignored fighter sweeps, a *staffel* of bomb-carrying Me 109s was now included in every *jagdgeschwader*. This meant that no formation could in future be ignored – because the defenders would be unable to predict whether bombs would fall upon them. This first raid was a success, surprising Fighter Command – although Douglas led the Big Wing on an uneventful sweep over London. That evening Douglas flew to 12 Group HQ at Hucknall for another interview with Leigh-Mallory. So far as is known, no record of that conversation was ever made.

Over the next few days, the Big Wing flew further sweeps over the capital but without action. Within the corridors of power, though, the argument regarding tactics was hotting up. On 24 September, Air Vice-Marshal Douglas advised the Assistant Chief of the Air Staff (ACAS) (Tactics), Air Vice-Marshal Saundby, that he had received a number of criticisms from various sources regarding Park's tactics. Saundby instructed Group Captain H. G. Crowe, the Deputy Director of Air Tactics, to inquire into the matter. In due course, the ACAS was provided with both Park's reports on the fighting during August and September, and Leigh-Mallory's concerning the Big Wing's first few actions. When Park, however, reported on the battle, he pertinently wrote that

had 11 Group delayed in engaging the enemy until its squadrons had been assembled in wings of four or five squadrons, there would have been no opposition to the first wave of bomber formations, who would have had time to escape without interception. With the available force massed into a few wings of four or five squadrons, a proportion of the second wave would have been intercepted and severely punished. The third wave of enemy bombers would, however, have had unopposed approach to the vital points of London – as the 11 Group squadrons would have been on the ground re-arming and refuelling. After six months experience of intensive fighting, I have no hesitation in saying that we would have lost the Battle of London in September had 11

Group adopted as standard the use of wings of four or five squadrons – as has been advocated in certain quarters since that crucial battle was won.

In spite of the gathering support for big wings and criticism of Park's tactics, the fact is that these were actually flexible enough to include the use of wings when appropriate; it was, after all, Park who had first used big wings over Dunkirk. His report explained that 'the fighter squadrons from Debden, Tangmere and sometimes Northolt were employed in wings of three or in pairs to form a screen south-east of London to intercept the third wave of the attack coming inland, also to mop up retreating formations of earlier waves'.[26] The evidence suggests that Air Vice-Marshal Park perfectly understood fighter tactics and was, after all, the victor of these bitter daylight battles. Douglas, however, in spite of his close relationship with Leigh-Mallory and Woodhall, was, in the bigger scheme of things, merely a junior squadron leader and as such certainly not privy to discussions at the Air Ministry. Douglas firmly believed, as did his supporters, that his Wing had executed great damage on the enemy. He was simply sublimely happy to be in the company of fellow warriors – and be their leader. No longer was he intolerably sitting on the touchline – he was in his absolute element.

Towards midday on 27 September, some 300 enemy aircraft approached southern England between Dover and Lympne, heading for Chatham. The bombers, Ju 88s of I and II/KG 77, were late at their rendezvous and were without fighter escort; 120 Spitfires and Hurricanes fell on them: eleven raiders were lost. The frantic shouts for assistance brought numerous Me 109s and 110s hurrying to the scene, a huge combat developing over

'Hellfire Corner'. At 1155 hours, the Big Wing was scrambled with orders to patrol London – while 11 Group's fighters were engaged over the Kentish coast. Once more, the enemy's presence and chance of action much further south was simply too much for Douglas. According to official records, he led 19, 242, 310 and 616 Squadrons to patrol 'South of the Estuary'.[27] Over the Dover–Canterbury area, the Wing sighted a large gaggle of German fighters, just aimlessly milling around at 18–20,000 feet. Douglas, however, had climbed the Wing ever-higher – and had a height advantage of 3,000 feet. Attacking from up-sun, this was the perfect 'bounce'. Douglas:

> I chose an Me 109 which was passing underneath me and turned behind and above him and gave a short two-second burst with the immediate result that he became enveloped in thick white smoke, turned over and dived vertically. I did not follow it down, but as it was the first 109 shot down it was seen by Pilot Officer Crowley-Milling, Pilot Officer Bush and Flight Lieutenant Turner, in fact almost the whole Squadron. I also had my camera gun in action which will give further confirmation.[28]

No one saw the 109 actually crash, however, and no likely candidate is among the enemy aircraft known to have crashed on English soil that day. Douglas also fired at several more fleeting 109s, causing 'white vapour and black smoke' to issue from one. At such close range was his attack delivered that the windscreen of Douglas's Hurricane was covered in oil from the damaged enemy fighter. This 109 was last seen over the Channel, 'gliding down quietly and apparently under full control with his engine dead'; many Luftwaffe fighters would crash-land on the occupied French coast that afternoon, this machine no doubt among them.[29] During what was now a fast, cut-and-thrust combat, Pilot Officer Bush of 242 Squadron fired a long burst at an Me 109 which crashed into the sea. Pilot Officer Latta shot another down into the Channel. Pilot Officer Homer, however, became a 'flamer' over Sittingbourne and was killed.

When 310 Squadron's attack was delivered, Sergeant Kaucky attacked an Me 109, upon which a Spitfire dived and shot it down. Sergeant Komineck claimed a 109 which 'dived vertically into the sea some 5 miles SW of Dover' and a 'Do 17' probable – although the latter was undoubtedly an Me 110.[30] Flight Lieutenant Sinclair, however, was shot down and baled out, landing in a tree near Callam. 616 Squadron was attacked by high-flying Me 109s; Pilot Officer Holden claimed an Me 109 destroyed, and Sergeant Copeland a probable, but the squadron's weaver, Pilot Officer DS Smith, was shot down. Crash-landing near Faversham, he died of wounds the following day. 19 Squadron was also hit by 109s from above: Pilot Officer Burgoyne was killed and Sergeant David Cox baled out. Sergeant Jennings left a 109 enveloped in black smoke before breaking away, and Flight Sergeant Unwin engaged another 109 in a protracted dogfight of ten minutes: after a 30° deflection shot the enemy fighter stalled and span into the Channel. Back at Duxford, the Big Wing claimed thirteen destroyed, three probables, one possible and another damaged. The over-claiming ratio is likely to have been around 3:1. The fighting of 27 September was the heaviest since the major enemy assaults of mid-September; according to Douglas, '12 Group Wing as a whole did well'.[31]

On 28 September, the Big Wing twice patrolled over the Thames Estuary, although there was generally little aerial activity that day owing to poor visibility. Interestingly, although the incident went unrecorded on every document excepting Spitfire P7432's Aircraft Movement Card (Form 78), Pilot Officer Richard Jones of 19 Squadron was shot down that day:

When patrolling the Hawkhurst area at 29,000 feet, the Controller informed us that as there were apparently no enemy aircraft in the vicinity we could return to 'Pancake'. I was 'Arse-end Charlie' and relaxed slightly as we dived to 20,000 feet. Suddenly about 4 feet of my starboard wing just peeled off – my initial thought being that this was a poor show on a new aircraft. Then a loud bang and a hole appeared above my undercarriage. I was obviously the target of an enemy fighter up-sun. Immediately I took evasive action. Simultaneously my engine cut for good and I was suddenly in a high speed stall and spin. My radio was unserviceable so I was unable to alert the squadron, who returned to base blissfully unaware that I had been shot down.

I recovered from the spin at about 10,000 feet. The aircraft was not responding to the controls. I realised too that the hood was completely jammed. I subsequently crash-landed with a dead engine in one of only two suitable fields in a heavily wooded area just outside Hawkhurst. Unfortunately I did so among a flock of sheep and regret that several were killed. I was rescued by the army and taken to the Hawkhurst doctor who treated a flesh wound to my leg, then to their mess prior to safely returning to Fowlmere. My Spitfire had a broken propeller and radiator, a few holes and missing parts but was otherwise undamaged.[32]

In his logbook, Jones wrote, 'Shot down and crash-landed at Hawkhurst, Kent. Killed three sheep. What a bloody mess!!!'[33] Weavers were extremely vulnerable: Jones was lucky to survive.

The weather remained poor the following day. With the threat of invasion and the Luftwaffe's heavy daylight raids on southern England thwarted, on 29 September 616 Squadron was released from further Wing operations and remained at Kirton. Likewise 302 Squadron was no longer required, so the Duxford Wing reverted to its original three squadrons: 19, 242 and 310. If the aerial battle was beginning to quieten down a little, the same was not so in respect of the row about to erupt over the Big Wing. On 29 September, Park wrote directly to Dowding, stating that although 10 Group had co-operated perfectly, the situation with 12 Group remained unsatisfactory. The Big Wing roaming around on sweeps, as opposed to adhering to instructions, had, Park charged, confused 11 Group's controllers and his pilots in the air. On one occasion, Park required confirmation that the Wing was patrolling, as ordered, between the sector stations of Hornchurch and North Weald – but was told the 12 Group formation was 'somewhere near Canterbury'.[34] Moreover, on several occasions the Observer Corps had been confused by the Wing's appearance, leading to 11 Group fighters being vectored to intercept the 12 Group fighters. The letter was forwarded to Leigh-Mallory, who defended his actions and emphasised that the only time the Big Wing had operated over Kent was when requested to do so by 11 Group. This was untrue and rejected by Fighter Command HQ. Park was not, however, totally opposed to using wing formations when appropriate. On 28 September he explained this to his controllers. He also considered that the only way 12 Group's wing could be used effectively was by coming under the control of certain 11 Group sector stations on a daily basis. Park had identified, after five months of hard fighting, that wing formations were best suited to offensive fighting – not the defensive battle fought that summer, when time and flexibility were crucial. While Park tried to establish a solution to how best the Big Wing could be used, however, the Air Ministry was actually preparing a rebuttal of his chosen tactics. Having won the daylight battle, Dowding and Park now faced a powerful enemy from within.

On 14 October, Air Vice-Marshal Stephenson prepared an 'Air Staff Note on the Operation of Fighter Wings' – based not upon the many reports submitted by Park, detailing his changing tactics and ideas as the battle evolved, but on Leigh-Mallory's of 17 September. Park pointed out that Leigh-Mallory's report concerned the use of wing's on only five occasions – whereas 11 Group

> used wings of three squadrons in May, June, July, August and September, and are still using them when conditions of time, space and weather make them effective ... Our aim has been to engage the bombers BEFORE they reach vital objectives, using maximum force in time given – wings or pairs, or single squadrons, or even station commanders ... Duxford roving wings caused considerable confusion to London defences and prolonged Air Raid Warnings through wandering uninvited and unannounced over East Kent *after retreat of enemy*.[35]

The matter – now known as 'The Big Wing Controversy' – came to a head at a conference held in the Air Council Room on 17 October. Those present included certain of the RAF's most powerful moguls: Air Vice-Marshal Sholto Douglas, Air Marshal

Sir Charles Portal, and Air Marshal Sir Phillip P. B. Joubert de la Ferte. The AOCs of 10, 11 and 12 Group's – Air Vice-Marshals Brand, Park and Leigh-Mallory – were present, as was the AOC-in-C of Fighter Command himself: Air Chief Marshal Sir Hugh Dowding. Incredibly, a lowly junior squadron commander and fighter pilot also joined these officers of air rank: Squadron Leader Douglas Bader.

According to Brickhill, Leigh-Mallory had called Douglas, told him about the Air Ministry conference and said, 'I don't know whether I can get you in. It's rather high-level stuff, but I'm going to try because you're the only chap who has led the really big formations.'[36] Consequently on 15 October, Douglas disappeared on four days leave.[37] Dowding nor Park, however, were advised that Squadron Leader Bader would be attending – indeed, his attendance without the knowledge or consent of his AOC-in-C is astonishing. That Park was not invited to bring along any of his squadron commanders – who had borne the battle's brunt – was a clear indicator that the whole charade was a veritable *fait accompli*. During proceedings, Douglas espoused his belief that the formation leader should decide how and where to attack – not the Controller. Dowding, Brickhill wrote, 'seemed to be looking at him very severely'.[38] Years later, Dowding conceded that 'I should think I would have been, if that was what Bader found to be the most suitable way of running the Command'.[39] As the meeting wore on, it became clear to both the real architects of victory that those present were determined to push through the use of wings as standard operating practice. So busy had Dowding been that he had hitherto placed little importance on the meeting. Suddenly, however, it became clear that he had made an irrevocable error of judgement in allowing his group commanders so much latitude

– Dowding was unaware, however, of the complicit part played in the drama by Flight Lieutenant Peter MacDonald MP – but now it was too late. Air Vice-Marshal Douglas subsequently reported that the meeting had confirmed that wings of three or more squadrons were the correct response to large enemy formations. Correspondence from Dowding, Park and Brand objecting to the meeting's minutes were ignored, as was a lengthy paper by Park on fighter tactics. There would be worse to come.

Excluding Squadron Leader Bader, the young pilots of Fighter Command knew nothing of these high-level problems. Their battles revolved not around Whitehall but in the aerial battlefield over southern England. By the end of September, unable to sustain such crippling losses, the Do 17 and He 111 fleets were switched to night-bombing. The only bombers to thereafter venture over England in daylight were lone Ju 88s engaged on nuisance raids, or small formations of them escorted by fighters. The enemy fighter force remained active, however, and the possibility of fighter-bombers being included in these formations meant that these incursions could not be ignored. While the great daylight battles over London had passed, 11 Group Spitfire pilot Geoffrey Wellum remembered this as 'the most exhausting phase of all, because standing patrols were constantly required'.[40]

On 29 October, the three-squadron-strong Duxford Wing patrolled the Sheerness–Maidstone line twice without event. At 1615 hours, the Wing was scrambled again. Fifteen minutes later Douglas and his pilots were at 25,000 feet over Hornchurch, heading towards Sheerness. Two raids were incoming, it being feared that one or more of the sector stations north of the Thames would be attacked. 11 Group HQ at Uxbridge required Hornchurch to communicate the new patrol line to the Wing

– but it was unable to do so because of 'continuous R/T traffic between the Wing and Duxford'.[41] As the Duxford Wing merrily proceeded, two 11 Group squadrons were scrambled to meet the threat – but North Weald was bombed before the enemy could be intercepted by Park's squadrons. 12 Group was then requested to sweep over Kent and meet a raid incoming towards Biggin Hill – but Leigh-Mallory himself recalled his squadrons owing to bad weather; the opportunity to intercept these raids was therefore lost. Not surprisingly, this result led to an unwelcome rebuke from Fighter Command HQ: Leigh-Mallory 'must not neglect his own responsibilities in future'.[42]

Two days later, the Battle of Britain is officially considered to have concluded. While the historiography of the epic aerial conflict continually evolves, and historians hotly debate just how crucial or otherwise those sixteen weeks of high drama really were, the fact remains that Hitler failed to invade Britain in 1940 – which was his clearly stated intention. For Fighter Command, little or nothing seemed to have changed on 1 November: there was certainly no clear-cut finale to this particular battle. Indeed, the fighter forces of both sides continued to clash over the Channel until early 1941, when the weather closed in. A more pressing problem now, though, was the *nachtangriff* – the relentless pounding of British cities by night – to which, with airborne interception radar and dedicated night-fighting aircraft yet to arrive, there appeared no answer. Nonetheless, after the disastrous Fall of France and the evacuation from Dunkirk, many considered it nothing short of miraculous that Britain remained in the war – albeit at a cost of 544 Fighter Command aircrew and a great many others besides. Most importantly, Britain holding out that fateful summer ultimately made possible America's contribution to the war in Europe – and Churchill knew that without it Britain's chance of defeating Germany was slim indeed. Overy succinctly contextualised the Battle of Britain, which, he argued 'mattered above all to the British people, who were saved the fate that overtook the rest of Europe. The result was one of the key moral moments of the war, when the uncertainties and divisions of the summer gave way to a greater sense of purpose and a more united people. This was a necessary battle, as Stalingrad was for the eastern front.'[43] For this victory – for that is what is was – Air Chief Marshal Dowding and Air Vice-Marshal Park deserve full credit.

On 3 November, however, Air Vice-Marshal Douglas wrote to Dowding. What the latter was unaware of until then was that a week previously the Secretary of State for Air, Sir Archibald Sinclair, had visited Duxford. There the minister had spoken to Woodhall and Bader, both of whom enthused about the Big Wing. The day before the DCAS wrote, the Under-Secretary of State for Air, Harold Balfour, had likewise visited the famous 12 Group station and likewise spoken to Woodhall and Bader. Balfour confirmed what Sinclair himself had been told: the Wing was being requested too late and was under-used, and that Park jealously coveted 'his' Germans and resented 'poachers'. Moreover, Bader had emphasised that given time to gain height, he was 'absolutely certain' of 'taking enormous tolls'. Certainly on paper it already looked like he had. The DCAS also mentioned Mr Balfour's concern that Squadron Leader Bader may be disciplined for having been so outspoken. Dowding was not impressed. The information the two ministers had gleaned was wrong in its conclusions – as were the 'facts' upon which they were based. This approach, Dowding charged, was improper: 'There remains the question of the Under-Secretary of

State listening to the accusations of a junior officer against the Air Officer Commanding, and putting them on paper with the pious hope that that officer will not get into trouble ... Balfour has been in the service and ought to know better.' Dowding added that he blamed Bader for initiating much of the controversy, of whom he wrote, 'Whatever his other merits, suffers from a over-development of the critical faculties.'[44] Hinting at his realisation that the Leigh-Mallory–Woodhall–Bader triangle needed breaking, Dowding concluded that 'this might give an opportunity of moving young Bader to another station where he would be kept in better control. His amazing gallantry will protect him from disciplinary action if it can possibly be avoided.' Dowding was also forced to reiterate 12 Group's intended responsibilities. The bitterness between the neighbouring group commanders, in fact, was beginning to permeate their squadrons. Because of this on 6 November Dowding took an unprecedented step: control of combined operations between 11 and 12 Groups was removed from Park and Leigh-Mallory and given to Fighter Command HQ's operations room. On 17 November, Air Marshal Portal wrote to Dowding, informing him of Sinclair's direction that no disciplinary action was to be taken against Woodhall and Bader.

That same day, Dowding also learned that he was to be relieved as Fighter Command's chief. On 25 November he was succeeded by Air Chief Marshal William Sholto Douglas. On 27 December, Park was replaced as AOC 11 Group by Air Vice-Marshal Leigh-Mallory; the Victor of London became head of 23 Group, Training Command. The official account of the Battle of Britain, published by the Ministry of Information on behalf of the Air Ministry, made no mention of either Air Chief Marshal Dowding or Air Vice-Marshal Park.

This, though, is not a book about the so-called 'Big Wing Controversy'. Reams of documents survive, written in the hand of the political and service 'combatants' involved. The matter now has a historiography of its own – and, as always, historians remain divided over the Air Ministry's treatment of Dowding and Park. Some cite that both men had made political enemies and that the Big Wing argument provided a means of removing them. Others argue that the controversy was not the cause, that this was simply because Dowding's retirement was already overdue and Park was tired. Another view is that Dowding's inability to deal with German night attacks was his downfall, and that with the Battle of Britain won a change in command – ready to fight a more offensive battle – was naturally required. The truth, very likely, includes elements of all these things. Park, however, stated his opinion in 1968: 'To my dying day I shall feel bitter at the base intrigue which was used to remove Dowding and myself as soon as we had won the battle.'

Park later commented that 'Bader, for whose bravery and courage I have great admiration, was used ... to make room for ... Leigh Mallory'. Leigh-Mallory, of course, had indicated to Park some time previously his determination to see Dowding removed. Regarding Douglas's potential involvement in such a plot, Dowding said, 'I do not think Bader would ever have allowed himself consciously to become embroiled in such a move. It would probably have come to a shock to hear that Leigh-Mallory ever entertained such an idea. It was one thing to disagree with my views, and to express criticisms forcibly, but it was another altogether to intrigue against his own Commander-in-Chief, which is why I think the latter was out of the question.' Douglas was, the evidence confirms, an extremely outspoken individual and immensely strong character. Indeed, he had overtly criticised fighter tactics from the instant he arrived on 19 Squadron in February 1940. That he subsequently voiced criticism on a wider stage, shouting loudly from his soapbox regarding something he passionately believed in, was no surprise. Douglas's insubordination was innocent enough – even naïve – but the same could not be said of Woodhall and Leigh-Mallory. Indeed, that the latter had an axe to grind and personal ambition is indisputable. Whether the Big Wing argument was the entire cause of Dowding and Park's removal will always be a moot point, but it was certainly a significant factor – to which Squadron Leader Douglas Bader was pivotal.

In 1969, the book *Dowding and the Battle of Britain* was published. The author, Robert Wright, was a former night-fighter pilot and personal assistant to Dowding in the latter stages of the Battle of Britain. As such, Wright had personal knowledge and experience of what had gone on, and interviewed Lord Dowding – as he became, in the last years of his life. Wright's book was arguably biased towards his old boss and Air Vice-Marshal Park – but for the first time the 'base intrigue' was placed firmly in the public domain – provoking much interest and a strong reaction, not least from Douglas Bader. By then, Leigh-Mallory was dead, having been killed in a wartime flying accident, so was not alive to either defend himself or publish his account. Brickhill's *Reach for the Sky* was released in 1954, when Douglas first read of MacDonald's meeting with Churchill. At first he simply refused to believe it, berating the publisher as to what rubbish it was and forcefully stating that he, MacDonald's CO, had no knowledge of it. Later, however, Douglas discussed these events with Balfour – from whom he discovered that his old adjutant had indeed personally involved Churchill.[45] It is likely that only then did Douglas even begin to appreciate the true effect of his wagging tongue during the Battle of Britain. Before his death in 1982, Douglas was interviewed by the British historian Alfred Price, and said,

You are the first author who has ever come to see me about it (the Big Wing Controversy). Despite everything published about my Wing you are the only one who has ever bothered to come and talk to me about it, and after all I am the only chap left alive who can tell you. All, however, played on this so-called controversy between Leigh-Mallory and Park, and of course Dowding being sacked. I was only an acting squadron leader at the time, but I got fairly close to Leigh-Mallory. He was one of those warm people, he was a tremendously good commander and everybody who served with him was very fond of him. He would come over and say 'Well done' and all that sort of thing. What happened was that on 30 August 1940 we got off a squadron, just twelve of us, and we had everything in our favour: height, I knew where they were and we had the sun. We shot down a few without any problems whatsoever. When we were writing out our combat reports afterwards, Leigh-Mallory rang me up and said, 'Congratulations, Bader, on the Squadron's fine performance today,' and so I said, 'Thank you very much, Sir, but if we'd had more aeroplanes then we would have shot down a whole lot more.' He asked what I meant and I explained that with more fighters our results would have been even better. He said, 'Look, I'd like to talk to you about this,' and so I flew over to Hucknall and told him what I thought. He agreed and created the Duxford Wing, under my leadership and comprising 242, 310 (Czech) and 19 Squadrons. Leigh-Mallory said to try the idea and see what we could do with three squadrons. There was actually no problem at all. We usually got off the ground in four minutes, at worst five. Now other people, who were ignorant and didn't bother to come and see me, assumed, and therefore stated in print, that the Wing took a long time to get off the ground. Not so.

The thing was that the battle should have been controlled from Fighter Command HQ, where they had a map of the whole country and knew the state of each squadron, instead of just the 11 Group control centre which focussed entirely on their area. The other point is that we never suggested that 11 Group should use wings, they couldn't, they were far too near the Germans. It was right for Park to use his squadrons as he did, and even if the battle had been controlled from Fighter Command HQ then I would not say that they should have been used any differently.

My point now is that all of these books have been written about the so-called controversy, but history has to be put right before it is too late. The point is that we should have been called for in good time, when the enemy was building up.

If there really was a controversy, why didn't we all know it was happening? There have been some appalling books written on the subject which malign me dreadfully, saying that I had done my best to torpedo Park and Dowding. It is absurd to suggest that a mere acting squadron leader would have such power. Some of the authors should have known

better. No one but you has ever come to see me about it, as I
have said.[46]

That Douglas personally held both Dowding and Park in only
the highest esteem cannot be doubted. When the ancient Lord
Dowding visited the set of the feature film *Battle of Britain* in
1968, it was Group Captain Douglas Bader who insisted on
pushing his former AOC's wheelchair. On 12 September 1975, the
Battle of Britain Fighter Association held a memorial service in
honour of Air Vice-Marshal Sir Keith Park, who had died earlier
that year. From the pulpit of the RAF's church of St Clement
Dane's in London's Strand, he said that

the late Air Chief Marshal Lord Dowding, Commander-in-
Chief Fighter Command, from 1936 until the end of 1940,
has often been acclaimed as the saviour of this country.
Rightly so, because in the pre-war years he laid down an
air defence system which in the event proved impregnable.
Nevertheless, the Battle of Britain had to be fought in that
high summer thirty-five years ago. It is right and proper for
me to say on this occasion something which I do not recall
has been said before. It is this. That great and vital air battle
had to be controlled, directed and brought to a successful
conclusion by the man whose memory we honour today.
The awesome responsibility for this country's survival rested
squarely on Keith Park's shoulders. Had he failed, 'Stuffy'
Dowding's foresight, determination and achievement would
have counted for nought ... During the battle this splendid
officer flew himself around in his Hurricane to see what was
going on. He had done the same during the Dunkirk episode

earlier in 1940. This was leadership indeed of the sort that was to become traditional in the Royal Air Force ... This is no sad occasion. Rather it is a time during which we can let our memories drift back to those halcyon days of 1940 when we fought together in English skies under the determined leadership of that great New Zealander we are remembering now ... Keith Park was one of us. We all shared the great experience. That is what we remember today. British military history of this century has been enriched with the names of great fighting men from New Zealand, of all ranks and in every one of our services. Keith Park's name is carved into that history alongside those of his peers.[47]

Many years before Douglas spoke those fine words of 11 Group's former AOC, on 29 January 1941, Park's successor, Air Vice-Marshal Leigh-Mallory, conducted a paper exercise. Using the circumstances of an actual attack made on the sector stations of Kenley and Biggin Hill on 6 September 1940, the new AOC 11 Group had orchestrated this experiment to prove the great worth of large fighter formations in defence. The enemy 'raid', however, was not intercepted while inbound and bombed both target airfields. Leigh-Mallory's fighters never even got off the ground.

14

WINTER OF CONTENT

The morale of the population under fire was naturally of enormous concern to the British government. On Christmas Eve 1914, in fact, the first German bomb had dropped on British soil – a small device which exploded harmlessly in a Dover garden. From that point onwards Britain could no longer rely upon being an island to distance the civilian population from military action. By the Armistice, German Zeppelins and twin-engined bombers had raided Britain over 100 times – killing 1,413 people.[1] For the first time in history London's underground railway network was used to shelter civilians from aerial attack – but the bombing, on occasion, provoked 'mass panic and near riots'.[2] The emergent air power doctrine between the wars consequently confirmed the bomber as supreme. Indeed, Bialer considered that 'the fear of aerial bombardment in interwar Britain was unprecedented and unique'.[3] Upon the outbreak of war in 1939, the MOI was re-established to 'present the national case to the public at home and abroad in time of war. To achieve this end it is not only necessary to provide for the preparation and issue of National Propaganda, but also for the issue of "news" and for such control of information issued to the public as may be demanded by the needs of security.'[4] In 1940, the MOI lost no time in producing a poster entitled 'Let Us Go Forward Together', showing Churchill's pugnacious image with a squadron of Hurricanes behind the Prime Minister. Vital to maintaining the morale of a population subjected to air attack was news of enemy losses – to which, of course, the fighter pilot, already glamorised by First World War exploits and seen as somehow exotic, was key. As Francis rightly argued, 'Given such star appeal, the flyer's decisive role in the British military effort between 1939 and 1945 was undoubtedly matched by an equally significant contribution to the propaganda war which accompanied it.'[5]

The legless Squadron Leader Bader, above all other RAF aircrew, was a potent source of morale-boosting news indeed for the MOI. On 15 July 1940, the *Mirror* published a front-page article, including a photograph of both Douglas and Thelma, entitled 'The Greatest Hero of Them All'.[6] Further articles followed concerning his inspirational leadership of 242 Squadron, gallantry in the air and, naturally, the award of his DSO. At the time, the Air Ministry's policy was to largely preserve heroic pilots' anonymity – but Douglas Bader was identified in the *Telegraph* on 16 September 1940.[7] The DSO and a score of ten enemy aircraft destroyed confirmed Douglas as both a fighter ace and bona fide war hero. This was the start of why he became, and remains, as Campion commented, 'arguably the best-known Battle of Britain pilot'.[8] With the Battle of Britain won, revelling in the camaraderie and adoration of his Canadian pilots, Squadron Leader Douglas Bader DSO was in his absolute element. In the months and years of war ahead, he would continue to be of great value not just in his fighter's cockpit and as a leader of men, but as an inspiration to the British people.

On 6 November, the Duxford Wing was patrolling between Dover and Deal when Me 109s of II and III/JG 26 swept westwards over the Channel on a *freie jagd*. Battle was joined but although claims were made, no enemy fighters crashed in England. Between 1427 and 1620 hours, forty-two more JG 26 Me 109s intruded. Over Canterbury, 310 Squadron was bounced: five Hurricanes were hit; two pilots baled out while the others crash-landed. Such was the ferocity of this attack that only Flight Lieutenant Willie McKnight of 242 Squadron brought his guns to bear, shooting down *Feldwebel* Schedit of I/JG 26. This enemy machine was also attacked by 19 Squadron's Flying Officer Haines. However, 242 Squadron's Sub-Lieutenant Gardner forced-landed his shot-up Hurricane and Pilot Officer Hart was killed by *Oberleutnant* Johannes Seifert, *Staffelkapitän* of 3/JG 26. 19 Squadron's Flight Lieutenant 'Farmer' Lawson, flying a new cannon-armed Spitfire, claimed a 109 which 'literally fell to bits'.[9] *Hauptmann* Rolf Pingel, *Gruppenkommandeur* of I/JG 26, shot down Pilot Officer Hradil of 19 Squadron, who crashed in flames off Southend's pier. Flight Sergeant 'Grumpy' Unwin claimed a German fighter but in turn his Spitfire was severely damaged, possibly by *Hauptmann* Gerhard Schöpfel, *Gruppenkommandeur* of III/JG 26. The Duxford Wing had not fared well in this engagement: two pilots had been killed, a further five aircraft destroyed with another damaged.

On 8 November the Wing was patrolling over Canterbury; Squadron Leader Brian Lane: 'Sighted Me 109s over Canterbury and turned to give chase. Hurricane squadron chased *us* and their leader put a burst into my engine!! Apparently CO of one of the North Weald squadrons. Blacked out, then minus oxygen forced-landed at Eastchurch OK. Jennings escorted me down and refused to leave me. Damn good of him.'[10] The speed and confusion inherent in aerial combat frequently and understandably led to both aircraft misidentification and such incidents of so-called 'friendly fire'; this was a far from uncommon experience as, in the heat of the highly charged moment, speed deceived the human eye. The offending Hurricane pilot was Squadron Leader Lionel Gaunce DFC, CO of 46 Squadron. Flying Officer Pat Wells was flying Hurricanes with 249 Squadron, which shared North Weald with 46: 'After this incident Squadron Leader Bader arrived from Duxford. He first approached the 249 Squadron dispersal but we told him that we knew nothing about it. He then taxied over to 46 Squadron. While he did so we telephoned to let them know that Bader was coming. I dread to think what happened when he got over there as he was fuming!'[11] If Douglas had previously considered 242 Squadron to be his own fiefdom, he clearly now considered that to apply to all squadrons in the Duxford Wing. Indeed, this fitted perfectly with what the Air Ministry would soon strive to create: *Esprit d'Wing*.

By this time, the German night Blitz was in full swing. Britain's nocturnal defences were woefully inadequate. Airborne interception radar remained in its infancy and the Bristol Beaufighter – which had greater speed and fire-power than the Bristol Blenheim Mk IF currently pressed into service as a night-fighter – was only just becoming operational. Consequently both Spitfires and Hurricanes were used as night-fighters – although neither had been designed as such. With two rows of exhausts glowing either side of their Merlin engines, situated in front the pilot, and small canopies, visibility was not good. Moreover, with a narrow track undercarriage, the Spitfire could be tricky to land at night – as Douglas had already discovered. Nonetheless, desperate measures were called for. 'Fighter Nights' were therefore launched that dreadful winter, during which Spitfires and

Hurricanes patrolled above British cities. Guided by searchlights and anti-aircraft fire, they sought out German bombers – but more often than not landed without having even so much as spied a raider. On the night of 14/15 November, the Luftwaffe, guided by radio beams, decimated the heart of the West Midlands city of Coventry. Only three of 242 Squadron's pilots were night operational: Bader, Turner and Ball. That night they patrolled above the burning city but, although they knew the raiders were discharging their deadly cargoes below, saw not one German bomber.

By 12 December, Big Wing supporter Air Chief Marshal Douglas was Commander-in-Chief of Fighter Command, and Air Vice-Marshal Leigh-Mallory AOC 11 Group. On that day, 242 Squadron moved to Martlesham Heath – in the Debden Sector of 11 Group. Given 11 Group's new AOC, this move was no coincidence. From Martlesham the squadron flew a seemingly endless round of patrols over the east coast and convoys. On 20 December, however, Fighter Command undertook an operation which was apparently inconsequential but which set the scene for the New Year: Flight Lieutenant Christie and Pilot Officer Bodie of 66 Squadron crossed the Channel at low level and attacked the enemy airfield at either Berck or Le Touquet. On Christmas Day, Douglas attended a conference of squadron commanders at Fighter Command HQ. 1941 would see a drastic change in policy: instead of continuing to fight a defensive battle, Fighter Command would be going on the offensive, 'Leaning into France'. This was exciting news indeed for our bloodthirsty and swashbuckling legless hero.

Air Chief Marshal; Douglas reported on these far-reaching plans:

Broadly speaking the plan, which we now adopted, visualized two kinds of offensive operations. In cloudy weather, small numbers of fighters would cross the Channel under cover of the clouds, dart out of them to attack any German aircraft they could find, and return similarly protected. In good weather fighter forces amounting to several squadrons at a time, and sometimes accompanied by bombers, would sweep over Northern France. The codenames chosen for these operations were respectively 'Mosquito' (later changed to 'Rhubarb' to avoid confusion with the aircraft of that name) and 'Circus'; but in practice it was necessary to restrict the name 'Circus' to operations with bombers, and fulfilling certain other conditions…

Rhubarb patrols began on 20 December 1940, and provided valuable experience alike for pilots, operational commanders, and the staffs of the formations concerned. I encouraged the delegation of responsibility for the planning of these patrols to lower formations, and many patrols were planned by the pilots themselves with the help of their Squadron Intelligence Officers.[12]

On 7 January 1941, having received a stern rebuke from Thelma for not telling her first when his DSO was awarded, Douglas's wife was the first to know that her husband had been awarded the Distinguished Flying Cross. The citation, published in the *London Gazette*, read that 'Squadron Leader Bader has continued to lead his squadron and wing with the utmost gallantry on all occasions. He has now destroyed ten hostile aircraft and damaged several more.' Although Douglas's personal score, like that of his squadron and the Duxford Wing, was questionable, no one could dispute the citation's first sentence. Once more Douglas was in the newspapers. Needless to say, Douglas lost no time in planning and personally leading 242 Squadron's first 'Mosquito' raid. On 9 January Douglas and Sergeant Richardson took off from Duxford, intruded over the French coast but found no targets. That same day, a wing of five RAF fighter squadrons swept over France – but was ignored by the Germans. It was an inauspicious start to the 'Non-Stop Offensive'.

On 10 January, 242 Squadron participated in 11 Group's first 'Circus'. These were, in fact, complex operations. Whereas a 'Mosquito' or 'Rhubarb' could be planned at squadron level, because of the large number of aircraft involved from various groups, a Circus had to be organised by Fighter Command. The object was that a swarm of fighters would escort a small number of medium bombers to attack a target in northern France. The fighter squadrons would be deployed thus:

Close Escort: Surrounding and remaining with the bombers at all times.

Escort Cover: Protecting the Close Escort fighters.

High Cover: Preventing enemy fighters getting between the Close and Escort wings.

Target Support: Independently routed fighters flying directly to and covering the target area.

Withdrawal Cover: Fighters supporting the return flight, by which time escorting fighters would be running short of fuel and ammunition.

Fighter Diversion: A wing, or even wings, eventually, creating a diversionary sweep to keep hostile aircraft from the target area during 'Ramrod' operations, this being similar to a Circus but involving the destruction of a specific target.

Circus No. 1 was despatched against ammunition supplies hidden in the Forêt de Guines. Blenheims of 114 Squadron were closely escorted by the Hurricanes of 56 Squadron, Forward Support being provided by the North Weald Hurricane squadrons: 242 and 249. 302 Squadron's Hurricanes and 610 Squadron's Spitfires flew Target Support; the Spitfires of 41, 64 and 611 Squadrons were High Cover, and finally 74 and 92 Squadrons' Spitfires brought up the rear. This represented some 120 fighters and six bombers. This was, of course, a complete reversal of the defensive role undertaken by Fighter Command – and an offensive one for which Hurricanes and Spitfires, intended as short-range interceptors, were not designed or intended. It was Fighter Command's pilots who now faced a two-way Channel crossing on a single engine with limited fuel, and combat either over the sea or enemy-occupied territory. On this initial operation, I and II/JG 53 responded and engaged the RAF fighters: one Hurricane and a Spitfire were destroyed for no German loss. This rather set the scene for the 'season' ahead.

Offensive operations suited Douglas's personality and temperament perfectly. This was exactly what this man of action required – not idling hours away while awaiting a scramble that rarely came. Rhubarbs also enabled Douglas to use his own initiative – typically he set to with enthusiasm. On 12 January 242 Squadron flew Fighter Command's first concentrated Rhubarb operations. On the first, Douglas and Flight Lieutenant Stan Turner machine-gunned a small vessel off Calais; two more pairs then strafed German vessels and troops at Gravelines. The Hurricanes, however, were bounced by the Me 109s of 8/JG 26: *Feldwebel* Helmut Bügelmann shot down and killed Pilot Officer Willie McKnight DFC. This was a sad blow to 242 Squadron, one which 'shattered everyone'.[13] The combat-experienced McKnight was exactly the kind of pilot Fighter

Command could ill afford to lose. Later that day, Pilot Officer John Latta was lost on a similarly senseless operation. Again, these sad events also set the scene for what lay ahead.

Against the backdrop of such operations, which really represented another new and bitter learning curve for Fighter Command, King George VI and Queen Elizabeth visited RAF Debden. Squadron Leader Bader and his pilots were presented to their Majesties. Many years later, the Queen Mother, as Her Majesty became, would make a point, as Patron of the Battle of Britain Fighter Association, of always dancing with Douglas at the annual reunion held at Bentley Priory. On that winter day in 1941, though, such peaceful days were a long way off and somewhere in the distance of a most uncertain future. Fighter Command was also changing. The requirement for large numbers of replacements had seen an end to the vice-like grip on commissions exerted by public schoolboys. Grammar schoolboys were now being commissioned into the RAFVR 'for the duration of the present emergency' and posted to both regular and auxiliary squadrons. Indeed, it was in the latter, hitherto socially elite squadrons that the change was most keenly felt; their composition now consisted of the same diverse mixture of personnel as regular squadrons: regulars, reservists and auxiliaries in addition to men from the Commonwealth, American volunteers and free men from the occupied lands. Nonetheless, a Cranwell background still marked such an officer out as a professional – and the 'associations of Cranwell' still bound that brotherhood closely.

On 12 February Douglas visited Broadcasting House in London and broadcast a morale-boosting account of 242 Squadron's activities in the Battle of Britain – this subsequently appearing in print, along with a collection of similar pieces by other airmen of note. As the winter wore on, 242 Squadron continued flying

Rhubarbs and Circus operations. Offensive in nature though these sorties were, the heady days of the Battle of Britain they were not. Weather, of course, plays an enormous part in flying, and what Fighter Command was really doing at this time was preparing for a sustained effort from the spring of 1941 onwards. 242 Squadron re-equipped with the improved Hurricane Mk IIC on 21 February. Even before the Battle of Britain, however, it was already apparent that the Me 109 was superior to the Hurricane, especially at high altitude – which was what really mattered. Park had, therefore, used his Spitfire squadrons in pairs to engage high-flying enemy fighters and protect his Hurricanes while they attacked bombers at medium height. Whatever improvements were made to the Hurricane it could never become a high-altitude fighter. What Fighter Command's front-line squadrons required were Spitfires – which was in hand.

What Douglas was unaware of at this time was that plans were afoot for all sector stations to accommodate a wing of three fighter squadrons. The Big Wing experience had indicated that such a formation required an overall leader. It was therefore intended to create a new post, that of Wing Commander (Flying). The Wing Leader, therefore, was cut loose from day-to-day administration and therefore able to concentrate on operational flying. Given Douglas's aversion to paperwork and corner-cutting, such a role would be perfectly suited to him. On 7 December 1940, in fact, Leigh-Mallory had drawn up a short-list of potential Wing Leaders: Squadron Leader DRS Bader DSO DFC was the first name on it. Early in March, Douglas was summoned by Leigh-Mallory, who revealed these plans. Fighter Command's two foremost stations were Biggin Hill and Tangmere, the latter situated on the south coast near Chichester. Douglas was given the choice of either. Biggin Hill, he thought, was far too close to the social distractions of London. He chose Tangmere; 'Sailor' Malan got Biggin Hill. The only downside from Douglas's perspective was that he was unable to take his beloved 242 Squadron with him. This was for two reasons: firstly because the new wings were all Spitfire equipped, and secondly because he would favour 242, which would have an adverse effect on the concept of *Esprit d'Wing*.[14] Douglas returned to Martlesham Heath and awaited formal confirmation of both his promotion to Wing Commander and posting. Understandably, 242 Squadron was unhappy at losing its popular CO. Indeed, before an audience with the king and queen at Debden, Flight Lieutenant Stan Turner 'jabbed his pipe into Leigh-Mallory's chest and said, "Look here, sir, you can't go and post our CO away, because we won't work for anyone else!"

"Turner", Bader balled, "Stop prodding the AOC with your pipe!"

Leigh-Mallory didn't seem to mind at all.'[15] Douglas had, of course, been appointed to command 242 Squadron upon the recommendation of Woodhall and Mermagen at what was a time of crisis. Upon his leadership the restoration of the squadron's morale and fighting efficiency rested. Whatever the rights and wrongs of the Big Wing, or 242 Squadron's actual score of enemy aircraft destroyed, that Douglas had achieved everything asked of him – and more – is demonstrable and recognised in the DSO. Moreover, the squadron had been awarded a total of ten DFCs – an incredible achievement considering how low morale had been after the Fall of France.

On 18 March, Douglas handed over command of 242 Squadron to Squadron Leader 'Treacle' Tracey – and set off in his MG, with his faithful batman, Stokoe, for Tangmere and new adventures.

15

TANGMERE WING:
BADER'S BUS COMPANY

On 18 March 1941, Wing Commander Douglas Bader reported to RAF Tangmere's Station Commander, Group Captain Jack Boret. Douglas discovered that the Tangmere Win's three Spitfire squadrons were 145, commanded by Squadron Leader Jack Leather DFC, Squadron Leader John Ellis DFC's 610 and Squadron Leader Billy Burton DFC's 616. 610 and 616 Squadron were based at Tangmere's satellite at Westhampnett (Goodwood); 145 at Merston. According to Brickhill, the 'Wingco' 'attached himself' to 616 Squadron because 'it had the least battle experience'.[1] More likely that was because Douglas already knew 616, which had flown in his Big Wing – and Burton was also a Cranwellian, which Leather and Ellis were not.

Inevitably, Douglas lost no time in flying one of 616 Squadron's Spitfire Mk IIs. His first flight as Wing Leader was the following day, a fifty-minute familiarisation flight. Never one to waste time, that afternoon Douglas led his new Wing on an uneventful channel sweep. Sergeant Alan Smith:

> Sitting in readiness at dispersal I heard the roar of a Spitfire as it dived low, climbed, did a half-roll and lowered its undercarriage while inverted, rolled out, side-slipped and made a perfect landing. Out of the cockpit climbed Wing

Commander Douglas Bader, who walked with his distinctive gait into dispersal. The Wing Commander introduced himself and said he would be leading the Tangmere Wing, and explained that he would do so with 616 Squadron. He obviously knew Flying Officer Hugh 'Cocky' Dundas and Pilot Officer Johnnie Johnson, and said, 'You'll be Red Three, Cocky, and you, Johnnie, will be Red Four.' Looking around he caught my eye and said 'Who are you?'

'Sergeant Smith, Sir,' I replied.

'Right, you fly as my Red Two and God help you if you don't watch my tail!'

I couldn't believe my ears, it was like God asking me to keep an eye on heaven for him! Flying with Douglas, Cocky and Johnnie was to become the greatest experience of my life and I considered myself quite the most fortunate pilot in the RAF.[2]

With his initials being 'DB', Douglas adopted the radio call sign 'Dogsbody'.

616 Squadron's 'A' Flight was commanded by Flight Lieutenant Ken Holden, a tough Yorkshireman, and 'B' by the twenty-year-old Flight Lieutenant Colin MacFie. Few of the squadron's other pilots, except Pilot Officer Lionel 'Buck' Casson, had much combat experience: the squadron had been decimated at Kenley in August 1940, and saw little action with the Big Wing. Based at Kirton before arriving in the Tangmere Sector on 26 February 1941, 616 had received and trained replacement pilots like Sergeant Smith.

At 1520 hours on 19 March, Douglas led 616 and 610 Squadrons off from Westhampnett, to patrol Hastings at 30,000 feet. 616 Squadron led, slightly below 610. Upon reaching Hastings the condensation trail height was found to be at 25,000 feet, so 610 descended below that altitude. This meant that any enemy aircraft above the Wing would create vapour trails and be readily seen. This formation, with 610 providing top cover, would become Douglas's standard operating procedure. Having made three sweeps out to sea, the Wing was ordered to Beachy Head. At 1620 hours, while re-crossing the English coast, two Me 109s attacked 610 Squadron from the rear. One of these assailants was destroyed. Pilot Officer Johnnie Johnson, Douglas's Red Three:

> We flew in line-astern formation, each squadron in sections of four. Cocky was Red Two, Bader, of course, Red One, and Pilot Officer 'Nip' Hepple brought up the rear as Red Four. As we climbed across the Channel I spotted three Me 109s only a few hundred feet higher than us, travelling in the same direction. They hadn't seen us and 145 Squadron, which had joined us from Merston and was higher than the 109s, were perfectly positioned to attack. I should have calmly reported on the R/T the number, type and position of the enemy. I did not do so. In my excitement I simply shouted 'Look out, Dogsbody!' This represented a warning of utmost danger, of being bounced. The other pilots took rapid evasive action, breaking in all directions. Our tight formation was reduced to a shambles, and we returned to Tangmere individually. Bader came into our dispersal and angrily inquired 'Now who's the clot who shouted "Look out"?' I admitted that it had been me. 'Very well. Now tell us what we had to "look out" for?'
>
> 'Well, Sir, there were three Me 109s a few hundred feet above ...'

'Three 109s! We could have clobbered the lot, but your girlish scream made us think there were fifty of the brutes behind!' This humiliating public rebuke hurt deeply, but was well justified. Douglas, though, was always quick to forgive and gave me an encouraging grin as he stomped out of dispersal. It was a lesson in leadership I never forgot.[3]

On 27 March, Douglas's initials were painted on the fuselage of Spitfire Mk IIA P7666. All Wing Leaders adopted this practice, to make them more readily identifiable in the air. On the engine cowling the Wing Commander had an artwork painted depicting Hitler sustaining a kick in the backside from an RAF flying boot. Such inspired nose art had adorned Douglas's 242 Squadron Hurricane (fuselage code letters 'LE-D'). Spitfire 'DB' also proudly sported a Wing Commander's rank pennant. The Wing Leader's section of four inevitably became known as 'Dogsbody Section'. On 2 April, Leigh-Mallory visited Tangmere to check on progress. Shortly afterwards Douglas began gathering his own men around him. John Ellis handed over command to Squadron Leader H. De C. A. Woodhouse AFC on 14 April, although this particular appointment was not a Bader selection and would be short-lived; Jack Leather was succeeded in command of 145 Squadron two days later, however, by Squadron Leader Stan Turner, Douglas's right-hand man in 242 Squadron. Sergeant Frank Twitchett: 'We had a first-class CO in Stan Turner, a craggy Canadian who stood no nonsense from anybody but treated his pilots, regardless of rank, with absolute fairness. I, for one, had much admiration for him.'[4] That afternoon Leigh-Mallory returned to Tangmere by air and held a conference with Douglas and his squadron commanders. Sergeant Peter Ward-Smith flew Spitfires with 610

Squadron: 'When Wing Commander Bader took over at Tangmere we realised that something big was the offing, but never an air offensive on the Big Wing scale.'[5]

On 21 April, the Tangmere Wing escorted eighteen Blenheims to Le Havre. The bombers, however, were unable to locate their target. Running low on fuel, the Spitfire pilots had no choice but to abandon the Blenheims to their fate. Sergeant Bob 'Butch' Morton, 616 Squadron: 'When our fuel was getting near danger point, Bader waggled his wings as a signal to us and set off for England. On the crossing I fear we concentrated more on our fuel gauges than keeping lookout.'[6] 616 Squadron was subjected to a fleeting attack by *Leutnant* Votel of I/JG 2, who shot down and killed Morton's number two, Sergeant Sellars. On 22 April, Group Captain Boret was succeeded as Tangmere Sector Commander by none other than Group Captain Woodhall. Leigh-Mallory now had his old Duxford team back together – setting the scene for high drama.

Already, Wing Commander Bader was making his presence felt; Sergeant Bob Morton:

My first sight of Wing Commander Bader was sitting on the radiator of Billy Burton's car, holding a shotgun, while the CO drove him erratically across the airfield in search of rabbits! At this time I had a coat of arms painted on my Mae West: argent, on a pale azure, three crowns for Hull, on a chief of the second the tail of a Spitfire diving into a cloud; the motto was 'Spotto, Squirto, Scrammo', or 'I spot, I shoot, I remove myself.' It was highly commended by Wing Commander Bader. Outside our 'A' Flight hut soon appeared a notice: 'Bader's Bus Company: Daily Trips to the Continent.

Return Tickets Only!' The 'trip' turned out to usually take place twice daily, the 'Bus Company' bit derived from the Wing's radio call sign of 'Greenline Bus'.[7]

Pilot Officer Buck Casson:

I had first met Bader at Coltishall on 3 September 1940, when he tried to tick some of us off for having our top buttons undone in true fighter pilot style. I came to know him briefly during early 1941, when 616 occasionally joined up with 242 Squadron as a 12 Group Wing flying from either Duxford or Wittering. Of course I came to know him much better at Tangmere from March 1941 onwards. We enjoyed playing golf together at Goodwood. At the house in Bognor Regis where he was billeted with Thelma, called 'The Bay House' but known to we pilots as 'The Bag House', we carried him to the pool where he swam extremely well. He always wanted company so we often went over there for drinks and a chat.[8]

Billy Burton's young wife, Jean: 'I had already met the Baders the previous summer in Norfolk. During the summer of 1941 got to know them really well, largely due to their generous open-house entertaining at "The Bay House" during the evenings, which Billy, members of the Wing and I frequently attended.'[9]

Sergeant Alan Smith:

Whenever we flew over France on fighter sweeps or escorting bombers, we were always the last to return to base. Mission completed and everyone else going home, Douglas would hang around looking for a Hun to engage so long as we had ammunition and enough fuel to get us back to base. As soon as we crossed over the English coast, Douglas would slide back his cockpit cover and out would come his pipe, which he lit and puffed away upon contentedly. I could not help but reflect that he was virtually sitting on his petrol tank![10]

Pilot Officer Johnnie Johnson: 'Oh yes, Bader used to light a match in the cockpit, "Swan Vestas"; he'd be there puffing away, couldn't see him for smoke sometimes! Douglas was very "salty", you know, always effing and blinding. Our Controller, Woodhall, would shout up and say, "Come on, Douglas, I've got WAAFs down here," and Bader would just reply, "Oh it's alright, Woody, I'll just come and see 'em later and apologise!"'[11]

Flying Officer Hugh Dundas:

I was shot down during the Battle of Britain, baling out and injuring my shoulder. When I resumed operations 616 Squadron was contributing to the five squadron strong Big Wing. Given my earlier experience I was not unnaturally a little anxious. On our first patrol, Bader's voice came over the radio. To my amazement this legless man, flying into battle, was calling up Woodhall to arrange a game of squash! I was absolutely astonished! This calmed my nerves no end. With such a man leading us, how could I come to any harm? His arrival at Tangmere and decision to lead the Wing with 616 Squadron was welcome indeed from my perspective.[12]

The Tangmere Wing continued flying Rhubarbs, sweeps and Circus operations. Douglas continued to enthusiastically discuss tactics. On the evening of 7 May, Douglas gathered certain of his officers around him, sitting up in the mess until late. Flying Officer Dundas: 'We expressed our dissatisfaction with formations adopted in the past ... the half pints went down again and again while we argued the toss.'[13] Dundas suggested that four aircraft flying in line abreast, some 50 yards apart, could never be bounced from behind. Those on the right would cover the tails of the Spitfires on the left and *vice versa*. No enemy could therefore approach unseen, but if attacked the formation could break upwards, one pair to port, the other to starboard. This was identical, of course, to the tactics German pilots had developed during the Spanish Civil War and rapidly adopted as standard. It is difficult to understand, therefore, why Fighter Command took so long to imitate the enemy. The vic had rapidly been found virtually suicidal, and individual squadrons had been experimenting with their own tactical formations for some time. These generally seem to have involved some kind of line-astern formation – not abreast, like the German *schwarm*, comprising two pairs, leader and wingman. Nursing a hangover at breakfast the following morning, Dundas regretted his inspirational suggestion: 'Not being a drinker, "DB" strode into the mess with his buccaneering gait and was clearly in rude health. He told me that he had considered my idea and had decided to try it out. I nodded in weak agreement but was somewhat startled when he added "This morning"!'[14]

Douglas led off a section of four Spitfires, comprising two pairs: Dundas and himself, and 610 Squadron's Squadron Leader Woodhouse and Sergeant Maine. The section climbed to 26,000 feet over mid-Channel and prowled up and down, just south of Dover, inviting trouble. Six Me 109s of Stab/JG 51 – coincidentally led by Major Werner Mölders, who had invented the *schwarm* in Spain – soon appeared tailing the Spitfires and at the same height. At what he guessed to be the optimum moment, Douglas broke both pairs around to reverse the situation. As Dundas levelled out, resuming the section's original course, there was no sign of the enemy – but then rounds raked his machine. Thick smoke engulfed his cockpit. Dundas opened his hood and limped back to crash-land at Hawkinge. During the break, tracer had also flashed past Maine, who shook off his assailant before firing at an Me 109 and hitting its fuselage. Maine was then hit by anti-aircraft fire but broke again and attacked a 109 at point-blank range – which crashed into the sea.

Back at Westhampnett, Douglas debriefed. Despite Dundas having been shot down, the benefits of the line abreast formation in preventing a surprise attack were evident. The fault laid with Douglas, who had mistimed the break, leading to several of the 109s remaining behind the Spitfires as they levelled out. Moreover, instead of breaking in opposite directions, the two pairs should have turned in the same direction. Once the correct timing was achieved, all involved agreed that this new formation, the aircraft occupying similar positions to the fingers of an outstretched hand, was the future. Over the years, it has frequently been written that Wing Commander Bader was entirely responsible for the so-called 'Finger Four' – which was soon adopted not just by the Tangmere Wing but throughout Fighter Command. The fact is, though, that this was really a joint initiative with a twenty-year-old flying officer named Hugh Dundas. Pilot Officer Johnnie Johnson:

The RAF version of the 'Finger Four' was really Cocky Dundas's idea. We had all seen the Germans flying in these loose formations of German fighters, lean and hungry-looking, with plenty of room between them, like a pack of hunting dogs. Prior to going to Tangmere, we of 616 Squadron were not flying vics but pairs. Then Bader arrived and at first we flew in three fours, the loose fours being in line astern, and then Dundas suggested that we should fly fours in line abreast. Consequently, after a little experimentation, we adopted this in May 1941. Bader was actually the first man to talk to us about tactics. He had the ability to dissect an air battle and learn from it. It was therefore people like Bader and Malan who dictated tactics.[15]

As the offensive sorties continued, so did changes to the Tangmere Wing. On 4 June, Squadron Leader Woodhouse was succeeded in command of 610 Squadron by Ken Holden, hitherto the commander of 616 Squadron's 'A' Flight and with whom Douglas was impressed. Flight Lieutenant Denis Crowley-Milling:

Douglas found 610 Squadron at Westhampnett to be in poor shape with low morale. He promoted Ken Holden to command, and brought in both Flight Lieutenant Lee-Knight and myself from 242 Squadron as flight commanders, having already taken Stan Turner from 242 to command 145. From then on, we never looked back: sweeps over Northern France twice daily, escorting a few bombers, often Stirlings, to ensure a German reaction. As usual, Douglas Bader maintained a running commentary from the time we approached he French coast to the time we left on return. Also coming over the ether as we saw the French coast approaching was Stan Turner: 'Okay chaps, put your corks in!', or in other words 'Now is the time to look out for German fighters but don't be scared!' The Germans listening on the ground to this radio chatter must have thought it an order to activate some special equipment! There were, of course, numerous encounters with the Me 109s of Adolf Galland's JG 26, based around St Omer. For us it was the first time we had taken the fight to the Germans in a big way, so we were very inspired by it all and our morale was very high.[16]

On 9 June, Leigh-Mallory's Duxford team was completed at Tangmere when Flight Lieutenant Peter MacDonald MP arrived to take up duties as station adjutant. While 'Boozy Mac' shovelled paper, the air war over Northern France increased in intensity. Douglas, however, was frustrated that the German fighters were not being brought to battle – especially when the Biggin Hill Wing enjoyed some success. Returning from a subsequent Wing Leaders' Conference at 11 Group HQ, according to Brickhill, Douglas ranted, 'Malan got two today and his boys got a few more. It's damn well time we found some!'.[17] Pilot Officer Johnnie Johnson:

To say that Douglas was enthusiastic would be an understatement; he was very bloodthirsty, you know, just couldn't get enough of it. He'd come stomping into dispersal and say to our CO, Billy Burton, 'What are we doing today, then, Billy?' and Billy might respond, 'Well the Form "D" (Operational Order) has come through, Sir, but we're not on it. The other Wings are, but not us.' Bader would say, 'Right, we'll see about that! I'll have a word with bloody "LM"!' Then he would ring the AOC and, lo and behold, we'd be on ops![18]

Sergeant Ron Rayner would, in due course that summer, fly with 41 Squadron in the Tangmere Wing:

A Circus was quite a sight as it assembled. There would be this mass of Spitfires over Beachy Head, going round and round in circles over the English coast until everyone was together. It resembled – and became referred to as – a 'Beehive'. Suddenly Bader would say 'Okay, we're going!' and the beehive would proceed towards France. From when a combat began to when we landed the R/T was chattering away constantly. Of course Spitfires had no cockpit heating at all and so we had to take steps to keep warm; my mother knitted me some woollen stockings which I used to pull up over my legs at high altitude. Flying a Spitfire was also a very physical business, requiring constant jiggling about of the control column. Regarding range, this depended on the use of the throttle, and of course combat used up more petrol. When attacked you would go into a steep diving turn, pushing the throttle forward for maximum boost as you did so. Crossing the water with one engine was always a concern and we monitored our fuel gauges very carefully. After an operational flight I suppose we were tired, but we were fit and just glad not to be in the infantry![19]

21 June saw Fighter Command's greatest effort thus far during the new air fighting season. In the morning, the Tangmere Wing flew as Target Support on a Circus to St Omer. A running battle developed with Me 109s of JG 26, Squadron Leader Burton and Sergeant Machachek sharing a 109. In the afternoon, Douglas led the Wing to cover Blenheims withdrawing from St Omer. Awaiting

the bombers, the Tangmere Wing patrolled over the French coast, around Desvres, and watched the Blenheims and their close escort leave France over Boulogne. Douglas:

> We stayed around above and behind the bombers and escort when I noticed two Me 109s in line-astern about to turn in behind my section of four. I told them to break left and twisted round quickly (metal ailerons) and fired a very close deflection burst at the first Me 109E at about 50 yards' range, about half to one second. My bullets appeared to hit him as his hood dispersed in pieces and the aeroplane pulled up vertically, stalled and spun right-handed. I foolishly followed him down with my eyes and nearly collided with a cannon Spitfire of another squadron in the Wing and then re-formed my section. I claim this as destroyed because a) I know it was and b) because Flying Officer Marples of 616 Squadron saw an Me 109 spinning down at the time and place, and Squadron Leader Turner of 145 Squadron saw a pilot bale out of an Me 109 at the time and place as also did one of his pilots, c) Flying Officer Machatek of 145 Squadron saw an Me 109 dive into the sea right alongside another which had been shot down by one of 145 Squadron, same time and place, and d) no one else claims the second Me 109 which I am sure was mine.[20]

At the end of this day's fighting, Fighter Command claimed twenty-six enemy aircraft destroyed, seven probables and six damaged – against the loss of six fighters and two pilots. In fact the Germans lost nine Me 109s destroyed and four damaged. As these battles took place over France, it was even more difficult than during the Battle of Britain to verify combat claims. 'Fighter Command,' argued Cox, 'continued to accept exaggerated combat claims ... and ... mistakenly believed it was winning a battle of attrition when it was in fact suffering severely.'[21] Throughout the war, in fact, both sides suffered from inaccurate intelligence on enemy losses, and neither RAF or Luftwaffe intelligence were appropriately sceptical regarding their pilots' claims. Nonetheless, typically, the Germans' claims on 21 June 1941 were far more accurate than the RAF's: fourteen destroyed – eight more than actual – whereas Fighter Command's score was inflated by some seventeen. Once more, over-claiming became a prevalent feature of Fighter Command's combat reports.

Sergeant Bob Morton:

To claim an aircraft destroyed one had to have seen one of three events: the aircraft concerned striking the ground, the pilot baling out, or the aircraft bursting into flames. The first was almost impossible; most of our fighting would be carried out above 10,000 feet and no one would be fool enough to keep his eyes on the aircraft he had shot at, or follow it down. The second took time to occur, and other aircraft were likely to be shooting at the attacker as the Germans always worked in pairs. As for the third, I never saw this happen – unlike the fanciful epic film *Battle of Britain* in which every German fighter attacked blew up! Of course for us, to lose any battle meant incarceration in Germany.[22]

Many claims were submitted for Me 109s diving vertically at high speed, trailing plumes of black smoke – but these were rarely seen to actually crash. The 109's Daimler-Benz 601 engine was fuel-injected. The standard German evasive tactic was therefore to dive – fast. This was because the fuel injection system, unlike the carburettor-fed Merlin, was not negatively affected by gravity. The 109, therefore, would always lose a pursuing Spitfire in a sustained dive. As the enemy pilot rammed forward his throttle, the engine, reacting to this sudden influx of fuel and in generating immediate extra power, produced a plume of black exhaust smoke – deceiving RAF pilots into thinking their targets were destroyed. In reality, once his assailant was shaken off, the German pilot would level out and resume the fray or hedge-hop safely home. Like Air Vice-Marshal Park during the Battle of Britain, the German controllers refused to commit their fighters to battle *en masse*. There were, of course, no targets in France of such strategic value that the Germans had to do so. Instead they would only attack when tactical conditions favoured them – usually when the beehive was heading towards the French coast and getting low on fuel. Their attacks would inevitably be from on high, often featuring fleeting dives through RAF formations, firing as they went and dubbed 'dirty darts' by Spitfire pilot Wing Commander David Cox. For all Brickhill's trumpeting that 'Leigh-Mallory's tactics began to pay' and that the RAF was 'knocking down three Germans to every two Spitfires',[23] the reality was very different.

Certainly the enemy *Kanaljäger* were a formidable enemy. The Western European coast was, in fact, defended by just two *Jagdgeschwadern*, each comprising three *gruppen* (wings) of three *staffeln* (squadrons), from the Netherlands to the Bay of Biscay. The Pas-de-Calais was protected by elements of Adolf Galland's JG 26 *Schlageter*, while Wilhelm Balthasar's JG 2 *Richthofen* was based around Cherbourg. These *Kommodoren* were briefed by the *Kanalfront Jagdfliegerführer* that their task was to inflict maximum losses on the enemy while preserving their limited forces in the process. In March 1941, a new Me 109 variant, the Franz, began replacing the angular Emil of Battle of Britain days. The Me 109F had redesigned flaps and ailerons and had a slightly greater wingspan, with round wing-tips. This was very different to the Me 109E, which had square wing-tips. With an almost elliptical wing, a streamlined nose profile incorporating a large spinner, and a tailplane which lacked the Emil's support struts, the more aesthetically pleasing Me 109F looked not unlike a Spitfire. With a service ceiling of 37,000 feet, top speed of 390 mph at 22,000 feet, and a range of 440 miles, this was an impressive aeroplane indeed. The 'F' was armed with two nose-mounted 7.9 mm machine-guns; initially the F-1 also had an engine-mounted 20mm Oerlikon cannon, but the F-2, which soon became available in quantity, used the 15 mm Mauser cannon. The F-2 was also fitted with an ingenious device which injected nitrous oxide, known as 'Ha Ha', into the engine, providing extra emergency boost. The 'F' represented the zenith of *Ein-hundert-Neun* development and was operated with enthusiasm by the *experten* on all fronts. Although the RAF's response, the Spitfire Mk V, was on the way, for the time being the new 'F' gave the enemy another advantage. Also, the German pilots now, of course, fought a defensive battle for which their fighter was intended and operated over friendly territory.

On 22 June 1941, Hitler unleashed Operation Barbarossa – and invaded the Soviet Union. The Non-Stop Offensive now increased in significance. Britain had to support Russia by tying down enemy forces and preventing their move eastwards. RAF operations, therefore, suddenly became politically as well as practically necessary. This also increased the pressure on JG

26 and JG 2, because so crucial to Germany's survival would the Russian war become that no reinforcements would be forthcoming.

On 25 June, the Tangmere Wing supported bombers on Circus 22, mixing it with German fighters on the return trip; Douglas:

As we crossed the coast at Gravelines at about 18,000 feet, my Section ran into four to six Me 109Fs milling around over Gravelines/Dunkirk area about 500 feet below. We flew into them and I gave one a short deflection burst and my Number Two, Sergeant West, followed in with another burst of two seconds. Sergeant West broke to port and lost sight of the enemy aircraft but I broke to starboard and saw it half roll and dive down and followed it down – giving it a half-second burst – seeing the pilot baling out about five miles off Gravelines in the sea. Then vectored 280° from this point, crossed over South Foreland and returned to Westhampnett at 1335 hours. This Me 109 was not visibly damaged although bullets were seen to strike, i.e. smoke etc.[24]

That afternoon the Wing was up again, on Circus 23. Douglas:

Climbed up to 21,000 feet and crossed French coast at Hardelot. Joined up with bombers underneath then flew east with them for a few minutes when numerous enemy aircraft were seen behind, below and to the north of us. Eventually was compelled to engage them and disregard the bombers, since they were all around us and we were flying down-sun. With the leading Section I engaged eight to nine Me 109Fs which were climbing east to west, i.e. towards

Boulogne. We were then at 20,000 feet and the enemy aircraft between 16,000 and 17,000 feet. We dived on to them and Flying Officer Dundas and his Number Two attacked two, who turned north and climbed. I attacked four Me 109Fs, with my Number Two, who were climbing in a slightly left-hand turn. I gave a short burst at one at close range from inside the turn and saw white, black and orange coloured smoke envelop the aircraft, which went down in an increasingly steep dive which finished up past the vertical. I did not follow the aircraft down and claim it as destroyed.[25]

Bader's victim was an ace, with five kills to his credit: *Oberleutnant* Heinz Gottlob of I/JG 26, who was so badly wounded that he never resumed operational flying.

So the daily round of offensive operations continued. On 2 July, the Tangmere Wing escorted bombers on Circus 29, to Lille. Near the target all three *gruppen* of JG 26 pounced on the beehive. Douglas:

I was leading 616 Squadron's first section. Sighted approximately fifteen Me 109Fs a few miles SW of Lille, so turned south and attacked them. They were in a sort of four formation, climbing eastwards. They made no attempt to do anything but climb in formation so I turned the Squadron behind them and attacked from about 2,000 feet above and behind. I attacked an Me 109F from quarter astern to astern, and saw his hood come off – he probably jettisoned it – and the pilot started to climb out. Did not see him actually bale out as I nearly collided with another Me 109 that was passing on my right in the middle of a half-roll. Half-rolled with him and dived down on his tail, firing at him with the result that glycol and oil came out of his machine. I left him at about 12,000 feet, as he appeared determined to continue diving, and pulled up again to 18,000 feet. My Air Speed Indicator (ASI) showed rather more than 400 mph when I pulled out. Found the fight had taken me west a bit so picked up two 610 Squadron Spitfires and flew out at Boulogne, round Gris-Nez and up to Gravelines where we crossed the coast again and found an Me 109E at 8,000 feet, and at which I fired from about 300 yards. No damage, but this one is claimed as 'Frightened'! The first 109 is claimed as destroyed since, although I did not actually see the pilot leave the aircraft, I saw him preparing to do so, and several pilots of 616 Squadron saw two parachutes going down, the pilot of one of which was shot down by Pilot Officer Hepple. The second 109 was seen by Pilot Officer Hepple and is claimed as damaged.[26]

On this day, Douglas was awarded a Bar to his DSO; the citation read, 'This officer has led his Wing on a series of consistently successful sorties over enemy territory during the past three months. His high qualities of leadership and courage have been an inspiration to all. Wing Commander Bader has destroyed fifteen enemy aircraft.'[27] Not all, however, would necessarily agree regarding 'high qualities of leadership' – but no one could deny the man's courage. The problem was actually twofold: firstly, Douglas, being the product of a hierarchical, elitist society, was unpopular among certain of the Wing's ground crews – men from a lower social strata; secondly, by exclusively leading the Tangmere Wing at the head of 616 Squadron, Douglas had not only created an elite within an elite, but equally was preventing Squadron Leader Burton – an extremely capable officer – from leading his own Squadron in the air. The first-hand testimony of survivors attests to these difficulties.

George Reid, a fitter with 616 Squadron:

When Wing Commander Bader arrived at Tangmere he was already a legend, there being quite a myth building up around him. While with 616 Squadron I came into direct contact with him and learned to both fear and dislike the fellow. He had a filthy mouth and lacked patience. He was a show-off and the most pompous man I ever met. On one occasion his Spitfire's wheels would not lock up correctly. There was a sweep at 3 p.m. and by this time it was already two of the clock. He came over in his car, stomped up to the Chiefy Sergeant and I, and raged – turning on high-powered filth from the mouth, and thumped his car bonnet with a stick. I actually thought he would strike Chiefy with that cane. In the end, the Wing Commander had to settle for a new Spitfire delivered by a female ferry pilot.[28]

Sergeant Harold Clowes was Tangmere's Link instructor: 'I never actually met Wing Commander Bader but once I heard him cursing the ground crew in a nearby hangar.'[29]

Harry Jacks served with 610 Squadron as a clerk:

While 610 Squadron operated out of Westhampnett there were a couple of events which caused Wing Commander Bader to blow his 'stack' and use very strong language to senior officers at Group HQ. On one occasion a signal was received ordering the Wing Commander to exchange his Vauxhall staff car for a smaller eight hp model, and second, another signal arrived ordering him to return to Group inventory one of his two aircraft, either his black-painted night-flying Hurricane or his Spitfire. It is my recollection that neither instruction was acted upon![30]

Sergeant Frank Twitchett flew Spitfires with 145 Squadron, based at Merston: 'We had a first-class CO in Stan Turner, but I cannot say the same for Wing Commander Bader. Obviously we admired the man tremendously but he did create problems through persistently basing himself at Westhampnett and flying solely with 616 Squadron. We very rarely saw him at all. In fact, despite having been with 145 for its entire tour at Tangmere in 1941, I can only recall having seen him twice.'[31]

Pilot Officer 'Buck' Casson, 616 Squadron:

Because Douglas always wanted company he frequently held court with Thelma at 'The Bay House'. Certain favoured pilots from the Wing would go over there in the evenings. We'd talk about tactics, that kind of thing, for hours on end – a subject for which Douglas's enthusiasm knew no bounds. I also used to play golf with him at Tangmere. I'd be enjoying a rare day off and receive a call from one of Douglas's staff, saying, 'The Wing Commander sends his compliments and invites you for a round of golf.' It wouldn't matter what you personally were doing, you'd just be expected to comply. It was a bit selfish of him, really.[32]

Pilot Officer Johnnie Johnson, 616 Squadron: 'Because Douglas always flew at the head of our Squadron, our CO, Billy Burton, was unhappy as he never got to lead his own Squadron. I do not think it was necessary for Douglas to do this. Later in the war, when I was a

Wing Leader, I flew with all of my squadrons in rotation, although I'd keep the same Number Two in each one. It would definitely have been better for the Tangmere Wing had Douglas done this too.'[33]

Pilot Officer Denis Crowley-Milling, having flown with Douglas in 242 Squadron and been brought in as a flight commander on 610 Squadron at Tangmere, was, like Johnson, very much a part of the Wing Leader's inner sanctum:

Squadron Leader Burton was certainly fed up on occasions as he was never given the opportunity to lead his own Squadron. Douglas Bader led it and he always had Johnnie Johnson and Hugh Dundas with him. I can understand both sides. Bader wanted pilots with him with whom he was familiar in combat, and they with him, while Billy Burton, a squadron leader, never had the status of that rank. You could say that he tried desperately to persuade DB to lead each of the three squadrons in turn, i.e. with different pilots around him on each operation. Burton failed for obvious reasons and it must have got him down. You must know the pilots you lead and depend on, both on the ground and in the air. Having said that, at no time was there any air of mutiny as suggested by Air Chief Marshal 'Bing' Cross in his book. There were of course, numerous encounters with Me 109s, mainly from Galland's JG 26 based around St Omer. Although it now appears that the losses were not actually in our favour, for us it was the first time we had taken the fight to the Germans in a big way, so we were very inspired by it all and our morale was very high.[34]

Sergeant Ron Rayner: 'At Merston we rarely saw Wing Commander Bader. He used to come stomping into dispersal to give us a peptalk, saying, "Don't go off on your own, do what I say and you'll be alright." I can still see him now, pipe in mouth, rocking from side to side to retain his balance. He would definitely have created more team spirit if he had not led solely with 616. For us, the most important thing was the squadron and our own CO, not the Wing or its leader.'[35]

So much for the reality of *Esprit d'Wing*.

By now, Fighter Command had received a new Spitfire – the Mk V. The new Merlin 45 engine produced a top speed of 359 mph at 25,000 feet, an altitude attainable in eight-and-a-half minutes, and in just under fifteen minutes the Mk V could reach its maximum ceiling of 35,000 feet. Significantly, the Mk VB was armed with two 20 mm Hispano-Suiza cannons and four .303 Browning machine-guns. The Battle of Britain tribulations of 19 Squadron with the experimental Mk IB had been resolved – the cannon was mounted upright, as the manufacturer intended, and blisters added to both wing surfaces to accommodate the ammunition drum. The inclusion of machine-guns in the armament package meant that the pilot enjoyed the best of both worlds: the greater destructive power of cannon but with the more rapid-firing machine-guns as back-up. Pilot Officer Johnnie Johnson: 'Of course that summer we faced the prospect of another Battle of Britain-type bombardment, but Douglas would rub his hands together and say, "Let me buggers come across! We've got the Wing and the cannon now! Bloody good show old boy! And if they don't come then we'll go over there, won't we?"'[36]

Perhaps surprisingly, however, Johnson added that 'Douglas, in fact, was averse to the cannon. Machine-guns have a much higher rate of fire, requiring less accuracy, and spray bullets all over the place. The pilot harmonised his guns, of course, so that the cones of fire converged at a set point, but really it was like a shotgun effect.

The cannon, with a slower rate of fire, obviously required more accuracy. DB's view was that the average squadron pilot was more likely to achieve success with machine-guns. He was wrong about that, because the combination of machine-guns and cannons meant that you had the best of both worlds, the spread and high rate of fire of machine-guns and the greater destructive power of cannon.'[37] So strongly did Douglas feel about this, in fact, that he personally refused to operate the Mk VB, preferring either the exclusively machine-gun-armed IIA or Mk VA.

On 4 July, the Tangmere Wing flew on Circus 32 to St Omer; Douglas:

Intercepted one Me 109F some miles south of Gravelines at 14,000 feet, while with a section of four. Turned on to its tail and opened fire with a short, one-second burst at about 150 yards. I found it very easy to keep inside him during the turn and closed quite quickly. I gave him three more short bursts, the final one at about 20 yards range; as he slowed down very suddenly I nearly collided with him. I did not see the result except one puff of smoke halfway through. Squadron Leader Burton in my Section watched, the complete combat and saw the Me 109's airscrew slow right down to ticking over speed. As I broke away the 109 did not half-roll and dive but just sort of fell away in a sloppy fashion, quite slowly, as though the pilot had been hit. Having broken away I did not again see the 109 I attacked, since I was trying to collect my Section together. I am, however, satisfied that I was hitting him and so is Squadron Leader Burton, from whose evidence this report is written.[38]

This Me 109E was destroyed: *Leutnant* Joachim Kehrhahn of I/JG 26 crashed at St Pol and was killed.

The afternoon of 6 July saw the Wing on its second trip over France that day, providing Target Support to six Stirlings bombing Lille. Douglas subsequently reported that

> during the withdrawal from Lille to Gravelines we were pestered by Me 109s starting to attack and then half-rolling and diving away when we made to engage. Of an initial three bursts I fired at three Me 109Es, I claim three as frightened (Pilot Officer Johnson subsequently destroyed number three). Finally, two Me 109s positioned themselves to attack from starboard quarter behind when my section was flying above and behind the bombers south of Dunkirk. These two were flying in line-astern and I broke my Section round on to them when they were quite close (250 yards away). They both did a steeply banked turn, still in line-astern, and exposed their complete underside (plan view) to us. I gave one a short burst (no deflection) full in the stomach from 100–150 yards and it fell out of the sky in a shallow dive, steepening up with white and black smoke pouring from it, and finally flames as well. The pilot did not bale out while I was watching. This is confirmed by Pilot Officer Johnson and Sergeant Smith in my Section, and is claimed as destroyed.[39]

Three days later, on Circus 41, 'Dogsbody' made more claims:

> Just after crossing the French coast (with bombers) at 18,000 feet I saw an Me 109 behind and above me, diving very steeply, obviously intending to get down below and behind bombers

and attack from underneath and then zoom away. I instructed my Section I was diving down, and dived straight through and under the Escort Wing converging on this Me 109 who had not seen me. He saw me as he was starting his zoom and turned right-handed, i.e. into me, and dived away. I was very close by then and aileroned behind him and gave him one to two second burst from 100–150 yards straight behind him. Glycol and heavy black smoke streamed out of his aeroplane and he continued diving. I pulled out at approximately 10,000 feet and watched him continue downwards. When he was about 2,000 feet I lost him and then saw a large flash on the ground where he should have hit. I am sure it was him but am claiming a probable only because when flying out over the same terrain I noticed sun flashes on glass in various directions, and as I did not actually see the 109 right into the ground these sun flashes must be recorded. Just after leaving the target area my Section was attacked from above and behind, and we turned into the attackers, Me 109Fs, who started half-rolling. I got a good squirt at one and glycol stream started. Did not follow him down and claim a damaged. Several others were frightened and I claim one badly frightened who did the quickest half-roll and dive I've ever seen when I fired at him.[40]

More action followed the next morning; Circus 42:

Was operating in a four over the Bethune area at 24,000 feet when we saw five Me 109s below us in a wide, loose, vic. We attacked, diving from above, and I opened fire at 200 yards closing to 100, knocking pieces off it round the cockpit and pulling up over the top. I saw flashes as some of my bullets struck (presumably De Wilde). Was unable after pulling up to see it again, but saw and attacked without result three of the same five (so it is to be supposed that two were hit), immediately after turning. My own aeroplane shielded my view immediately after the attack and I claim this one as probably only, because of the incendiary strikes and pieces coming off the cockpit.

Was flying with section of four northwards over 10/10ths between Calais-Dover. Sighted three Me 109Es below, flying south-west over the cloud. Turned and dived to catch them up, which we did just over Calais. The three 109s were in line abreast and so were my Section, with one lagging behind. I closed in to 150 yards behind and under the left-hand one, firing a two-second burst into its belly beneath the cockpit. Pieces flew off the 109 exactly under the cockpit and there was a flash of flame and black smoke, and then the whole aeroplane went up in flames. This was seen by Sergeant West and Pilot Officer Hepple of my Section. Time approximately 1250 hours, height 7,000 feet, position either south of Calais or over Calais.[41]

The Wing Commander's victim was *Leutnant* Herbert Reich of II/JG 26, who crashed, wounded, near Guines.

The pace of operations remained intense. On 12 July, Douglas led the Wing on Circus 46:

When orbiting the wood at Bois de Dieppe, about to proceed to St Omer at 26,000 feet, we saw approximately twelve to fifteen Me 109Fs climbing in line-astern from Dunkirk, turning west and south. I told my Section we would attack and told the two top squadrons to stay up as I thought I had seen more Me 109s above. We turned so that the enemy – who were very close and climbing across our bows – were down-sun, and I fired a very close deflection shot at the second last one at 100–150 yards' range. I saw De Wilde flashes in front of his cockpit but no immediate result as I passed him and turned across him and fired a head-on burst at the last Me 109 who had lagged a bit. A panel or some piece of his machine fell away and he put his nose down; as I passed over him I lost him. I then turned round 180° to the same direction as the 109s had been going but could not see them. I called my section together and, after a little, made contact with them. I then saw the beehive and bombers flying over the St Omer wood travelling south-east just below with a squadron of Spitfires above. I saw two Me 109Fs above the Spitfires and dived down to attack. These two flew away south more or less level and I closed up quickly on one which I shot from 100 yards dead astern and produced black smoke and glycol.

The second one was banking to the left when I attacked the first and he dived a little after the first. I got behind him with a good burst, followed him through 10/10ths cloud (about 100 feet thick) and gave him one more burst which set him on fire with a short quick flame under the cockpit, then black smoke, then the whole machine caught fire around the fuselage. The pilot did not bale out. I pulled away at 9,000 feet and I reckon this aeroplane crashed between St Omer and Bethune. I went up to 14,000 feet and called my Section together, they were both above the cloud in the same area, and we had no more combat. I believe they had a fight at the same time. Of the four Me 109Fs one was definitely destroyed and the other three are considered damaged. The one which disappeared through the cloud layer emitting black and white smoke I consider was more likely a probable.[42]

The Tangmere Wing's first commitment of the day was to escort six Blenheims, but the Spitfires were five minutes late, the bombers seven minutes early, so no rendezvous was made. Instead the Wing landed at Manston before taking off again on an impromptu 'Roadstead' to attack enemy shipping; Douglas:

Took off from Manston with Squadron Leader Burton at approximately 1340 after 242 Squadron on the expedition to bomb ship off Dunkirk. The weather was very hazy from about 1,000 feet upwards but clearer below. We flew from North Foreland and near Gravelines were attacked by an Me 109 out of the sun. We countered and Squadron Leader Burton had a shot at it. It flew low over the water to the French coast. We carried on up to Dunkirk and slightly past where we saw some flak and then a Spitfire (squadron markings XT) flying straight for home in a dive, being attacked by an Me 109. We immediately turned on the Me 109 which saw us and did a left-hand climbing turn back to France, but I got a very close short burst (half a second) at him from underneath and behind him. It definitely hit him and produced a puff of white smoke under his cockpit. I turned away immediately as I had no idea how many were about and did not want to lose Squadron Leader Burton. I claim this Messerschmitt as damaged but would like information from 242 Squadron who told me on landing back at Manston that they had seen two Me 109s go into the sea in that area. We flew back to Manston after this and landed among 242 Squadron, who arrived back at the same time. I claim a damaged aircraft just around Dunkirk out to sea, which may be a destroyed one. I never saw this Messerschmitt after breaking away because visibility was poor.[43]

That evening, Douglas led the Wing on another Circus. After crossing the coast over Le Touquet the Wing was constantly engaged by Me 109s – which almost immediately split the Spitfires into sections of four or pairs. Another fifty Me 109s were seen holding back, their leader clearly timing the moment to attack. The 610 Squadron diary recorded that 'all engagements were terrific dogfights'.[44] One of 610's pilots crash-landed at Bexhill with shrapnel in one arm and a cut eye. 'Dogsbody' and Sergeant Raine shared an Me 109 destroyed, Pilot Officer Grey claimed a probable and Sergeant Twitchett damaged another. Sergeant Breeze's Spitfire was damaged but he managed to glide home across the Channel and crash-land at Beachy Head. 616 Squadron met 'plenty of enemy fighters'.[45] Douglas and Flying Officer Dundas shared an Me 109 destroyed, Flight Lieutenant Casson destroyed another and damaged two more, while Pilot Officer Johnson winged a third. There would be no let-up in the scale and intensity of fighting, in fact, for the rest of the season.

On 28 July, the composition of the Tangmere Wing changed significantly: Squadron Leader Stan Turner's 145 Squadron was relieved at Merston by 41 Squadron, commanded by the Olympic hurdler Squadron Leader Don Finlay. Flight Lieutenant Archie Winskill:

On arrival at Tangmere as a young flight lieutenant I found Bader a very charismatic leader and a truly impressive individual. A Wing briefing went something like this: Wing Commander Bader would waddle into the briefing marquee in his usual peg-legged style, halt in front of the thirty-five pilots present, stare at us for a few seconds, take his pipe out and in a loud, confident, voice say, 'Okay, chaps, St Omer today – return tickets only! Press tits at 1300 hours.' Then he would waddle out. We would have followed him to the ends of the earth! After taking off the squadrons of the Wing would gradually form up while climbing easterly along the south coast, reaching the Wing formation at 20,000 feet over Beachy Head. We would then head south to the target area. As we crossed the French coast the Me 109s were waiting for us. As sweeps were usually flown at mid-day, the 109s usually had the added advantage of the sun's position. To keep a wing of thirty-six Spitfires together, pilots can fly at no more than three-quarter throttle, thus the 109s had the height and speed advantage. Wing Commander Harry Broadhurst's theory for sweeps at that time was to fly high and at full throttle once you had crossed the French coast – a much sounder principal. With Bader, once he had spotted the enemy, there was a semblance of directing his squadrons and deploying them in the air for the attack, but on the whole when he sighted the first 109s he was after them, the Wing just breaking up and it being every man for himself.[46]

The next day, the Wing flew many Rhubarbs; Sergeant Ron Rayner of 41 Squadron:

Rhubarbs were eventually used only when the weather was unsuitable for fighter sweeps. It was just so that, regardless, we could continue with some offensive activity. Two Spitfires used to cross the Channel to France, shoot up a target of opportunity and return. I wouldn't say that we achieved a great deal, these attacks were more of a nuisance value. We would try and find a train or German troops, or sometimes shoot up a 'staff car' – although I have often wondered since whether on occasions these were perhaps French civilian vehicles. My logbook records that on one occasion I flew a Rhubarb and 'Shot up Le Havre'! That was a long flight, 160 miles across the sea. Navigational aids were somewhat rudimentary, and so on the return flight we received no assistance from the ground until we had crossed the English coast. That was one of the reasons why these sorties were so unpopular with pilots, the fact that they were flown in poor weather compounding the problem.[47]

Indeed, many experienced pilots were lost on these futile sorties, as indeed they were throughout the so-called Non-Stop Offensive – dubbed the 'Non-sense Offensive' by the Germans. Adding to the Bader myth, Brickhill wrote that the offensive achieved its objective: 'Göring was pulling fighter squadrons out of Russia.'[48] That is not so. JG 2 and JG 26 held their own against the Fighter Command effort over France in 1941 – and never lost the tactical initiative or upper hand. By the end of 1941, in fact, Fighter Command had claimed the destruction of 176 enemy aircraft destroyed and seventy-four probables; in reality the Luftwaffe had lost but forty-four machines. 41 Squadron's Flight Lieutenant Winskill was among those RAF pilots shot down over France and on the run – making it home via the Pyrenees: 'While I was hiding on a farm in the Pas-de-Calais, I was visited by a British agent, Sidney Bowen, who was from an escape organisation based in Marseilles. He asked why more Spitfires were crashing in France than 109s – I had no answer for him.'[49] Fighter Command was losing the day-fighter air war over France by a ratio in excess of 2:1.

Not surprisingly, after such intensive operational flying over what was a protracted period, Douglas was tired. Typically he refused to slacken the pace and continued driving himself. Pilot Officer Johnnie Johnson: 'The signs were there. Douglas's reactions were getting slower in the air, and he was becoming increasingly greedy, you know. His awareness and judgement was impaired.'[50] Pilot Officer Bob Beardsley of 41 Squadron wrote of a sweep to Lille on 7 August:

On this sortie I was leading a section of four, our rear cover. We were the low squadron of the Wing, and as I looked to my rear left I saw an Me 109 closing on my port sub-section, so close that the cannon orifice in the propeller boss was very apparent! The attacking aircraft had not fired, but I called the Wing Leader to tell him that we had been attacked by 109s. To my amazement, Wing Commander Bader responded, 'Only Hurricanes, old boy!' The next second the whole Wing was engaged – I saw no more 'Hurricanes'! When the lead squadron was attacked, Bader did actually say, 'Sorry, old boy!'[51]

At Biggin Hill, Wing Commander 'Sailor' Malan had recognised that he too was exhausted – and asked to be relieved. That was a very great thing to do. He went off to teach air fighting – in which his experience was immeasurable. This is what Douglas should have done, but such a thing was completely contrary to his incredibly driven character. At the end of July, however, Leigh-Mallory realised that Douglas too was tired – and more valuable long-term if rested. Douglas's somewhat forceful personality resisted even his AOC – who backed down; Johnson: '"LM" knew that Douglas was tired but he basically *refused* to go. Thelma was worried too and tried to persuade him to come off. He wouldn't listen to anyone, not even the AOC, who gave in and agreed to let him continue until the end of the "season".'[52] Even the press were concerned; Brickhill: 'The *Daily Mirror* columnist "Cassandra" wrote that Bader had done enough, was too valuable to lose and should be taken off operations. He read it angrily ... The Wing was the thing and the battle an intoxicant that answered his search for a purpose and fulfilment.'[53] That was undoubtedly so, but remaining on operations was irresponsible and self-serving. The story goes that on 8 August, Flight Lieutenant Peter MacDonald MP insisted that Douglas take a few days off and booked rooms for Thelma, Douglas and himself for a golfing break at St Andrew's starting on 11 August.[54] As with so much else connected with Brickhill's account, it is unlikely that this is true, given that MacDonald was actually posted away from Tangmere on 1 August.[55]

Although he was blissfully unaware of the fact, the night of 8 August 1941 would be the last that Wing Commander Douglas Bader DSO* DFC would spend in England for nearly four long years.

16

'BREAK! FOR CHRIST'S SAKE BREAK!'

On the morning of Monday 9 August 1941, the teleprinter clattered away at Tangmere as the Form 'D' came through from 11 Group HQ, detailing the Wing's task for that day. This was another complex Circus, No. 68, involving many aircraft to Gosnay. The Tangmere Wing was to provide Target Support. For Wing Commander Bader and the Westhampnett Spitfire squadrons, 616 and 610, Target Support was a routine sortie, although not, of course, without the usual hazards. Squadron Leader 'Elmer' Gaunce DFC's 41 Squadron had arrived at Merston just two weeks previously; the squadron had already flown numerous practice sweeps when based at Catterick and at least one offensive patrol over France from Redhill. Circus 68, therefore, represented nothing other than a typical sortie and was not beyond the capabilities of any of the Tangmere Wing's three Spitfire squadrons.

Sergeant Alan Smith, Wing Commander Bader's usual 'Dogsbody Two', had a head cold and so was unable to fly. Imminently to be commissioned, and as his name was not on the board, Smith prepared to go into London and buy a new uniform. His place as the Wing Leader's Number Two was taken by a New Zealander, Sergeant Jeff West, a pilot with one-and-a-half Me 109s destroyed and one damaged to his credit. Clearly West was not without experience: frequently that summer he had flown as wingman to Flight Lieutenant E. P. Gibbs, until that officer was shot down over France on 9 July.

For this Target Support sortie to Gosnay, 'Dogsbody' Section therefore consisted of:

Dogsbody	Wing Commander Douglas Bader
Dogsbody Two	Sergeant Jeff West
Dogsbody Three	Flight Lieutenant Hugh Dundas DFC
Dogsbody Four	Pilot Officer 'Johnnie' Johnson

Also leading 'Finger Fours' within the 616 Squadron formation of three sections, would be the squadron commander, Squadron Leader Billy Burton (Yellow Section), and the 'B' Flight Commander, Flight Lieutenant Lionel 'Buck' Casson (Blue Section). Across the other side of the airfield, Squadron Leader Ken Holden DFC and 610 Squadron also prepared for the morning sortie.

Take-off came at 1040 hours, 'Dogsbody' Section leading Westhampnett's Spitfires for yet another sortie into very hostile airspace. High over Chichester, Squadron Leader Holden swiftly manoeuvred 610 Squadron into position above and slightly to port of 616. As Target Support, the Wing had no bombers to meet prior to setting course for France, although the Spitfires were still routed out over Beachy Head. As the Wing left Chichester, however, there was no sign of 41 Squadron.

The Beachy Head Forward Relay Station recorded the Tangmere Wing's R/T messages that day. As the Wing neared 'Diamond' (Beachy Head), 41 Squadron had still not appeared. Group Captain Woodhall, at Tangmere, was the first to speak, making a test call:

'Dogsbody?'

'OK, OK.'

Bader then made R/T test calls to the commanders of both 610 and 41, using their first names as was his usual practice:

DB: 'Ken?'

Ken Holden (KH): 'Loud and clear.'

DB: 'Elmer?'

There was no response from Squadron Leader Gaunce, which provoked an acerbic remark from the Wing Leader to 'Woody'. Unable to wait, 616 and 610 Squadrons set course for France and Gosnay, adopting their battle formations in the process. Still climbing, Wing Commander Bader waggled his wings insistently, indicating that 'Dogsbody Three', Flight Lieutenant Dundas, should take the lead. Dundas slid across, tucking his wing-tip just 2 or 3 feet from Bader's. From this close proximity, Dundas saw the Wing Leader mouth two words: 'Airspeed Indicator', meaning that this all-important instrument on Spitfire Mk VA W3185 was unserviceable. The Wing had to climb at the right speed to ensure Time on Target at the appointed time, which was crucial. Dundas gave a thumbs up and moved forward to lead the Spitfires to France. On the rear of his hand he had fortunately written the time at which the Wing was due over the French coast in addition to the speed which had to be maintained. The twenty-one-year-old Flight Commander then 'settled down to concentrate on the job',[1] climbing the formation to 28,000 feet.

Then, more radio messages:

DB: 'Ken and Elmer, start gaining height.'

KH: 'Elmer's not with us.'

Then an unidentified, garbled voice on the R/T, believed to be Squadron Leader Gaunce.

DB: 'Elmer from Dogsbody. I cannot understand what you say, but we are on our way. You had better decide for yourself whether to come or go back.'[2]

Following the last radio transmissions, at least the Wing was now aware that more Spitfires were bringing up the rear, even if some distance away. The Spitfires cruised over the Channel towards France, with 610 Squadron above and behind 616. Dundas led the Wing over the French coast right on cue (although there is conflicting evidence regarding whether the coast was crossed south of Le Touquet, known as the 'Golf Course', or Boulogne, slightly further north). This crucial timing observed, Bader accelerated ahead and informed 'Dogsbody Three' over the R/T that he was resuming the lead. The Spitfires' arrival over the coastal flak belt was greeted by dangerous little puff-balls of black smoke which made the formation twist and turn. 'Beetle' (Tangmere Control) then called 'Dogsbody', informing him that the beehive itself was 'on time and engaged'.[3] As the Spitfires forged inland, therefore, some distance behind them the bombers and various cover wings were now bound for France and action.

Slightly below the condensation trail level, a 610 Squadron pilot reported seeing contrails 'above and to our left'.[4] Squadron Leader Holden consequently led the squadron higher still while 'Beetle' (B) reported,

B: 'Dogsbody from Beetle. There are twenty plus 5 miles to the east of you.'

DB: 'OK, but your transmitter is quite impossible. Please use the other.'

B: 'Dogsbody is this better?'

DB: 'Perfect. Ken, start getting more height.'

KH: 'OK, Dogsbody, but will you throttle back? I cannot keep up.'

DB: 'Sorry Ken, my airspeed indicator is u/s. Throttling back, and I will do one slow left-hand turn so you can catch up.'

KH: 'Dogsbody from Ken, I'm making "smoke" (contrails) at this height.'

DB: 'OK, Ken, I'm going down very slightly.'

Beetle then advised 'Dogsbody' of more bandits in the vicinity. 616 Squadron's Flying Officer Roy Marples (RM) saw the enemy first: 'Three bandits coming down astern of us. I'm keeping an eye on them, now there are six.'

DB: 'OK'.

B: 'Douglas, another twelve plus ahead and slightly higher.'

RM: 'Eleven of them now.'

DB: 'OK, Roy, let me know exactly where they are.'

RM: 'About 1 mile astern and slightly higher.'

B: 'Douglas, there is another forty plus 15 miles to the north-east of you.'

DB: 'OK Beetle. Are our friends where they ought to be, I haven't much idea where I am.'

B: 'Yes, you are exactly right. And so are your friends.'

RM: 'Dogsbody from Roy. Keep turning left and you'll see 109s at nine o'clock.'

DB: 'Ken, can you see them?'

KH: 'Douglas, 109s below. Climbing up.'[5]

By this time, 616 and 610 Squadron had progressed into a very dangerous French sky indeed, Beetle having already reported some seventy-two 'bandits', representing odds which outnumbered the Spitfires by nearly 3:1. Clearly this was not to be an uneventful sortie. Tension mounting, the Spitfire pilots switched on their gunsight reflectors and gun buttons to 'Fire'. Anxiously they searched the sky, an ever-watchful eye being kept on the 109s positioned 1,000 feet above the Wing, waiting to pounce. Bader himself dipped each wing in turn, scrutinising the sky below for the 109s reported by Ken Holden.

DB: 'I can't see them. Will you tell me where to look?'

KH: 'Underneath Bill's section now. Shall I come down?'

DB: 'No, I have them. Get into formation. Going down. Ken, are you with us?'

KH: 'Just above you.'[6]

As Dogsbody Section dived on the enemy, Flight Lieutenant Casson followed with three other aircraft of 'B' Flight. Dogsbody Three, Flight Lieutenant Dundas, had 'smelt a rat' in respect of the *schwarm* of 109s that Dogsbody Section was now rapidly diving towards. Finding no targets to the Section's right, Dogsbody Four, Pilot Officer Johnson, skidded under the section and fired at an Me 109 on the left. By this time the whole of Dogsbody Section was firing, although Dundas, still unhappy and suspecting a trap, had a compelling urge to look behind. Suddenly Pilot Officer 'Nip' Hepple shouted over the R/T, Blue 2 here. Some buggers coming down behind, astern. Break left!'[7]

The Spitfire pilots hauled their aircraft around in steep turns. The sky behind Dogsbody Section was full of Me 109s, all firing – without Hepple's warning the Spitfires would have been instantly nailed. As the high 109s crashed into 616 Squadron,

Squadron Leader Holden decided that it was time for his section to join the fray and reduce the odds. Informing Flight Lieutenant Denis Crowley-Milling of this decision, Holden led his Spitfires down to assist. Flight Lieutenant Casson, following Bader's section, was well throttled back to keep his flight together. Also attacking from the rear, Casson managed a squirt at a *Rotte* of 109s. Flying Officer Marples, Number Three in Casson's Section, then shouted a warning of even more 109s diving upon the Wing – while Squadron Leader Billy Burton urged the Spitfires to 'Keep turning', thus preventing the 109s (which could not out-turn a Spitfire), getting in a shot. Suddenly the organised chaos became a totally confused maelstrom of twisting, turning fighters: 'BREAK! FOR CHRIST'S SAKE BREAK!' The Spitfires immediately 'broke' – hard. Pilot Officer Johnnie Johnson remembered,

There was this scream of 'Break!' – and we all broke, we didn't wait to hear it twice! Round. Then a swirling mass of 109s and Spitfires. When I broke I could see Bader still firing. Dundas was firing at the extreme right 109. There was some cloud nearby and I disappeared into it as quick as possible! I couldn't say how many aircraft were involved, suffice to say a lot. It seemed to me that the greatest danger was a collision, rather than being shot down, that's how close we all were. We had got the 109s we were bouncing and then Holden came down with his section, so there were a lot of aeroplanes. We were fighting 109Fs, although there may have been some Es among them. There was an absolute mass of aeroplanes just 50 yards apart, it was awful. I thought to myself, 'You're going to collide with somebody!' I didn't think about shooting at anything after we were bounced ourselves, all you could think about was surviving, getting out of that mass of aircraft. In such a tight turn, of course, you almost black out, you cannot really see where you are going. It was a mess. I had never been so frightened in my life, never![8]

Chased by three Me 109s, the closest just 100 yards astern, Pilot Officer Johnson maintained his tight turn, spiralling down towards the safety of a nearby cloud which his Spitfire dived into with over 400 mph on the clock. Pulling back the throttle and centralising the controls, the altimeter stabilised, but, speed having dropped to less than 100 mph, the Spitfire stalled. Beneath the cloud, Dogsbody Four recovered control. Having requested and received a homing course for Dover, he headed rapidly for England. Over the R/T, Pilot Officer Johnson could still hear 616 and 610 Squadrons' running battle:

'Get into formation or they'll shoot the bloody lot of you!'

'Spitfire going down in flames, ten o'clock.'

'YQ-C (616 Squadron Spitfire). Form up on me, I'm at three o'clock to you.'

'Four buggers above us,' this from Hepple.

'All Elfin aircraft (616 Squadron) withdraw. I say again, all Elfin aircraft withdraw.'

'Use the cloud if you're in trouble,' from Billy Burton.

'Are you going home, Ken?' also from Burton.

'Yes, withdrawing,' from Holden.

'Ken from Crow. Are you still about?'

'I'm right behind you, Crow.'

'Are we all here?'

'Two short.'

'Dogsbody from Beetle. Do you require any assistance?'

'Beetle from Elfin Leader. We are OK and withdrawing.'

'Thank you Billy. Douglas, do you require any assistance? Steer three-four-zero to the coast.'⁹

The silence from 'Dogsbody' was ominous. Flight Lieutenant Casson remembered:

I watched Wing Commander Bader and 'A' Flight attack and break to port as I was coming in. I was well throttled back in the dive, as the other three had started to fall behind and I wanted to keep the flight together. I attacked from the rear, and after having a squirt at two 109s flying together, left them for a single one which was flying inland alone. I finished nearly all of my cannon ammunition up on this boy who finally baled out at 6,000 feet, having lost most of his tail unit. The other three 'B' flight machines were in my rear and probably one of the lads saw this.

I climbed to 13,000 feet and fell in with Billy Burton and three other aircraft, all from 'A' Flight. We chased around in a circle for some time, gaining height all the while, and more 109s were directly above us. Eventually we formed up in line abreast and set off after the Wing.

Billy's section flew in pairs abreast, so I flew abreast but at about 200 yards to starboard. We were repeatedly attacked by two Me 109s which had followed us and were flying above and behind. Each time they started diving I called out and we all turned and re-formed, the 109s giving up their attack and climbing each time.

About 15 miles from the coastline I saw another Spitfire well below us and about half-a-mile to starboard. This machine was alone and travelling very slowly. I called up Billy on the R/T and suggested that we cross over to surround him and help the pilot back as he looked like a sitting duck. I broke off to starboard and made for the solitary Spitfire, but then, on looking back for Billy and the others, was amazed to see them diving away hard to the south-west for a low layer of cloud into which they soon disappeared. I realised then that my message had either been misunderstood or not received. Like a greenhorn, I had been so intent upon watching Billy's extraordinary disappearance to the left, and the lone Spitfire to my right, I lost sight of the Me 109s that had been worrying us. I remember looking for them but upon not discovering their position assumed that they had chased Billy instead. I was soon proved wrong, however, when I received three hits in both fuselage and wing. This occurred just broke for some cloud at 5,000 feet, which I reached but found too thin for cover, and was pursued by the 109s.

I then picked out two more 109s flying above me and so decided to drop to zero feet, fly north and cross the Channel at a narrow point as I was unsure of the damage sustained and the engine was not running smoothly. I pressed the teat and tried to run for it, but the two Me 109s behind had more speed and were rapidly within range, while the other two flew 1,500 feet above and dived from port to starboard and back, delivering quick bursts. Needless to say I was not flying straight and level all this time!

In the event I received a good one from behind, which passed between the stick and my right leg, taking off some of the rudder on its way. It passed into the petrol tank but whether the round continued into the engine I do not know. Petrol began leaking into the cockpit, oil pressure was dropping low, and with the radiator wide open I could smell the glycol overheating.

As the next attack came, I pulled straight up from the deck in a loop and on my way down, as I was changing direction towards the sea, my engine became extremely rough and seized up as white glycol fumes poured forth. There was no option but to crash-land the aircraft. I tried to send 'Dogsbody' a hurried message, then blew up the wireless and made a belly landing in a field some 10 miles south of Calais. The 'Goons', having seen the glycol, were decent enough not to shoot me up as I was landing, but circled about for a time and gave my position away to a German cavalry unit in a wood in a corner of the field. One of the pilots waved to me as he flew overhead, and I waved back just before setting fire to the aircraft. Due to the petrol in the cockpit, and because I was carrying a port-fire issued for this purpose, igniting the aircraft was easy. No sooner had I done this than a party of shrieking Goons armed with rifles came chasing over and that was the end of me!

What eventually happened to the lone Spitfire which I went to help out I have no idea. As the 109s followed me, I assume that he got away okay, I certainly hope so.

I will never forget that day, one which I have gone over so often in my daydreams.[10]

Flight Lieutenant Casson had been the victim of Hauptmann Gerhard Schöpfel, *Gruppenkommandeur* of III/JG26:

My IIIrd *Gruppe* attacked a British bomber formation, after which my formation was split up. With the British on their homeward flight, I headed alone for my airfield at Ligescourt, near Crecy. Suddenly I saw a flight of Spitfires flying westwards. I attacked them from above and after a short burst of fire the rear machine nosed over sharply and dived away. While the other aircraft flew on apparently unaware, I pursued the fleeing Spitfire as I could see no sign of damage. The British pilot hugged the ground, dodging trees and houses. I was constantly in his propwash and so could not aim properly. Because of the warm air near the ground my radiator flaps opened and so my speed decreased, it thus took me a long time to get into a good firing position. Finally I was positioned immediately behind the Spitfire and it filled my gun-sight. I pressed the firing button for both cannon and machine-guns, but – click! I had obviously exhausted my ammunition in the earlier air battles. Of course the British pilot had no way of knowing this and I still wanted to strike terror in him for so long as he remained over French soil. I thus remained right behind him, at high speed. Suddenly I was astonished to see a white plume of smoke emit from the Spitfire! The smoke grew denser and the propeller stopped. The pilot made a forced landing in a field east of Marquise. I circled the aircraft and made a note of the markings for my victory report, watched the pilot climb out and waved to him. Just before being captured by German soldiers, he ignited a built-in explosive charge which destroyed the centre-section of his aircraft.

I returned to my field and sent my engineering officer to the site to determine the reason for the forced landing. He found, to my amazement, that the Spitfire had taken a single machine-gun round in an engine cylinder during my first attack. Had I not pressed on after running out of ammunition and therefore forcing the pilot to fly at top speed, he would probably have reached England despite the damage. Just a few weeks before, in fact, I myself had made it back across the Channel after two of my engine's connecting rods had been smashed over Dover. On this occasion over France, however, the British pilot, a flight lieutenant, now had to head for prison camp while I recorded my thirty-third victory.[11]

While Casson was to spend the rest of the war as a prisoner, Schöpfel running out of ammunition had clearly saved his life. With petrol splashing into the cockpit, another hit would no doubt have ignited the Spitfire into a blowtorch. Luck, it would appear, played no mean part in survival.

Returning to the French coast, Pilot Officer Johnson saw a lone Me 109 below. Suspecting it to be one of the three which chased him into the cloud just a few minutes previously, Johnnie anxiously searched the sky for the other two: the sky was clear. From astern, Dogsbody Four dropped below the 109 before attacking from its blind spot, below and behind. One burst of cannon shells sent the enemy fighter diving earthwards emitting a plume of black smoke. Pilot Officer Johnson came 'out of France on the deck, low and fast',[12] his Spitfire roaring over waving civilians, just feet above their fields. At the coast, German soldiers ran to their guns but in a second the fleeting Spitfire was gone. Climbing over the Channel, 'Dogsbody Four' realised that something might have happened to Wing Commander Bader: 'As I was crossing the Channel, Group Captain Woodhall, who obviously knew that there had been a fight from the radar and R/T, repeated, "Douglas, are you receiving?" This came over the air every five minutes or so. I therefore called up and said, "Its

Johnnie here, Sir, we've had a stiff fight and I last saw the Wing Commander on the tail of a 109." He said, "Thank you, I'll meet you at dispersal."'[13]

The silence from Dogsbody over the R/T clearly meant one of two things: either that his radio was unserviceable, or he had somehow been brought down. Flight Lieutenant Denis Crowley-Milling of 610 Squadron recalled that

the greatest impression I have is the silence on the R/T. Douglas always maintained a running commentary. Had the worst happened? The colourful language and running commentary had suddenly ceased, leaving us all wondering what had happened. Was he alive or dead? Had his radio failed? I know we were above thick cloud on the way home and asked the Tangmere Controller to provide a homing bearing for us to steer. This was way out in accuracy, however, and unbeknown to us we were flying up the North Sea, just scraping in to Martlesham Heath with hardly any fuel remaining – it was indeed a day to remember![14]

So confused had been the fighting, so numerous the aircraft in this incredible maelstrom over St Omer, that only Wing Commander Bader himself had the answers to the questions regarding his present state and whereabouts. Douglas later wrote,

The Tangmere Wing Leader did everything wrong. I signalled 'attacking' and dived down too fast and too steeply. I was tense, and my judgement had gone for some reason which I did not recognize at the time. One never did. I behaved as I had done on my first glimpse of an enemy over the sea off Dunkirk in May 1940. I closed so fast on the 109 that I had no time to fire, and barely time to avoid cutting him in half with my Spitfire. I continued diving and levelled out at 24,000 feet. I pulled myself together and had a look around. Nothing in sight, I was alone in the sky. It was always the same. One moment the sky was full of aeroplanes, the next it was empty. I was debating whether to carry on towards the target and hope to find the others or whether to follow my own advice to my pilots when alone, which was to get down to ground level and fly home, when I noticed a couple of miles in front and at the same height three pairs of 109s. There was no doubt in my mind what to do. They had come up from St Omer or Merville and were target bound.[15]

Douglas had indeed done 'everything wrong'. He should, in fact, have turned about shortly after take-off and immediately after his ASI went unserviceable. In his selfish pursuit of action, Dogsbody had wasted precious seconds by not despatching Holden's Section to intercept the enemy that 610 Squadron's CO had sighted – but which he himself could not immediately see. Then, alone over France, Wing Commander Bader committed the cardinal sin of not diving and hedge-hopping home – but once more allowed greed to get the better of his judgement.

Douglas, alone over France, now prepared to attack:

I dropped down just below them and closed up. If they saw me and turned I would dive vertically for a few thousand feet and then go home. No 109 could stay with a Spitfire in a dive [this, for technical reasons previously explained, was not so]. They did not see me. I destroyed the back one of the middle pair with a short burst from close range. As he dived away on fire I closed up on his companion in front, and was just opening fire when I saw the two 109s on my left turning towards me – I decided to go home. A few bits were falling off my 109, but I'd nearly been caught that way before when I'd thought I just had time to finish an enemy off and got a cockpit full of bullets instead.

I then made my final mistake. The rule is as old as air fighting: always turn towards your enemy, never turn your back on him. If you do, you lose sight of him and present him with you as a target. The two enemy on my right were still flying straight which was why I turned right towards them, intending to pass over the top of or even behind them, and then dive away for home in the opposite direction. At this stage there was no problem. But the bad judgement that had dogged me all day finally fixed me. I banked over right-handed and collided with the second 109 ... I felt rather than heard a noise behind the cockpit, saw the tail of a 109 out of the corner of my eye passing behind me and then got the impression that someone was grasping the tail of my Spitfire. Down went the nose vertically; I pulled the stick back and there was nothing there ... I looked behind and there appeared to be nothing behind the cockpit. In other words, the complete back end, elevator, and fin had disappeared. Time to leave.[16]

At 24,000 feet, Douglas was unable to consider escape due to the lack of oxygen outside the cockpit at that height. His dilemma, however, was that the doomed fighter was already travelling in excess of 400 mph, so would soon be subjected to forces so great that baling out would become impossible. Yanking the canopy release mechanism, the hood was sucked away, the cockpit immediately being battered by the airflow. Without legs though, would he be able to thrust his body upwards to get out? As he struggled to get his head above the windscreen, he was nearly plucked out of the cockpit, but halfway he became stuck – the rigid foot of his artificial right leg jamming in the cockpit, the grip vice-like. Ever downwards the fighter plunged, the pilot helpless and continuously battered by the rushing wind, half in and half out of his crashing aeroplane. Desperately gripping his parachute's 'D' ring, Douglas struggled furiously to get out. Eventually, at about 6,000 feet, the offending artificial leg's restraining strap broke. Free at last, the pilot was plucked out into mid-air; as the Spitfire continued its dive, he experienced a moment of apparently floating upwards. That terrible buffeting having thankfully ceased, in the silence he was able to think – hand still gripping the 'D' ring, he pulled; there was a slight delay before the parachute deployed and then he was really was floating, gently to earth beneath the life-saving silk umbrella.

At 4,000 feet Wing Commander Bader floated through a layer of cloud, emerging below to see the ground still far below. Alarmed by the roar of an aero-engine, he saw an Me 109 fly directly towards him, but the bullets he must have half-expected never came as the enemy fighter flashed by just 50 yards away. Such a parachute descent – made due to enemy action or some other mishap while flying actively – was often the first a pilot would actually make, there being no formal parachute training. Consequently, Douglas had never before had to consider the practicalities of landing with artificial legs, or indeed on one such leg, as he drifted earthwards. Having had some minutes to ponder this matter, suddenly French soil rushed up to meet him and he hit the ground hard, in an orchard near Blaringhem, to the south-east of St Omer. For Wing Commander Douglas Bader, the air war was over: his personal period of operational service had lasted just eighteen months. As Douglas said, 9 August 1941 was 'a lousy day indeed'.[17]

Pilot Officer Johnson recalled the scene back at Westhampnett: 'Group Captain Woodhall was waiting for me on the airfield, and when Dundas, West, Hepple and the others came back the consensus of opinion was that the Wing Commander had either been shot down or involved in a collision.'[18] In his flying logbook, Johnson wrote that on this penetration over France there had been 'more opposition than ever before'.[19] Squadron Leader Burton's logbook recorded, 'Had a bad time with 109s on way out and had to get into cloud.'[20] As the clock ticked on, it became clear from fuel considerations that the two Spitfires reported missing during the radio chatter over France were unlikely to return to Westhampnett. Reasoning that if flying damaged machines the pilots might land at one of the coastal airfields, Tangmere telephoned each in turn, receiving negative responses from all.

Douglas Roberts was a Radio Telephone (Direction Finding) Operator at the Tangmere 'Fixer' station located on West Mailing airfield in Kent: 'We were told that Wing Commander Bader was missing and so listened out for several hours. Our system was basic when compared to modern equipment today, but nevertheless very efficient. The aerial system was a double dipole which, when rotated, would indicate either a true bearing or a reciprocal. Despite our diligence, nothing was heard from "Dogsbody".'[21]

Had either of the two missing pilots reached mid-Channel, then there was an excellent chance that they would be picked up by air-sea rescue. If their dinghies had drifted closer to the French coast then it was more likely that the Germans would get to them first, unless their positions could be discovered and a protective aerial umbrella established. Consequently Dundas, Johnson, Hepple and West were soon flying back over the Channel, searching. At Le Touquet, Dundas led the section north, parallel to the coast and towards Cap Griz-Nez. Avoiding flak from various enemy vessels, especially near the port of Calais, a steep turn at zero feet returned the Spitfires to Le Touquet. At one point Hepple broke away to machine-gun a surfacing submarine, but otherwise the only item to report was an empty dinghy sighted by Sergeant West. To Johnnie Johnson, that empty, life-saving rubber boat was somehow symbolic of their fruitless search. With petrol almost exhausted, the section landed at Hawkinge. No news had yet been received of either missing pilot. As soon as the aircraft were refuelled, the 616 Squadron pilots took off, intending to head back across the Channel to France. Shortly after take-off, however, Group Captain Woodhall cancelled the sortie, fearing that a second trip was too risky as the enemy might now be waiting. Swinging round to the west, Dundas led the Spitfires back to Westhampnett. For Dundas, the thought of Bader dead was 'utterly shattering'.[22] Buck Casson's loss was also a serious blow to Dundas's morale: they had joined the squadron together at Doncaster and, until that day, were the last remnants of the old pre-war pilots. When the fact dawned on him that he was now the only member of the old guard left, Dundas found this a 'terrifying thought'.[23] Regarding Bader, as a loyal lieutenant, Dundas felt some degree of responsibility. He drove back to Shopwyke House 'alone and utterly dejected'.[24]

With no news other than the fact that her husband had apparently vanished, Group Captain Woodhall had the unenviable duty of driving over to The Bay House and informing Thelma that Douglas was missing. John Hunt, a young Intelligence Officer, was already there, having arrived to give some support only to discover that Thelma had yet to receive the bad news, which Woody tempered by stating that Douglas Bader was indestructible and probably a prisoner. Later, Dundas arrived and with Jill, her sister, persuaded Thelma to take some sherry – which she only brought up again. As Dundas drove back to Shopwyke House he cried. Back at the mess, he and Johnson shared a whole bottle of brandy. Despair had overtaken the inner sanctum.

Just as the Target Support mission had been routine for the Tangmere Wing, so too was the interception by JG 26. Having urgently responded to the *Alarmstart*, it was 109s from the *Schlageter Geschwader* that the Tangmere Wing had fought that day high above Bethune. After the action, which developed into a running battle between Bethune and the French coast, the German pilots claimed a total of seven Spitfires destroyed. In reality the figure was five, three Spitfires of 452 (Australian) Squadron having also failed to return, lost somewhere between Bethune and Mardyck. However, although JG 26, the only Luftwaffe unit to engage Spitfires that day, only lost two 109s during the engagement, the RAF pilots claimed a staggering twenty-two destroyed, ten probables and eight damaged.

Among the successful German pilots was JG 26's *Kommodore*, *Oberstleutnant* Adolf Galland, who had recorded victory number seventy-six, a Spitfire north-west of St Pol, at 1132 hours. Shortly afterwards, *Oberleutnant* 'Pips' Priller, *Staffelkapitän* of 1/JG 26, arrived at Audembert to tell Galland about this captured legless *adler*, urging Galland, 'You must come and meet him.'[25] While in hospital, at the Clinique Sterin in St Omer, Bader was actually visited several times by two JG 26 pilots; he shared a bottle of champagne with them in the doctor's room and concluded that they were 'types' whom he would have liked in the Tangmere Wing. Previous accounts have stated that the Germans recovered Bader's missing leg from his Spitfire's crash site, but in fact French eyewitnesses confirm that the artificial limb in question fluttered down on its own and landed close to Wing Commander Bader's parachute. The villagers handed the article in to the German authorities, after which Galland's engineers made running repairs on the leg to afford the Wing Commander some mobility. A few days later, Galland sent his *horsch* – staff car – to fetch Bader for a visit to the *Geschwaderstab Schwarm*.

While visiting JG 26, Douglas was interested to know what had happened when he was brought down. His explanation was a collision with an Me 109, although he had not actually seen the aeroplane with which he had supposedly collided. Galland was puzzled, however, as none of his aircraft had been involved in such a collision. One 109 pilot had been killed: *Unteroffizier* Alfred Schlager, who crashed at Aire, some 10 miles south-east of St Omer. The Germans therefore conceded it was possible that Bader may have collided with Schlager, who had not survived to make any report. More likely, though, so far as Galland was concerned, was that Wing Commander Bader had been shot down by one of two pilots, either *Oberfeldwebel* Walter Meyer (6/JG 26) or *Leutnant* Kosse (5/JG 26) who had recorded their eleventh and seventh victories respectively above the area of St Omer that morning. According to Adolf Galland, for Bader it was an 'intolerable idea' that his master in the air was an NCO pilot.[26] Tactfully, therefore, a 'fair-haired, good looking flying officer' was selected from the victorious German pilots and introduced to

Bader as his champion.[27] Kosse was the only officer of that rank to make a claim that morning, and so it is likely that it was he who Bader met at Audembert. However, neither German pilots' victory report was conclusive. As Galland later wrote, 'it was never confirmed who shot him down'.[28]

Among the officers present at the reception thrown for Bader by JG 26 was *Hauptmann* Gerhard Schöpfel:

> My meeting with Wing Commander Bader was memorable and one which I well recall. Our *Oberst* Joachim-Friedrich Huth had lost a leg in the First World War, and when the report about Bader being shot down reached him he was sure that spare artificial legs existed in England. There followed a number of telephone calls, during which Bader's capture was reported to the Red Cross, and it was decided that an RAF aircraft should be offered free passage to deliver the spare legs to our airfield at an appointed time and date. So far as I know, this was initially confirmed by England.[29]

When the Red Cross announced that Wing Commander Bader was a prisoner, on 14 August there was absolute euphoria within Fighter Command, and in particular, of course, at Tangmere. George Reid, of 616 Squadron's ground crew, felt differently: 'So far as I am concerned, after Wing Commander Bader was shot down, a happy feeling settled on 616, Westhampnett, Tangmere and, I daresay, Chichester. Good days arrived, the sun came out and life was grand.'[30] Flight Lieutenant Crowley-Milling remembered that

> the loss of Douglas Bader had left us all stunned. A few of us, including Dundas and Johnson, were with Thelma Bader in

their married quarters at Tangmere when the telephone rang. After speaking, Thelma came back to join us and very calmly said, 'Douglas is safe and a prisoner.'

When the signal was received from Germany offering free passage for an RAF aircraft to deliver Wing Commander Bader's spare legs, Group Captain Woodhall responded so enthusiastically that he even offered to fly a Lysander to Audembert himself. However, the Air Ministry rejected the proposal out of hand.[31]

Gerhard Schöpfel recalled events across the Channel: 'On the appointed time and date for an RAF aircraft to arrive with the legs, I was at the *Geschwader-gefechtsstand* in Audembert, having flown in from my base at Ligescourt, home of my III/JG 26. Soon after our meeting, Bader wanted to inspect one of our Me 109s. Galland invited him to climb into a *Geschwader-maschine* and Bader commented that he would like to fly it, but of course this could not be allowed.'[32] Many photographs were taken by the Germans of this visit, which numerous non-flying JG 26 personnel would later recall as the most memorable incident of their entire war. Among the snapshots is a photograph of Douglas sitting in the cockpit of a 109, a German officer stood on the wing. In *Reach for the Sky*, and consequently many other books, the object in this officer's left hand has been described as a 'pistol' – other photographs from the same series show that in fact *Oberst* Joachim Huth is holding his gloves! Schöpfel continued that 'when told of our arrangement via the Red Cross regarding his spare legs, he was not surprised when no plane arrived as he felt that high authority in England would take time to sanction such things. He hoped, however, that his own Wing would find a way. One or two days later, our radar announced a beehive approaching. The Blenheims flew over St Omer where they dropped a few bombs on our I *Gruppe*. Also dropped, however, was a crate containing Bader's legs which was attached to a parachute.'[33] Mobile once more, the Germans would soon rue the day.

At the end of the month, the 616 Squadron Operations Record Book concluded that August was

A disappointing one from the operational point of view owing to the poor weather conditions. Although sixteen offensive sweeps were carried out over France, their effectiveness was in several cases hampered by too much cloud, making it difficult for the squadrons in the Wing to keep together. Wing Commander Bader DSO (& Bar) DFC, and Flight Lieutenant Casson were shot down on August 9th and are now prisoners of war. This was a serious loss to the RAF, the Wing and the Squadron.[34]

August 1941 was, in fact, a 'disappointing' month for Fighter Command as a whole: ninety-eight Spitfires and ten Hurricanes were lost. However, JG 2 and JG 26 combined had lost just eighteen pilots; the loss ratio was exactly a staggering 6:1 in the Luftwaffe's favour. Certainly the Tangmere Wing would never be the same again without Dogsbody. According to Adolf Galland, however, 'it was never confirmed who shot him down', even though Douglas 'particularly wanted to know who it was and if possible to meet his master in the air'.[35] This is deserved of further explanation.

In addition to 616 Squadron's grievous loss, both 315 and 603 Squadrons also suffered one Spitfire damaged each. JG

26 provided the sole German opposition to Circus 68, the *Geschwaderstab* and all three *Gruppen* making contact with the enemy. This represented 100–120 Me 109Es and Fs, a substantial force indeed. Consequently the German pilots made claims for seven Spitfires destroyed – the actual RAF losses being five Spitfires destroyed and four damaged. The German victory claims were as follows:

Pilot	Victory No.	Unit	Opponent	Time & Location
Oblt J. Schmid	16	*Geschwaderstab*	Spitfire	1125 hrs, 10 km E of St Omer
Obfw. W. Meyer	11	6/JG26	Spitfire	1125 hrs, St Omer
Obfw. E. Busch	6	9/JG26	Spitfire	1125 hrs, location not known
Uffz. H. Richter	n/k	*Geschwaderstab*	Spitfire	1130 hrs, N of Dunkirk
Obstlt A. Galland	76	*Geschwaderstab*	Spitfire	1132 hrs, NW of St Pol
Lt Kosse	9	5/JG26	Spitfire	1145 hrs, St Omer
Hptm. G. Schöpfel	31	StabIII/JG26	Spitfire	1145 hrs, E of Marquise

On the day in question, an Me 109F-2 of III/JG 26 crashed on take-off at Ligescourt, and an FW 190 crash-landed near Le Bourget, the latter incident not believed to be combat-related. The only other losses are as follows:

3/JG 26 Me 109F-4 (8350)
Crashed near Aire, *Uffz.* Albert Schlager killed.
II/JG 26 Me 109E-7 (6494)
Pilot n/k, baled out near Merville.

Douglas's personal impression was that he had collided with an enemy aircraft. Certainly Johnnie Johnson graphically described the close proximity of the enemy, the maelstrom of fighters being just '50 yards apart' – but Bader was not lost during those initial seconds of mayhem. Having levelled out from the diving charge, Dogsbody then went off alone, stalking a section of Me 109s. When repatriated in 1945, Wing Commander Bader reported that after his subsequent attack, 'in turning away right-handed from this, I collided with an Me 109 which took my tail off, it appeared as far up as the radio mast but was actually only the empennage'.[36] However, in a letter dated 5 August 1981, he wrote that his 'impression was that I turned across a 109 and that it collided with the back of my Spitfire, removing the tail. On the other hand, if the pilot of the Me 109 had fired his guns at that moment, he could have blown my tail off. The result would have been the same.' The crucial question that must therefore be asked is, did Wing Commander Bader collide with an Me 109, or was he actually shot down? None of Galland's pilots had been involved in a collision, however, so the only candidate for such an occurrence was JG 26's single fatality: *Unteroffizier* Albert Schlager, whose aircraft crashed near Aire-sur-la-Lys. The evidence, though, confirms that Schlager was not involved in a collision, but actually shot down by Pilot Officer 'Nip' Hepple, whose combat report stated,

I was Yellow Three when 616 Squadron took off from Westhampnett at 1040 hours. Shortly after crossing the French coast south of Boulogne the Squadron went into a left-hand orbit. After a few minutes about twenty Me 109Fs were seen to the east of us and several thousand feet below, climbing up over white cloud. Wing Commander Bader went into attack in a steep dive, when I got down to their level the E/A had split up.

I climbed up to the right and saw an Me 109F come up in front of me. He appeared to be on the top of a stall turn and so I gave him a long burst, closing to point blank range. I saw on the side of his a/c, as he turned to the left, a large '6' just behind the cross on the fuselage. He then went into a very slow gliding turn to the left and I had a vivid view of his hood flying off and the pilot jumping out of his machine. I watched him falling and turning over and over until he had dropped down to some low white cloud; his parachute had still not opened so I assume he was killed. This a/c is claimed as destroyed.

The camouflage was a dirty grey and black, in addition to the usual cross there was a '6' behind it. The tail was painted orange and the spinner black and white.[37]

To assist recognition in the air, German fighters were specifically marked on the fuselage with either a thick horizontal or wavy line adjacent to the black cross. In the case of I Gruppe, however, no such marking was carried, and Schlager's 109F was of I/JG 26's 3rd Staffel. Hepple remarks on the number six painted on the fuselage, but makes no mention of any line marking, which would have been highly visible. Hepple's reference to an 'orange' tail was more likely red, and specifically the vertical rudder. Unfortunately we do not know what identifying colour 3/JG 26 used at this time, which could assist with identifying Hepple's victim, and nor are we aware of what individual number Schlager's aircraft was. The German pilot, however, baled out, and Hepple makes no reference to seeing a parachute open: Schlager's parachute failed to open and he died as a result. It is reasonable to credit Schlager's demise to Hepple's guns, and not a collision with Wing Commander Bader (moreover and conclusively, in more recent times, enthusiasts excavated the crash site of Schlager's 109, recovering the tail wheel assembly. This proves that Schlager's aircraft did not lose its tail unit, as did Wing Commander Bader's Spitfire). The only other 109 down that day was at Merville, some 14 miles south-east of Blaringhem, a distance in itself not altogether ruling out this aircraft as a collision contender. However, the pilot baled out safely and must have subsequently reported on the incident, details of which presumably did not include a collision. 452 Squadron's pilots also claimed two Me 109Es destroyed in their fight, so the enemy fighter of that type down at Merville was most likely one of them – Flight Lieutenant Brendan 'Paddy' Finucane DFC claimed an Me 109E in the 'Gosnay–Bethune area',[38] and Flight Lieutenant 'Bluey' Truscott an 'E', his first-ever combat claim, between 'Mardyck-Bethune'.[39]

Douglas himself conceded that he did not see the Me 109 which he thought he had struck, a collision being just his 'impression' of the destructive forces acting upon his Spitfire at that time. The same effect could have been achieved had the Spitfire been hit by 20 mm cannon shells. If Wing Commander Bader was actually shot down, though, who was responsible? Looking at the table of German combat claims, and bearing in mind that Dogsbody, although not lost in the initial charge, was nevertheless hacked down within the opening few minutes of the engagement, only one claim stands out: that of *Oberfeldwebel* Walter Meyer of 6/JG 26, who claimed his eleventh victory over St Omer at 1125 hours. However, that Meyer was Bader's victor is a theory slightly diluted by the claim for a Spitfire destroyed at the same time but at an unknown location by 9/JG 26's *Oberfeldwebel* Busch. 9/JG 26 was a part of *Hauptmann* Schöpfel's IIIrd *Gruppe* which, according to the *Kommandeur*'s account, had actually intercepted the beehive proper, some minutes after the initial skirmish in question. It appears unlikely, therefore, that Busch's claim relates to the same engagement in which Wing Commander Bader was lost.

When researching Douglas Bader's biography, Lucas, working with Henry Probert, the then head of the MOD's Air Historical Branch (AHB), examined German claims. Both men were sufficiently satisfied with the timing of Mayer's claim to conclude that he was responsible. Although making a connection between Bader and Mayer, Lucas wrongly referred in print to 'Max Mayer'.[40] Lucas and Probert also wrongly assumed that Flight Lieutenant Casson had been shot down in the same area as Wing Commander Bader. Thus they decided that *Leutnant* Kosse, who claimed a Spitfire over St Omer at 1145 hours, had shot down Casson. In reality, Casson was shot down by *Hauptmann* Schöpfel – who even had a photograph taken of the downed Spitfire. Regarding Kosse's claim, it is unlikely, in fact, that this pilot even fought the Tangmere Wing. The Tangmere Spitfires, as the Target Support Wing, were first to arrive over the target area. Kosse recorded that his combat had occurred at 1145 hours, some twenty minutes after the initial 'bounce' during which

Oberfeldwebel Meyer destroyed a Spitfire at 1125 hours. A time-lapse of twenty minutes therefore represents a long interval. By 1145 hours, the Tangmere Wing was re-crossing the French coast, this being confirmed by the fact that Casson was shot down near Marquise, just 3 miles from the coast at exactly that time. As Schöpfel went to some trouble to obtain evidence for his victory report, such as even flying low over the crashed Spitfire to record its code letters, we can, I think, accept his timing as accurate. In view of these times, and the fact that the Tangmere Wing was heading home at 1145 hours, it is likely that Kosse actually engaged Spitfires of 452 Squadron.

During exhaustive research into this engagement, Lucas and I corresponded; he wrote,

> When having dinner at Douglas Bader's house in the country, Adolf Galland told me categorically that DB had been shot down over the Pas-de-Calais in 1941. Galland stated that there had not been a collision. I can say in fact that, in my own humble experience, receiving a volley or two of cannon shells from an Me 109 could certainly sound like a collision with a London bus! I put this view to Douglas, who responded, 'In that case, old cock, because it was me, why didn't they have the bugger responsible goose-stepping down the Under-den-Linden?'[41]

What no one had considered was the unthinkable: the famous Tangmere Wing Leader had actually been shot down by one of his own pilots.

On 9 August 1941, Flight Lieutenant Buck Casson was also captured. He did not, therefore, return to Tangmere to report on the incident. However, in 1945, at Douglas Bader's request, Buck wrote to his former Wing Leader regarding his own experiences of that fateful day. The account in question has already been reproduced in full earlier in this chapter, but I would particularly draw to the reader's attention the following extract: 'After having a squirt at two 109s flying together, I left them for a single one flying inland alone. I finished nearly all of my cannon ammunition up on this boy, who finally baled out at 6,000 feet, having lost most of his tail unit.' Who did Casson shoot down?

We know that JG 26 lost but one Me 109 in this engagement, and that Schlager crashed at Aire was confirmed by the discovery of an identification plate when that crash site was excavated in 2003. A tail wheel was also recovered, proving that the tail section of that aircraft was still very much attached upon impact. Buck could not, therefore, have shot down Schlager. Neither do I believe that Buck shot down the Me 109E lost by II/JG 26, because Merville is just too far away to be relevant. What cannot be discounted, however, is that the circumstances described by Casson are exactly those which befell Wing Commander Bader, i.e. that his tail unit was badly damaged and he baled out at about 6,000 feet. One might ask why Douglas Bader himself did not question this when Buck wrote to him in 1945, but at that time the pilots concerned no doubt considered that they had been involved in a hectic dogfight with the aircraft of both sides being shot down all around; certainly this is reflected by the RAF's gross over-claiming on the day in question. Had Casson ever submitted an official report, which would have been made available to the general public during the 1970s, perhaps the connection would have been made then? That Wing Commander Bader was the victim of 'friendly fire' would certainly explain why the German combat reports were so inconclusive. Furthermore, as the pilot possibly responsible had absolutely no idea himself of what had happened, and indeed was also captured that day, these two factors could also help explain the mystery. The truth only became apparent, in fact, when, having possessed a copy of Casson's letter to Douglas since 1987, the circumstances became obvious to me when researching the incident in 1995. In the heat of the moment such mistakes frequently occur – especially in aerial combat, given the speed and confusion involved.

Shortly after making my discovery, I put the evidence to key survivors. Air Vice-Marshal Johnnie Johnson: 'I would be very surprised if an experienced and careful fighter pilot such as Buck Casson would make such a mistake, but do agree from his description of events that he has almost certainly seen DB come down.'[42]

Group Captain Sir Hugh Dundas: 'Nothing is certain, nor ever will be.'[43]

Air Marshal Sir Denis Crowley-Milling: 'Absolute rubbish!'[44]

Squadron Leader Casson's own opinion on the matter was clear: 'I was an experienced fighter pilot and well knew what a 109 looked like. I shot down a 109 that day.'[45]

Having flown throughout the Battle of Britain and during that long summer of offensive operations in 1941, Buck most certainly would have seen many Me 109s. Indeed, he had shared one destroyed on 22 June and probably destroyed another on 19 July. But if his trigger finger did make a mistake in the great confusion and heat of the moment, it was perfectly understandable, not least given the prevalent chaos and marked similarities in appearance between the Spitfire and Me 109F – the latter still a comparatively new shape in the sky.

It is also worth reporting how, back in 1981, the tale took on yet another twist. Lucas wrote that in March 1981, Sir Douglas Bader opened the Schofield Air Show, Sydney, where, by chance, he was introduced to former Luftwaffe fighter pilot 'Max Mayer'. The pair exchanged pleasantries, but no more. The following day Bader was apparently astonished to read in the press an article based upon an interview which Mayer had given a journalist after his meeting with Sir Douglas and in which he claimed to have shot down the Tangmere Wing Leader.[46] Lucas, having researched to some extent the German records, assumed that this was actually *Oberfeldwebel* Walter Meyer (note the difference in spelling of the surname) who claimed the destruction of a Spitfire over St Omer at 1125 hours on the day in question. What Lucas did not know was what had happened to *Oberfeldwebel* Meyer: on 11 October 1942, Meyer had collided with his *Rottenflieger*, crashed and was hospitalised; he did not recover, and died of tuberculosis in January 1943. Burns, typically using Lucas's biography as his principal source, accepted the information that 'Max Mayer' had shot down Bader. Burns claimed that the 'Australian Fighter Mafia' had unsuccessfully attempted to trace Mayer.[47] Why there should have been any difficulty, I cannot understand.

So who was 'Max Mayer'? Having contacted Sydney's *The Daily Telegraph Mirror* in 1995, I received a copy of the article in question, written by a C. J. McKenzie. Mayer claimed to have shot Bader down with 'one cannon burst, which ripped away the tail of Bader's Spitfire'. Mayer continued, 'I saw him spiralling down, I saw his face. I followed him down because I had to confirm the kill. When I saw his parachute coming up I turned away. I reported where he had crashed.' McKenzie was advised by one of Bader's entourage not to 'bring that up or you'll get an argument'.

Mayer claimed that it was the second time he and Bader had shaken hands, the first having been in the Clinique Sterin in St Omer: 'He was surprised when he found out it was me. He was a Wing Commander. I was a mere *Leutnant*. He was very warm towards me and we shook hands strongly.'[48]

Already it was possible to identify major inaccuracies in Max Mayer story, not least that Walter Meyer had died in 1943! Firstly it would be impossible, of course, to identify a pilot's face in the circumstances discussed. Secondly, Mayer gives the impression that at the time, so far as the Germans were concerned, his claim was accepted. Refer again to Adolf Galland: 'It was never confirmed who shot down Douglas Bader.' Furthermore, whereas Mayer claims to have been a *Leutnant*, Walter Meyer was an NCO. Martin Maxwell Mayer also claimed to have destroyed thirty-four enemy aircraft, a tally including victories not only on the *Kanalfront*, but also over Russia and North Africa. Such a score had, he stated, won him the coveted Knight's Cross. Anyone checking the list of fighter pilots who were *Ritterkreuztrager* would discover no reference to a Martin Max Mayer. After the Second World War, Martin Maxwell Mayer claimed to have flown with the French Air Force in Algiers, but amateur military historian Professor Bernard-Marie Dupont, himself a former French Army officer, confirms that there is no record of such a pilot, a non-French national, having flown with the French Air Force.

In August 1995, I located C. J. McKenzie himself, now retired, who supplied a copy of a letter from Douglas to 'Max Mayer':

Dear Max Mayer,
    You will recall that we met on Saturday, March 28th, at

the Schofield Air Show near Sydney. We were both pleased to meet each other because we were ex-fighter pilots (on opposite sides) and we had an agreeable conversation for some minutes.

The next morning, March 29th, I read an article in one of the newspapers quoting an interview with you, during the course of which you said that you had shot me down over France on August 9th, 1941 and had followed me down until you saw me bale out. Having read that, I was hoping to see you that day, so that we could discuss it. None of us could find you on Sunday. We tried on the Monday to contact you, but were unsuccessful. Then I left to go elsewhere in Australia. Dolfo Galland, who commanded JG 26, has become a great friend of mine since the war. He cannot tell me about the incident on August 9th 1941.

My impression was that I turned across an Me 109 and that it collided with the back of my Spitfire, removing the tail. On the other hand, if the pilot of the Me 109 had fired his guns at that moment, he could have blown my tail off. The result would have been the same.

Please write and tell me your account of this incident, if you can remember it. You told the Australian press that you followed my Spitfire down until you saw me bale out. I imagine you knew it was me because you saw, when I baled out, that one leg was missing. I know that you had lived in Australia for 25 years but cannot think why you did not tell me all this when we talked to each other on March 28th. We could have had a tremendous laugh about it and really enjoyed it.

I shall greatly look forward to hearing from you,
Best wishes,
Yours sincerely,
Douglas Bader[49]

McKenzie observed that Douglas had

> put more 'spin' on his meeting with Mayer than Shane Warne
> puts on a 'leggie'! Bader met Mayer at Mascot Airport (our
> Sydney Kingsford Smith International), not at the Schofields
> Air Show. It had taken me some time to tee-up the meeting
> and Bader knew precisely who he was meeting and why.
> I introduced Mayer in those terms. He knew also why I
> was there, why the photographer was there, yet he seems
> to express surprise at the story of 29 March. He says, after
> reading the story, 'I was hoping to see you that day so we
> could discuss it.' What day does he mean? And discuss what?
> He says further that he tried to find Mayer on the Sunday
> and Monday. He had only to phone *The Sunday Telegraph*
> to have been put in contact with Mayer. The meeting
> between the two was brief, not as Bader says 'an agreeable
> conversation for some minutes'. Indeed, I was embarrassed
> by Bader's attitude. It is not always easy in words to give the
> right tone to something said. Bader's use of the word 'Kraut',
> instead of 'German', surprised me. The way he said it was, in
> my view, intended to be insulting or at least denigrating. Max
> Mayer died some years ago.[50]

There is no doubt that 'Martin Maxwell Mayer' was not the man he
claimed to be, nor indeed the man who shot down Douglas Bader.

Whatever happened that day over France now so long ago, the fact remained the Tangmere's apparently invincible leader had fallen – if not to enemy action, he was nonetheless a prisoner of war (POW). Exactly one month later, the award of a Bar to Douglas's DFC was gazetted. The citation read that 'this fearless pilot has recently added a further four enemy aircraft to his previous successes; in addition he has probably destroyed another four and damaged five hostile aircraft. By his fine leadership and high courage Wing Commander Bader has inspired the Wing on every occasion.'[51] Beneath the 'Bader's Bus Company' sign on 616 Squadron's pilots' hut, a wag added 'Still Running'. At Tangmere the war went on – for Douglas more adversity awaited behind the barbed wire.

17

AN UNAPPEASABLE PRISONER

On 9 August 1941, a thirteen-year-old French schoolboy, Artur Dubreu, was watching the action from his village at Steenbecque, near St Omer:

I remember the incident vividly. I saw a lot of planes, it was mid-morning on a sunny day. There was a big dogfight and many contrails in the sky. I saw an aircraft coming down very fast and then a parachute opened. The aircraft crashed in a field and a cloud of black smoke and debris rose over the site. Due to the wind the parachute drifted slightly; it was the first parachute I had ever seen, in fact, so I remember it very well. I wanted to see the pilot, so I ran after the rapidly descending canopy. The parachute seemed to land very fast, but the pilot hit some trees in an orchard which took the shock. The pilot was just sitting there, silk billowing around him. I was horrified to see that he only had one leg, which was twisted at an unnatural angle. There was no blood and, although he seemed to be stunned from the landing, he did not appear otherwise concerned about his legs. I could not understand it at all. I was the first on the scene but before I could help a German officer ran into the field, took charge and told me to clear off, which I did as i was very frightened on the soldiers. The Germans then carried the pilot to their waiting car.[1]

The Germans had certainly won a prize that day, but for Douglas the prospect of being a prisoner – and not fighting the enemy in the air – was an intolerable one. Douglas was taken to Chambre 21 in the Clinique Sterin at St Omer. There, as previously described, he was visited by certain of Galland's officers and subsequently entertained by JG 26. Indeed, the Germans expertly repaired Douglas's damaged artificial leg and returned it to him – which Galland would later have occasion to regret.

On 17 August, after his visit to III/JG 26 at Audembert, a female French auxiliary nurse, Lucille Debacker, handed him an astonishing note: a Frenchman would be waiting outside the hospital every night from midnight to 0200 hours, poised to guide 'Le Colonel' to a local safe house. Incredibly, the note was even signed by the author, Madame Maria Hiècque – the matriarch of a working-class family residing at the Quai du Haut-Pont, a long row of terraced dwellings overlooking St Omer's canal. A friend of the family, Gilbert Petit, a railway worker, subsequently broke curfew on a nightly basis and awaited 'Le Colonel'. Douglas was animated by this development but received bad news: he was to be taken to Germany. On the night of 20 August, he knotted bed sheets together, lowered his makeshift rope from his ward's window – and promptly descended to disappear into the French night. Meeting Petit, the unlikely pair made their way through the blacked-out streets, avoiding a German patrol. It was physically trying for Douglas, but eventually they reached sanctuary. The exertion, however, had left him in great pain from severely chafed stumps. As he drifted off to sleep, concealed in an upstairs room, the ever-optimistic Wing Commander thought, 'That's foxed the bloody Huns. I'll be seeing Thelma in a couple of days!'[2]

At noon the following day, Douglas heard a beehive passing overhead and was moved by the French populace's enthusiastic reaction. What he did not know was that the operation being flown was a special one: to drop, along with bombs on St Omer airfield, a new pair of legs for him. His escape had, in fact, already caused Galland some discomfort: 'This was very unpleasant for me ... and Command made a most embarrassing inquiry into his escape. Even his visit to our air base, for which I had not asked permission, came up in the course of a stern investigation.'[3] So far as Madame Hiècque was concerned, however, 'Les Boche sont tres stupides!' – the old lady delighted in seeing numerous German soldiers searching St Omer for the escaped RAF war hero. Although Douglas expressed great concern regarding the likely fate of his helpers if discovered, his host was supremely confident that they would not be discovered. Fortunately Quai du Haut-Pont was a fair distance from the Clinque Sterin; the Germans, convinced that the legless escapee could not walk far, restricted the radius of their search accordingly. Nonetheless, Madame Hiècque's confidence was misplaced: when the hospital staff were inevitably questioned, one terrified young auxiliary, Hélène Léfèvre, broke down and betrayed the patriots. A neighbour was soon banging a warning on the canal-side hide-out's front door as German soldiers swooped. Douglas was rapidly bundled into the small back garden and hid beneath a pile of straw in the chicken run. Within minutes jackboots were crunching through the house. Seconds later a bayonet was being thrust into the straw – with no choice, Douglas dejectedly stood up with hands raised in surrender.

Douglas's main concern was the fate of Madame Hiècque and her fellow conspirators. All but Gilbert Petit were discovered, arrested by the Gestapo and interrogated at St Omer's *Kommandanteur*. Remanded in custody and later found guilty at a military tribunal on 9 September, all were sentenced to death. Local feeling, however, ran high, provoking innumerable pleases for leniency – including one such appeal from Marshal Pétain, the leader of Vichy France. Consequently the Germans commuted the sentences to fifteen years' imprisonment for Lucille Debacker, and ten each for Leon and Maria Hiècque. Leon saw out the war in Diez Lahn jail, the two females in Fortress d'Anrath. Remarkably, all survived the ordeal. The involvement of Gilbert Petit, however, was never discovered – who simply continued working at St Omer's railway station as though nothing had happened.

Flight Lieutenant Denis Crowley-Milling:

I was shot down over France on 21 August 1941 – one of eighteen Spitfire pilots lost by Fighter Command that day. Fortunately I was taken in by the French Resistance and hidden in St Omer at the same time Douglas was on the run. There I heard of a plan to break him out of hospital. I asked to stay and help. Unfortunately the scheme became impossible when Douglas, who was unaware of it, escaped by other means only to be recaptured. It was a pity, because the Resistance's plan could have worked.[4]

'Crow' was more fortunate: guided down the 'Line' by the infamous Harry Cole, a pre-war Cockney confidence trickster who became a double-agent, he safely returned to England and resumed operational flying.

The furious Germans had received an early indication that Douglas Bader would be a very difficult prisoner indeed. Denied the mobility of his artificial legs, Douglas was driven to Lille before being packed off, under guard, on a train to the Luftwaffe interrogation centre, Dulag Luft, at Oberusal, near Frankfurt. Douglas became obsessed with the prospect of escape, berating his fellow prisoners that to do so was their duty. Such attempts, he argued, were valuable to the war effort by tying down German resources. Unfortunately, however, a plan to tunnel out of the camp would not include Douglas – his refusal to salute enemy officers of junior rank led to his rapid transfer to Oflag VIB at Lubeck. This was a camp for officer aircrew – where Douglas continued hatching escape plans and being generally bloody-minded so far as any co-operation with the Germans was concerned. In October 1941 the whole camp was moved to Warburg, near Cassel. 'Goon-baiting' became Douglas's favourite past-time – much to his guards' discomfort. While at Warburg there was some solace: he learned that he had received a Bar to his DFC, making him only the third man in history to win such for both the DSO and DFC. Lieutenant David Lubbock of the Fleet Air Arm was a fellow prisoner who involved Douglas in various unsuccessful escape attempts:

Douglas would stomp around the camp, then pretend to fall over and have to fix his legs. The thing was that we were digging a tunnel and filled his tin legs up with displaced soil! When he fell, Douglas would take his legs off and in so doing scattered the soil around him. Those legs also came in handy when we were caught trying to get through the wire. In a rage a German guard smashed the butt of his rifle down on the foot nearest to him. It happened to belong to Douglas, and I will never forget the look on that guard's face as Douglas burst out laughing![5]

Early in May 1942, Douglas was transferred to Stalag Luft III at Sagan – later to become the scene of the dramatic, tragic, so-called 'Great Escape' (another wartime epic written up by Brickhill as a popular post-war book). Douglas was uncompromising in his 'goon baiting' – his fellow officers, Mackenzie observed, viewing his behaviour with 'a mixture of awe and exasperation'.[6] Nonetheless, there were inspired and popular examples of real Bader charisma; Pilot Officer Roger Boulding had been shot down and captured while flying Spitfires with 74 Squadron:

It was snowing hard and we were playing snowballs. Wing Commander Bader was enthusiastically joining in the fun. A young German *leutnant* then came rushing over with a note from the *Kommandant* for the '*Ving* Commander'. Bader, quick as a flash, said, 'Be a good chap and hold that for me will you?' – holding out his snowball for the German. Instinctively the German took it and then, not knowing what to do but realising that he had made a complete fool of himself, just stood there holding it – while several hundred prisoners had hysterics! It was little things like that that made you realise what kind of man Douglas Bader really was.[7]

At Sagan, Douglas had been reunited with his old pre-war flight commander and aerobatic partner, Wing Commander Harry Day, who as Senior British Officer (SBO) present did his best to keep the peace between the RAF prisoners – and appease the ever-restless Wing Commander Bader. Neither job was easy – the latter was doubtless the more difficult task. His irascible behaviour led to another move, this time to Stalag VIIIB at Lamsdorf. Needless to say, the Germans failed to achieve this without incident, as Wing Commander Bob Stanford-Tuck recalled:

> Douglas staged a sort of sit-in in the centre of the camp, removing his legs to make it more difficult for them to move him. The guards were by then shaking with rage as they pointed their guns at him. I was certainly frightened for his life. Anyway, Douglas got the message and decided that he must leave. They had an escort laid on, and, unbelievably, he went down the ranks telling them what was wrong with their dress! I'll never forget hearing someone gasp in astonishment 'Good Lord, he's actually *inspecting* the buggers!'[8]

Aeneas 'Don' MacDonnell – the Laird of Glengarry in addition to having been an excellent Spitfire squadron commander during the Battle of Britain – wrote that after Douglas's departure, 'our guards relaxed and we settled down to undercover activities without the constant risk of their being blown by the Germans reacting to Bader-provoked nonsense'.[9] That, of course, was the flip-side to Douglas's more direct and nuisance-making personal continuance of waging war against Nazi Germany. Douglas's new camp was huge. Among the 20,000 prisoners incarcerated there was Sergeant Peter Fox – another Spitfire pilot captured in 1941: 'Douglas Bader and I were frequently in adjacent cells, in what the Germans called "Protective Custody", but known to us as the "Cooler". We devised a way of passing cigarettes to each other. On one occasion, as I passed some through the hatch to Douglas, or so I thought, the cigarettes were accepted but a German voice said, "Danke"!'[10] Persistent trouble, however, led to Douglas being transferred once more, on 18 August 1942: to the bad boys' prison at the notorious Oflag IVC – better known simply as Colditz Castle.

Four hundred Polish, Dutch, British Czech and French 'bad boys' were incarcerated at this supposedly escape-proof fortress built atop a high, rocky outcrop jutting into the River Mulde, 30 miles from Leipzig. This was a high-security prison for incorrigible Allied officers – and yet boasted one of the highest numbers of successful escape attempts. No matter how hard the Germans tried, the prisoners' ingenuity somehow managed to circumvent their security measures. Some schemes were incredibly adventurous – such as the glider built in the ancient castle's attic, although the war ended before this risky flying machine was launched from the rooftop. There Douglas was reunited with his old Cranwell friend and former squadron commander, Squadron leader Geoffrey Stephenson – whose trouble-making path had likewise led to Colditz. Douglas, according to fellow inmate Jack Pringle, was 'fanatically anti-German, and baited them at every opportunity'.[11] Lord Charles Linlithgow, a Scots Guards captain, remembered that 'Douglas disguised himself as a civilian laundry worker, intending to leave with the weekly laundry truck. But by now the guards were so paranoid about Douglas Bader that they actually lined up the laundry workers and went along the line, tapping their legs with a stick: a hollow "clonk" revealed … Douglas!'[12] Colonel Philip Pardoe: 'Having convinced the *Kommandant* that he had difficulty taking exercise in the Colditz yard, because it was cobbled, permission was granted for Douglas to walk to the nearby village and back, accompanied by a guard. On these walks he would bribe the guard to look away while he swapped our Red Cross cigarette rations for corn, which Douglas then stuffed into his hollow legs and brought back to Colditz. There we used it to make very welcome bread.'[13]

Douglas joined in cricket and stool-ball in the Colditz exercise yard with his fellow prisoners and continued antagonising the Germans at every opportunity. He remembered that 'we were all together at Colditz. We combined together, that was the point. We were wholly anti-German and dedicated to it. Unlike the other camps, there were very few new arrivals, new recruits who had just been shot down, to bring in the news. We were mostly long-standing prisoners, united by the concept of escape, even if it couldn't be effective, and by the resolve to challenge. That was the reason for our being there and that's why we all combined so well.' Interestingly, Douglas was offered the opportunity to go before a Swiss Commission for consideration of repatriation – the Germans no doubt being equally anxious to get this troublesome prisoner off their hands. This prospect, however, Douglas commendably rejected out of hand on the grounds that not having been wounded he had no right to this privilege.[14] The issue of repatriation, however, and Douglas's attitude towards it, negatively impacted on one Alec Ross, a bandsman of the Seaforth Highlanders and the Wing Commander's Medical Orderly; it also provided a further indication of the extent to which Douglas was a product of the hierarchical society of his time. Ross had become Douglas's batman at Lamsdorf and accompanied his master to Colditz. There Douglas relied upon the faithful Ross for such things as piggy-back rides up and down the long and narrow castle stairways. Ross later said that 'in all the time I knew him I don't think he said "please" or "thank you" to me. I was only a little squirt compared to him … He was the boss. Wherever he was he liked to be the head one. When he shouted you ran to do whatever he wanted.'[15] As a non-combatant, Ross was entitled to repatriation, which was arranged for him by the Germans via the Red Cross in 1943. He told Douglas, '"I'm going home!" but his lord and master furiously responded, "No you're bloody not! You came here as my skivvy and that's what you'll stay!" I had to stay another two bloody years when I could have gone home with the rest of my mates.'[16] This was, as Mackenzie observed, 'breathtakingly insensitive'[17] – and incredibly self-centred and selfish to the extent of beggaring belief. Brickhill described Ross as 'faithful':[18] in reality the batman clearly had no choice to be otherwise.

Back home, though, reports about Douglas still appeared in the British press. Cuttings were often sent to him by his friend Denis Crowley-Milling, who, in 1942, wrote to Douglas that he 'saw New Year in with Thelma; we drank your health!'[19] Accompanying that note was a cutting from the *Express*:

Bader sends for leg No. 7. Lack of exercise in a German camp has caused Wing Commander Douglas Bader to 'grow out of' his artificial legs and an urgent request has come from him to the Red Cross. New legs are to be rushed to Germany by air, sea and land. When they arrive, Bader will have had five new legs since he was taken prisoner by the Germans, after being shot down in August. The first new leg was dropped over northern France by a member of Bader's squadron. It was to take the place of the one Bader damaged landing by parachute. He used the new leg to make a four-day escape from his prison hospital, and got 100 miles towards England. After that the Germans took one leg away every night and gave it back each morning. In October two legs in a box weighing 37lb went by the Red Cross to Bader via Lisbon and Geneva.[20]

Douglas, therefore, continued to be a weapon in the propaganda and morale war, his story continually inspiring people. As in the foregoing report, however, the actual facts were frequently exaggerated to make better copy – during his escape from the Clinque Sterin, for example, Douglas had not 'got 100 miles towards England' – he never actually left St Omer. Importantly, though, Douglas was increasingly becoming an inspiration and example to the amputee disabled community, as indicated by this letter he received while a prisoner from Norman Rowley, a youngster from Yorkshire: 'I am sorry that they took your legs away so that you cannot escape. My Mum says she will do that to me, too, if I don't be good and come home at the proper time. I have got one leg now and am getting on all right like you said. One day soon I will get the other one. With love from Norman.'[21]

Although war news was hard to come by for the prisoners in Colditz, a tangible indication of the Allies' progress came one day in 1944: a huge formation of American B-17 Flying Fortresses droned overhead towards Germany. Seeing no German fighters, Douglas shouted, 'Wo ist die Luftwaffe?', other prisoners repeating this provocative chant.[21] The air war had, in fact, changed considerably since the days when Douglas led the Tangmere Wing. The German FW 190 fighter had soon afterwards appeared in numbers of the *Kanalfront*, outclassing the Spitfire Mk V until the IX tipped the balance back in the RAF's favour. By then Johnnie Johnson, one of Douglas's protégés of Dogsbody Section, was a Wing Leader himself, at Kenley. Having entered the war following the surprise attack against its Pacific Fleet by Japan on 7 December 1941, America had poured aircraft and troops into the Allied war effort. The following year had seen the first daylight forays over enemy-occupied France by American heavy bombers which, in the absence of a suitable long-range offensive fighter, were escorted by Spitfires – not least Johnson's Canadian Wing at Kenley. The Spitfire's limited range, however, led to heavy American losses, but the 'Yanks' pressed on until the matter was resolved by the in-theatre arrival of dedicated escort fighters such as the Mustang, Thunderbolt and Lightning – able to escort the B-17s all the way to Berlin and back. In North Africa the Allies developed tactical air power, flying in support of ground troops, this being subsequently put to great effect during the Allied invasion of Sicily, Italy, and, of course, the liberation of France when that great day came on 6 June 1944. Gone, therefore, were the great fighter battles of 1940 and 41; gone were the Big Wings. Instead very small tactical formations of pairs, sections or flights became the order of the day, as Allied fighter-bombers stalked the battlefields seeking enemy troops, armour and transport. In the east, the Germans had suffered a catastrophic defeat at Stalingrad in 1943, since when the Soviets had advanced ever westwards. On the night of 23 March 1945, the western Allies at last crossed the River Rhine and began the final battle for Germany.

On 12 April 1945, American troops surrounded Colditz Castle. Unaware that it was a prison camp, however, they began shelling it – the blast from one round knocking Douglas over and forcing the prisoners to take cover. They quickly fashioned and hoisted a Union Jack, after which the barrage ceased – but fighting continued throughout the surrounding town all that night. The following morning, however, Colditz was liberated by the American Army. During the course of the infamous Oflag IVC's existence, there had been at least 300 escape attempts, of which thirty-two were successful – more than at any other camp. Immediately in the liberating troops' wake came American reporters – to whom Douglas presented himself. A female among their number, Lee

Carson, arranged for Douglas to be the first prisoner out of the foreboding prison. Pausing overnight at Naumburg, he ascertained from a British Army intelligence major that Spitfires were further north. '"Can I get to them?" Bader asked. "I'd like to grab one and get another couple of trips in before this show folds up."'[23] Clearly not even nearly four years of deprivation and incarceration had mollified Douglas's blood-lust and thirst for action and glory. From Paris the Americans connected Douglas with Thelma by telephone. Naturally Thelma was extremely anxious to see her husband again after those long and uncertain years of separation. In response to the question regarding when this was likely to be, and in yet another example of insensitivity beyond incredulous, Douglas answered, 'A few days, darling. I'm looking for a Spitfire. I want to have a last fling before it packs up.'[24] The war was virtually won – in a few days' time American and Russian forces would meet on the River Elbe. The only reason for Douglas to once more take to the skies as a combat pilot was purely to satisfy his insatiable appetite for action – and marked him as among only the most selfish and bloodthirsty human beings on the planet. By then Tubby Mermagen was an air commodore at Rheims, but refused Douglas's request and packed him off straight back to England in an Avro Anson.

Flying into Northolt, reporters were soon clamouring at the main gate for an interview with the legless war hero. On his third morning back in England, Douglas drove to Ascot but even his long-awaited private reunion with Thelma was ruined by the sudden appearance of more journalists. The years in captivity had not dimmed Douglas Bader's bright star – they had made him 'a legend'.[25] Like many repatriated prisoners, though, Douglas had difficulty adjusting. After three weeks spent as quietly as possible with Thelma in a Devon hotel, Douglas enjoyed a welcome home dinner at a Belgravia club with fellow Fighter Command luminaries. Reunited with his personal flying logbook, Douglas recorded at last his final operational flight and his personal score against the enemy as thirty machines destroyed. Officially his tally was twenty-two-and-a-half – although, due to the nature of air fighting and over-claiming, like many other aces, the actual number was no doubt somewhat less. Concerned about the fate of those brave French people who had helped him in St Omer, Douglas was relieved to discover that all had survived – and even, in an enigmatic act of humility, wrote to the French government requesting that the twenty-year prison sentence meted out to Hélène Lefevere was reduced to five.

The war in Europe finally ground to a halt on 8 May 1945, when Germany signed an unconditional surrender on Luneberg Heath. The war still raged in the Far East, however – and Douglas was anxious to get there and fight the Japanese. The Air Ministry, however, vetoed this possibility, not least because Douglas's stumps would be troublesome in that climate; there was clearly no end to the man's zeal. Due to his rapid departure from Colditz, he had in any case left behind his spare pair of legs. By now Ross was also back in England, so Douglas tracked him down and called to confirm that his former batman had brought them back with him. Upon discovering that Ross too had left the legs behind, the furious Wing Commander Bader verbally abused the bandsman and slammed down the phone – never to speak to his 'faithful' batman ever again.[26] Francis's conclusion that Douglas Bader was 'an insensitive bully' appears well founded.[27]

Across the Channel, the Tangmere Wing's old adversary, Adolf Galland, had risen to General of Day Fighters and as such was now an important prisoner. The last time the pair met it was Douglas who was a prisoner. Galland described their first post-war meeting, which appropriately occurred at Tangmere: 'This time I stood before him as a prisoner and he offered me his box of cigars. Our roles were reversed. Bader concerned himself in the most charming way about my personal comfort, but next morning he suddenly vanished again, as he had done once before.'[28] Given the hospitality he had shown Douglas at Audembert in 1941, and considering the trouble subsequently arising from the St Omer escape attempt, Galland was surprised that this was not reciprocated – leading him to conclude that 'in 1945 the war went on despite the unconditional surrender. War is no game of cricket.'[29]

On 6 and 9 August 1945, America dropped two atomic bombs on Japan. The unprecedented destructive capacity of these weapons immediately shifted the balance of world power in favour of the West – and, of course, America. On 15 August, Japan finally surrendered – bringing the war to an end at last. The post-war world would be very different to that which produced Douglas Bader and those of his ilk. A man born and bred for war, Douglas ended the conflict as not just a national but an Allied hero. Uncertain though his future was once more, as was the world's future generally, Douglas Bader would make an indelible mark upon it – and in so doing make an infinitely greater contribution to humanity than ever achieved with arms. A whole new world of opportunities now awaited the legless dynamo.

18

REACH FOR THE SKY

On 1 June 1945, Group Captain Douglas Bader became the new Commanding Officer of the Day Fighter Wing of the Central Fighter Establishment – at Tangmere. It would prove an unhappy time. The role and deployment of fighter aircraft had changed enormously since the heady days of 1940 and 1941. Ground attack had increasingly become the main activity for Spitfires, Typhoons and Tempests. Of this, however, Douglas had no experience – nor of the new Gloster Meteor jets now replacing piston-engined fighters. His ideas and experience were dated. Those he commanded felt they had little in common with this Battle of Britain relic – and he with them. The discontent was such that the AOC-in-C, Air Chief Marshal Sir James Robb, had no choice but to post Douglas, on 20 July, to North Weald as Station Commander. While there, Douglas once more delighted in flying Spitfires, his logbook even indicating a couple of trips across the Channel to St Omer – once for an emotional reunion with the Hiècques and Lucille Debacker – but while reflecting on the glory days of battles with JG 26, it was a peaceful sky through which his Spitfire Mk IX scythed. On 15 September, a mass fly-past over London was organised – and Douglas, inevitably, was chosen to lead it. Along with many others who had fought hard throughout Britain's 'Finest Hour' were, of course, the Tangmere inner sanctum: Dundas, Johnson, Turner and Crowley-Milling, all of whom had survived the war as Wing Leaders. Indeed, Johnnie Johnson was arguably the Wing Leader *par excellence* in addition to being the RAF's top-scoring fighter pilot of the war with thirty-eight-and-a-half victories. Douglas knew, though, that the halcyon days were over, and that this was the last time he would ever lead a massed formation of fighters.

There were two spectres peering over his shoulder. Firstly, to achieve high rank meant overseas service. His stumps, he knew, were fine for short visits but not for a protracted posting. As ever, Douglas refused to settle for the middle ground – even in the service he loved so much; it was to the highest peak of personal advancement or nothing. Secondly, he knew that the peacetime service was unlikely to maintain his unrestricted flying category, bringing him full circle to those miserable days of over a decade before. Had Leigh-Mallory still been around, that may have been different – but Air Chief Marshal and Lady Sir Trafford Leigh-Mallory had been killed in a flying accident shortly before the war ended. His experience at Tangmere had clearly indicated how much the service had changed; indeed the 'strawberries and cream' pre-war flying club atmosphere had disappeared forever from the RAF. So far as the service went, Douglas was a man and product of those times – not this new age.

After the war, Peter MacDonald, Douglas's former adjutant, returned to the House of Commons. With utmost vigour he and others did their best to persuade Douglas to join them, and stand for the Conservative seat of Blackpool North. Although he gave the proposition serious consideration, ultimately Douglas declined on the grounds that he was his temperament was unsuited for a life in politics. Moreover, aviation was a part of his very being – and a life without flying remained unthinkable. Shell Oil – the company which had taken Douglas in the wake of his first retirement from the

RAF – offered him a job as an executive in the Aviation Department. Douglas felt compelled to and did accept this offer – not least because a light aircraft came with the job. On 21 July 1946, Group Captain Douglas Bader retired from the RAF for the second and final time. His decorations now comprised three DSOs, three DFCs, and the French *Legion d'Honneur* and *Croix de Guerre* – and he had been mentioned in despatches three time. That he had no legs confirmed the unparalleled achievement involved.

Shell provided Douglas his own Proctor aircraft, in which he enjoyed an early flight with none other than American Air Force war hero Lieutenant-General James Doolittle – a vice-president of the company. In 1947, Doolittle arranged a tour of America for Douglas to visit and inspire US servicemen who had lost limbs during the war. With passion and enthusiasm Douglas embraced the project – and thus began a whole new public service of inspiring the worldwide amputee disabled community. War had made Douglas Bader. His story had been manna from heaven to Britain's propagandists. An early indication of his fame and public interest was provided by the media's response to his repatriation in April 1945. Shell knew that Douglas Bader's involvement was a huge public relations coup. Everywhere Douglas went there was press interest in what he was doing – which was inevitably some inspirational thing or other, whether involving a large number of amputees or just the forlorn individual coming to terms with losing a limb or more. So began, in fact, a whole new, parallel – and perhaps unexpected – voluntary career as an example to and champion of disabled people all over the world. Everywhere, amputees were inspired by his mantra: 'Never let that thing get you down – and never let it be an excuse. You've got to live with it, but you can always master it. Don't listen to anyone who says you can't do this or that. That's all nonsense. And make up your mind that you'll never use crutches or a stick. Then have a go at everything. Join in all the games you can. Go anywhere you want to go. Try anything.'[1]

Times, however, were changing. The Conservative-dominated Britain of the 1930s, for example, was gone forever. In 1945, in spite of Churchill's enormous popularity as Britain's war leader, Clement Attlee's Labour Party won the General Election that year. The socialists immediately set about creating the welfare state, restricting education and nationalising key industries, public transport and the Bank of England. The truth was that although Britain had emerged victorious from those long years of struggle, it was financially exhausted. The immediate post-war period saw a shortage of food and clothing, meaning that rationing and 'austerity' continued into the 1950s. Nonetheless, that decade saw virtually total employment, and the majority of Britons had never been so well off. On the wider stage, however, although Britain remained a leading European power, America had emerged leader of the Free World, and the Soviets soon retired behind the Iron Curtain – heralding the Cold War between democracy and communism. Crucially, Britain's Empire was rapidly waning: in 1947, India won independence, and British influence in Africa continued to decline. Large-scale immigration brought increasing numbers of Afro-Caribbeans and Asians to Britain – transforming post-war Britain into an ethnically diverse and multi-cultural society. The loss of Empire and changing demography was a difficult time for Britons. The British contribution to victory in the Second World War, however, is, Dawson argued, 'one of the supremely popular moments in British history'.[2] It was this supreme moment which provided post-war and austere Britain with a mythic reminder of the country's great past. Austerity Britain saw publication of a plethora of wartime memoirs, histories – and films.

Douglas's story, of course, was screaming out to be told – but the legless and very *English* war hero refused point blank to add to the ever-burgeoning list of august autobiographies. Someone – an author – was required to write the Bader story.

Paul Chester Jerome Brickhill was an Australian journalist in Sydney before the war. After war broke out he joined the Royal Australian Air Force, successfully won his pilot's brevet in Canada, and joined 92 Squadron, flying Spitfires in the Western Desert. In 1943 he was shot down over Tunisia and captured – the following year he was incarcerated in Stalag Luft III, Sagan, when the so-called Great Escape took place. After the war, Brickhill lost no time in applying his journalistic experience to producing popular narratives of inspirational wartime stories. His first book, *Escape to Danger*, a work co-authored with Conrad Norton, appeared in 1946. Four years later came his first best-seller: *The Great Escape*. A year later came *The Dam Busters*, chronicling Operation CHASTISE, the famous raid on three German dams led by Wing Commander Guy Gibson of 617 Squadron. Douglas and Thelma Bader had both read these books, and agreed that their story should be written by Brickhill.[3] It is not known whether the Baders approached Brickhill or vice versa, but in 1952 the author began researching for his written portrayal of the Bader legend. The resulting book, *Reach for the Sky*, was published in 1954 – the year austerity measures ended – by British Davis Cup tennis players Ian and Billy Collins, who were Douglas's friends.[4] The book had exactly the required effect, on every level. During the first few weeks of publication alone, some 172,000 copies were sold. The critics loved the book, the *Daily Mail* confirming it as a story to 'stir a glow in English hearts'. No one, however, could have predicted that Brickhill's book would become a perennial and huge global seller, published in numerous languages. Among those who avidly devoured the French edition, in fact, was Arthur Dubreu, the thirteen-year-old schoolboy who had seen Douglas's parachute descent on 9 August 1941; only then, however, did he realise exactly which famous RAF pilot he had seen that day. This global success, however, was unpredicted when Douglas had signed a deal waiving all rights to royalties arising from book or film right sales. Instead he received a one-off payment of £10,000, enabling the Baders to buy a home.[5] Douglas was pleased with Brickhill's work – although, as this book has demonstrated, there were certainly some departures from the actual record and regarding which he must have been aware. Interestingly, publication of the book provided an opportunity for Douglas to meet Churchill, a particular personal hero of his. The occasion was arranged by 242 Squadron's former adjutant, Peter MacDonald MP; Douglas presented the wartime British Prime Minister with a signed copy of Brickhill's best-seller.

In the same year that saw *Reach for the Sky* become an international publishing phenomenon, Brickhill's *The Dam Busters* was made into a box-office hit. Like books, films trumpeting Britain's triumphal contribution to Allied victory were being churned out for an apparently insatiable audience. The pivotal moment of Britain's war, of course, had been its 'Finest Hour' – and the Battle of Britain was already well on the way to receiving a hallowed and mythicized status in popular memory. *Angels One Five*, which presented a very stiff upper-middle class lip, told the story of Pilot Officer 'Septic' Baird, a Hurricane pilot. The Spitfire and Battle of Britain had already been highly romanticised by Leslie Howard's wartime classic *First of the Few* (1942). Nonetheless, it was *Angels One Five* and 'especially *The Dam Busters*' which, considered Medhurst, influenced the 'securing of the myths and spectacle of the RAF war, which prepared the way for that seminal text of romanticised distortion *Reach for the Sky*'.[6] The film rights were actually purchased by independent film-maker Danny Angel, for £15,000, even before he had read Brickhill's book. It is worthy of note, however, that due to the one-off payment Douglas had already received, he made not one penny from either the film rights or the subsequent, massively successful film directed by Lewis Gilbert and financed by Rank.

Richard Burton was originally tipped to play Douglas in the film but turned the role down. Instead Kenneth More was chosen: 'I admired Douglas Bader. He was to me a Rudyard Kipling figure; you don't find them anymore. I understood him. He was a harder man than I am. To me he represented everything that every Englishman wants to be: courageous, honest, determined – but knows he hasn't the nerve or capacity to be. He has got his faults – who hasn't? He was difficult, impulsive, strong-headed; he was all these things. But I felt that someone had to give him to the world.'[7] That More certainly did. During his research for the part, More met Douglas twice, firstly over lunch before golfing at Gleneagles. The pair got on – and most importantly Douglas trusted the actor. Naturally Douglas wanted the film to be accurate. Some of his friends became involved and were close to the film-makers. Group Captain Harry Day, for example, became Technical Advisor. It was a good job, as Air Marshal Sir Denis Crowley-Milling remembered, 'When Angel discovered that I had been shot down and hiding in St Omer at the same time Douglas was in hospital there, he immediately came up with the ridiculous idea that the story should be changed to show me leading an attempt with the French Resistance to break Douglas out. We swiftly put a stop to that nonsense!'[8]

Douglas was adamant that everyone who had played a part in his life story should be faithfully represented – which is simply impossible in a film of 136 minutes. Composite characters and the 'telescoping' of certain events were therefore required. For example, Cambridge graduate Lyndon Brook, who had already starred alongside Gregory Peck in *The Purple Plain* (1954), became 'Johnny Sanderson' – a composite character based upon Geoffrey Stephenson. After the Woodley crash, it was not the Australian Jack Cruttenden portrayed lifting Douglas from the wreckage, as in fact had happened, but 'Sanderson'. This was a great worry to Douglas. Some of his RAF friends were included by name, however: Stan Turner was played by Lee Patterson, 'Woody' Woodhall by Howard Marion Crawford, and Crowley-Milling by Basil Appleby. 242 Squadron's Engineering Officer, Warrant Officer West (Michael Ripper) also appeared, as did Dowding (Charles Carson) and, of course, Leigh-Mallory (ironically played by former 11 Group Battle of Britain Controller Ronald Adam). Cleverly, 'Sanderson' was also used as a narrator to link scenes together. Certain medical staff were also included: Nurse Brace (Dorothy Alison), Mr Joyce (Alexander Knox), and Robert Desoutter (Sydney Tafler). Naturally a crucial character was Thelma Bader – played by former Royal Shakespeare Company and ENSA actress Muriel Pavlow (who in 1953 had starred alongside Alec Guniness in *Malta Story*). With Douglas's life, Brickhill's book, and a cast, the scene was set for high cinema drama.

The film was shot at Pinewood Studios near London and RAF Kenley, and released in July 1956. Set against a backdrop of sun-drenched cumulus clouds, this text introduces the film: 'Douglas Bader has become a legend in his own lifetime. His courage was not only an example to those in war but is now a source of inspiration to many in peace.' The next text-over was in response to Douglas's concern that certain people would take offence at having been left out: 'For dramatic purposes it has been necessary in this film to transpose in time certain events in Douglas Bader's life and also to re-shape some of the characters involved in this story. The producers apologise to those who may have been affected by any changes of omissions.' The first scene shows a young Bader en route to Cranwell by motorcycle, ending up in a ditch when 'buzzed' by a low-flying Avro 504. A ruined bowler hat brings Cadet Bader to the attention of the Flight Sergeant – and a knowing wink shared with 'Johnny Sanderson'. Cranwell antics are well-covered, as is the Woodley crash and aftermath. The film's most powerful scenes are undoubtedly those in which More recreated Douglas's unyielding determination to master his new artificial legs. These scenes, more than anything else in the film, made it not just another war or flying movie but one about courage and determination in the true British mould. After covering how Douglas left the RAF, worked for Shell and married Thelma, the camera focusses on his return to the RAF, how he won the respect of and inspired 242 Squadron, the Battle of Britain and Duxford Wing. Naturally the impression provided is that Douglas's tactics were revelatory (although there is no hint of controversy) and that he was a crucial leader of the Few. The action then shifts to Tangmere, sweeps over France, and Douglas's parachute-descent into captivity. His escape from the Clinique Sterin and recapture was included, giving due acknowledgement to Douglas's brave French friends. Typically, in common with the mood of the period, German prison camp guards are portrayed as buffoons, and a great scene is when More stomps along a line of German soldiers, inspecting them – much to the delight of onlooking prisoners. The film concludes with our hero leading the 1945 Battle of Britain fly-past, and this voice-over by Lyndon Brook: 'This is a story of courage. It has no end, because courage has no end. It is the story of a man made famous by war, but for whom the war was only an episode in a greater victory, fought for and won in silence and pain, the victory of man's own spirit, creating strength and hope out of disaster.' Inspirational words indeed – and a tonic for a Britain emerging from austerity and into an uncertain post-war future.

The film's première was attended by the Duke of Edinburgh – but not Group Captain Douglas Bader, who, in fact, only watched the film on television some years later and declared it 'rather good'.[9] It was certainly an entirely sympathetic depiction – which became the biggest box-office success of 1956. Indeed, the *Daily Mirror* considered Gilbert and Angel's work to be 'one of the greatest British films ever made and one of the most inspiring'. Like the fateful crash in 1931, the film was also a defining moment in Douglas's life. Millions of people watched the film worldwide in 1956 and when re-released in 1959, and have since done so on television and at their leisure since videos and DVDs became available. As Mackenzie wrote, 'Bader had been converted into the kind of unblemished champion once seen in the *Boy's Own Paper*: little wonder that he subsequently ended up number one in a schoolboy poll of favourite heroes.'[10] It was not just schoolboys, though, who were impressed by the story of this pipe-smoking British air ace with no legs and an awkward gait: the international amputee community was immensely inspired by the story – and overnight Douglas Bader became their champion. Indeed, this epic story of courage even moved the Kainai tribe at a reservation near Alberta, Canada. At a special ceremony there in 1957, Chief Jim Shot Both Sides bestowed a great honour on the legless Englishman by making him 'Chief Morning Bird'.

It was now that Douglas really began his greatest contribution to humanity. At Richmond he was a frequent visitor to the Star and Garter Home, demonstrating how he worked his artificial legs; he was active in the British Limbless Ex-Servicemen's Association; believing in practical aid for the disabled, not patronisation, he became an influential member of a Ministry of Health committee; a member of the British Council for Rehabilitation, Douglas fought to educate employers 'in the advantage of using such persons'. Together with Thelma, Douglas toured the world, becoming an unofficial ambassador for Britain. There were, however, problems. The Baders had struck up a friendship with the British Prime Minister Harold Wilson, and Douglas visited Rhodesia and spoke with the Premier, Ian Smith – a fellow wartime Spitfire pilot. When, in 1965, Smith's Unilateral Declaration of Independence broke ties with the motherland, Britain imposed sanctions and took the matter to the United Nations. Speaking on the matter at a South African Air Force Association dinner in Pretoria, Douglas said, 'I'm ashamed of being British, the way the British Government have treated Rhodesia. And I've a good mind to take out a Rhodesian passport.'[11] The incident indicated that, as ever, Douglas was one to speak his mind and was ever a loose cannon; friendship with the Wilsons progressed no further. People the world over, and the press in particular, were interested in anything he had to say. A committed Conservative with Victorian values, Douglas's insistence upon restoring the death penalty, stopping immigration into Britain, banning betting shops and describing members of the Campaign for Nuclear Disarmament as 'a rabble' rather confirmed his unsuitability for politics. These views also confirmed him as a throwback to days of Empire – but those halcyon days were now replaced by an increasingly tolerant and enlightened age. Nonetheless, on 2 January 1956, Group Captain Bader had been appointed a Commander of the Most Excellent Order of the British Empire (CBE) for services to the disabled – a richly deserved award.

Douglas was also very active in wartime aviation circles, attending reunions and dinners all over the world. He simply loved the company of fellow aviators and, indeed, their adoration. In 1952 he accepted an invitation to write a foreword to the autobiography of one-legged German dive-bombing legend Hans Ulrich-Rudel. Douglas had briefly met Rudel, whom his foreword described as 'a gallant chap'. When the press reported Rudel's antecedents as a committed Nazi and his publisher's links to the British Union of Fascists, Douglas remained unmoved.[12] Two years later he contributed the foreword to Adolf Galland's wartime memoir; he wrote that

> now, ten years after the end of the Second World War, seems to me to be a suitable time for this book to be published in English. We can view it in truer perspective than perhaps when the Nuremburg Trials were fresh in our minds. To Galland's great credit, he keeps to his subject and does not attempt, like others before him, to examine or seek to justify German politics. He fought for his country, which happened to be Germany, so he was on the other side. By any criterion, Galland is a brave man, and I personally shall look forward to meeting him again at any-time, anywhere, and in any company.

This post-war reconciliation, though, failed to prevent another outburst of embarrassing Bader rudeness: at a German fighter pilots' reunion in Munich, Douglas exclaimed to Galland, his host, 'My God, I had no idea we left so many of the bastards alive!'[13] A visit to St Omer, however, went off much better. The occasion was the award of France's *Legion d'Honneur* to the now ancient Madame Hiècque. Douglas was delighted to attend – especially when he was surprised by being made an honorary citizen of St Omer. A shadow, however, fell over the globe-trotting Baders in 1967: Thelma, a heavy smoker, was diagnosed with throat cancer.

The cinema-going public's appetite for war films continued unabated – and such were compulsive weekend viewing on the television screens now a common feature of every home. The problem so far as portrayals of the British war effort were concerned, though, was that the small British film industry was in decline and all big-budget movies were financed and made in America. Consequently the Battle of Britain story, although featured in such black-and-white films as *Angels One Five* and *Reach for the Sky*, had a difficult and slow passage to the silver screen. In 1965, Ben Fisz – a Polish wartime fighter pilot turned independent film producer – decided to make a film called *Battle of Britain*. In collaboration with successful producer Harry Saltzman and director Guy Hamilton, Fisz persuaded United Artists to finance the film – a colour epic made with airworthy Spitfires, Hurricanes – and German fighters and bombers currently operated by the Spanish Air Force. By 1968 filming, in Spain, France and at both Pinewood Studios and Duxford airfield, was in full swing. Certain of the Few were engaged as British technical advisers, and Lieutenant-General Adolf Galland joined those on the German side. The intention was to make a fair picture of the sixteen-week-long battle – departing from 1950s films in which the Germans were ridiculed. The Big Wing Controversy, however, soon became a concern, and Douglas Bader's on-set attendance became 'inevitable'.[14]

It was imperative that Dowding and Park, both of whom were still alive, were happy with the film. On 26 May 1968, the eighty-six-year-old Dowding, crippled with arthritis, visited the Duxford set. There Group Captain Douglas Bader insisted upon pushing his former Commander-in-Chief – whom he had caused a very great deal of trouble – around in his wheelchair. During this tour of proceedings, Dowding was heard to remark that 'the Battle may have gone considerably better if junior officers had not exercised undue influence over their seniors at certain critical moments'.[15] Douglas ignored the remark and made clear to all that Dowding was the hero of the hour. When introducing the old man to the actor Robert Shaw, Douglas said, 'If it hadn't been for him, old boy, we might be digging salt out of a Silesian salt mine. Those bloody Kraut aeroplanes over there with all that language written all over them – that's what we would be speaking. At least I wouldn't, I'd probably be dead, but your generation would.' Shaw and fellow actor Christopher Plummer decided that Bader was 'obviously the type of hero' they 'never really imagined existed in real life'.[16] Dowding went away happy, and wrote in positive terms to his old friend Park, who had returned to his native Auckland. Ultimately the Big Wing Controversy was sensitively dealt with – although the scene depicting a meeting between the two opposed group commanders with their boss never took place; not once during the Battle, in fact, did Dowding get them together – had he done so, the controversy may never have arisen, or at least been nipped in the bud.

Douglas joined Shaw in giving an interview to the BBC – although the actor failed completely to get a word in edgeways, listening to Douglas with incredulity, having not hitherto appreciated that anyone really spoke like this:

Interviewer: 'Douglas Bader, here we are, surrounded by German aircraft on an RAF field which must be quite a shock to you. Now there are people who say, after quarter of a century, why make this film, why bring it all up again? What do you feel about it?

DB: 'Well it's history, old boy, one must show history. If you can show history in a film it's better than in the history books, and it'll be in those things anyway. By all means let's show it in a film, but all I beg *Battle of Britain* producers not to do is to make it so that the Germans win the Battle of Britain, because they didn't. They may try to make out that they did now it's all over, but they didn't in fact.'

Interviewer: 'In a word, Douglas, what's your message as we stand here at this time on your old airfield, surrounded by the Hurricanes which you flew out of here ...'

DB: 'Not Hurricanes, Spitfires which I flew out of here, Me 109s which I shot down out of here ...'

Interviewer: 'And all those 109s around here – what message do you hope that the film and these planes and you can give now, this year, about the Battle of Britain? Everything is sweetness and light between Britain and Germany now. Is it right to bring it up, remind everybody of the old war and old animosity?'

DB: 'Well, why not? Why not film history? Surely the lessons one learns is that one forgives but that one doesn't forget. It's as simple as that.'

Interviewer: 'When you were up there in your plane fighting, Douglas, what were you thinking?'

DB: 'Well, I was thinking about what I was going to do when I got back in the evening. That's what I was thinking about old boy.'

Interviewer: 'Even when you were up in the air?'

DB: 'Yes.'

Interviewer: 'Was it us and them, or was it your machine against their machines?'

DB: 'No, it was the aeroplanes one sort of felt badly about. I loathe those crooked swastikas. What was it Churchill said: "The crooked cross of Nazi infamy." That's what one hated. Coming into our skies and dropping bombs on our country and so on. It wasn't personal. You can't hate a chap you can't see, although we all hated the idea of Hitler and the things he did. I mean he was identifiable – but the aeroplanes were just aeroplanes and when you saw them go up in smoke one was delighted and one never thought about anyone being inside them, you know.'

Interviewer: 'Were you surprised when you found all these old machines assembled here?'

DB: 'Very surprised to see them here at Duxford, old boy. My old station. They wouldn't have been if the Socialist Government hadn't disbanded RAF Fighter Command. Did you see that picture in the newspapers the other day of these 109s flying over the cliffs of Dover on their way here? I remember thinking that if the Government hadn't disbanded Fighter Command a fortnight ago, those K ... those planes wouldn't have flown over the cliffs of Dover – even now. We'd have gone out and we'd have shot the bleeders down.'

Interviewer: 'Thank you, Douglas Bader.'[17]

The author and film critic Leonard Mosley was present:

Bader turned and put his hands to his nose and sniffed them. 'You know, even if I was blind, I'd know I'd been in a bloody Kraut kite. You can tell them by their smell.' He stumped away, waving a hand. 'I can't wait to see the film,' he shouted, 'It's going to be good. Historical. Only don't let the Krauts win it. We won the Battle of Britain – not them!' Robert Shaw looked after him for a long moment and then turned away. 'I never knew people *talked* like that,' he said.[18]

The film was screened in 1969 to mixed reviews, but remains both the most ambitious visual attempt to recreate the Battle of Britain and a defining moment in fortifying the Battle of Britain myth to a whole new generation.

That year also saw Douglas retire as Managing Director of Shell Aviation. The company's parting gift was most generous: the Beech 95 Travelair aircraft that he had often flown on company business. With such a wealth of aviation experienced, Douglas easily established himself as an independent consultant; he also contributed articles on aviation subjects to British national newspapers, and joined the Civil Aviation Authority's board and that of fellow Battle of Britain pilot Paddy Barthropp's Belgravia-based executive car-hire company. In retirement, although Thelma was ill, the Baders continued travelling the world. Douglas also carried on playing golf with distinction, his handicap being a remarkable four. As a golfing celebrity he was frequently in demand, playing with many equally famous people, among them boxing champions Henry Cooper and Alan Minter, the actor Sean Connery, Hollywood screen legend James Stewart, and British and US Open Champion Tony Jacklin. In retirement, therefore, Douglas remained as busy as ever and continued to make his presence felt – wherever he went.

On 24 January 1971, Thelma died – ending a thirty-seven-year marriage, one which had begun with highly questionable prospects. A memorial service was held at St Clement Danes, organised by

Air Marshal Sir Denis Crowley-Milling – there was a capacity congregation. The following day, newspapers proclaimed 'the Few Salute Thelma Bader'. Without his life-partner and soul mate, Douglas energetically threw himself into various activities – not least golf. In 1960, Douglas had begun partnering one Joan Murray, who was now competing at championship level; they made a formidable combination. Joan was also an equestrian and among the original volunteers of the Riding for the Disabled charity – of which Douglas was an honorary vice-president. The pair shared much common ground, therefore, and married on 3 January 1971. Together Douglas and Joan continued working for the disabled in various ways, making their home together in an old farmhouse near Newbury in Berkshire.

The war, though, and Douglas's part in it, was never far away. Lord Longford, chairman of Sidgwick & Jackson, commissioned Douglas to write the story of the Spitfire and Hurricane. The book, *Fight for the Sky*, was published in 1973. As the dust-jacket stated, 'Group Captain Douglas Bader has become a legend in his lifetime. Legendary too are Britain's most famous fighters, the Spitfire and Hurricane. Perhaps no one is better suited than Douglas Bader to tell their story.' That was certainly true. Since the book and film *Reach for the Sky*, in the public's mind Douglas, more than any other, epitomised the wartime fighter pilot – and was the one they were most interested in. Turner – a Bader biographer and ardent admirer – undertook 'Special Research' for the project. Accounts of their personal experiences and specialities were included from various RAF aces – including Group Captain Hugh Dundas and Air Vice-Marshal Johnnie Johnson; Wing Commander Laddie Lucas also contributed – another later Bader biographer who was married to Thelma's sister, Jill. The book's jacket bore a pugnacious photograph of Douglas, pipe in hand. Within, one particular photograph caption, accompanying a picture of a crashed German bomber, said it all: 'Dornier 17: normal view.'[19]

On 12 June 1976, Douglas was knighted for his 'unflagging' work for the disabled; a handwritten note was sent by Kenneth More: 'Well done, old love, it couldn't have happened to a nicer bloke!'[20] In 1977, Sir Douglas was made a Fellow of the Royal Aeronautical Society (FRAeS), and was given an honorary PhD from Queen's University in Belfast; he also became a Deputy Lieutenant of Greater London. Together with his exciting wartime decorations, the letters after his name confirmed a most successful life indeed.

Douglas's inspiration to the disabled, in fact, was often personal – raising their spirits from a low ebb. A friend of eighty-three-year-old Eastender Nellie Wallpole wrote to Sir Douglas, explaining that the old lady was a recent amputee and asking for a signed photograph. Douglas personally delivered one and stayed for tea. The photograph was signed, 'To Nellie Walpole: A brave lady.' As Nellie later said, 'When I look at that in the morning I know it's going to be a great day.'[21] In 1981, the courage of a four-year-old South African boy, Paul Ellis-Smith, moved Douglas to break his vow not to show his artificial limbs. Persuaded to pose by Joan – Lady Bader – Sir Douglas sat on the veranda of the Ellis-Smiths' Cape Town home, trouser legs rolled up, together with young Paul and another amputee, student Thys Nortje. Of Paul, Douglas said,

I went round to their house for morning tea and there was the little boy, running all over the place, as mobile as anything. In all my meetings with disabled people I've never seen anyone as mobile as that. I shall never forget the little boy. It was amazing the way he ran about, just as if he was on his own legs. You see, he had never known what it was like to walk on his own limbs, that's the point. It just goes to substantiate what I've always said: if you've got to have some awful catastrophe like that befall you, then the earlier in life it happens the better. It's when it happens later in life that the real problems are.[22]

For Paul's parents, the visit was a moving experience; the boy's mother, Meg, said that 'Douglas Bader is a strong and dynamic man … his presence filled the whole room immediately he walked in'.[23] What these South Africans had experienced at first hand was the 'Bader Factor' – that charisma, energy and enthusiasm that was so inspiring. Such humanitarian visits were, of course, in direct contrast to the interview given at Duxford during the making of *Battle of Britain* – making Group Captain Sir Douglas Bader a tantalising enigma.

On 2 March 1982, Douglas was present at a cocktail party at the Martini Terrace in London's Haymarket, arranged for people who had raised thousands of pounds for handicapped children. Just after Douglas handed over a cheque for £50,000 generated by the fund-raising group 'Sparks', of which he was president, to Action Research for the Crippled Child, the legless celebrity and knight was 'ambushed' by TV presenter Eamon Andrews. After weeks of careful research, throughout which time his family had steadfastly maintained secrecy, it was the turn of Group Captain Sir Douglas Bader on the long-running Thames Television series *This Is Your Life*. Back at the Royalty Theatre, Douglas was soon meeting family and friends, all of whom paid glowing tribute to than man whose story Andrews described as defying 'fiction' as an example of 'soul-stirring heroism'. Old Water Dingwall from St Edward's appeared, and even Madame Hiècque was filmed speaking from her bed. Better still, onto the stage walked Lucille Debacker herself – visibly moving 'Le Colonel'. Among the wartime luminaries was Dogsbody Section – Johnson, Smith, West and Dundas. The latter said, 'So long as Douglas Bader was there, morale was always sky-high ... two words describe Douglas Bader: bloody marvellous!' General Adolf Galland appeared, British film legend Sir John Mills, boxing champion Henry Cooper, all paid tribute – as did the indomitable Nellie Wallpole and Paul Ellis-Smith from their respective homes. Sadly, Kenneth More was suffering from Parkinson's disease and was unable to attend. Instead the actor who had become the cinematic face of Douglas Bader was represented by his wife, Angela Douglas, who read this message: 'My dear Douglas, you know very well why I can't be with you this evening. More's the pity! But I'm sending my old lady along to represent me. She's been in love with you for years anyway! Your inspiration and courage is, quite rightly, a legend. It was with me through the film and is with me still.' The most impressive tribute came from Clarence House: 'During the dark days of the Second World War, those of you who served in the Allied Air Forces brought hope and confidence to the people of this country through your courage, skill and determination. In times of peace you have been an inspiration to the young, and have given encouragement and support to many who have suffered physical misfortune. I send this evening my greetings and warmest good wishes for health and happiness in the years ahead. Elizabeth R, Queen Mother.' As the entirely positive and sympathetic programme concluded, Andrews presented Sir Douglas with his commemorative red album, as the Central Band of the RAF struck up rousing martial aviation music. Sadly, however, there would not be 'years ahead' but mere months.

On 4 September 1982, Joan's daughter Wendy Bickers, husband David and two infant children arrived at the Baders' Berkshire farmhouse, to stay overnight before heading to Cornwall and a late summer break. Douglas and Joan were due to go up to London that afternoon, for Douglas to speak at the ninetieth birthday party of Air Marshal Sir Arthur 'Bomber' Harris. Just after lunch Douglas donned his black tie and prepared to head off, the party due to start at 5 p.m. David:

It was a particularly hot afternoon and I noticed that Douglas was still looking a bit grey. He had suffered a heart attack two weeks earlier at an international pro-celebrity golf tournament. Over supper the previous weekend, Douglas had told us how he had driven into a bunker and while pitching out he had, so far as those following him, including Joan, were concerned, slipped over. In fact he had actually suffered a heart attack and was unconscious. Afterwards he told us that he heard two voices: one belonging to his friend the golfer Henry Longhurst, who had died a few years earlier, telling him to 'Come and join me', and Joan calling out 'Get up, Douglas!' Douglas said he told Henry 'I'm not ready yet', and got up. Typically, on the day in question, Douglas was driving up to London and Joan was driving back. Just after midnight the phone rang. Wendy answered it and returned to the bedroom stunned. 'Douglas is dead.' Apparently he had suffered another heart attack, just before the Hogarth roundabout between Hammersmith and Chiswick, as Joan was driving back to Newbury. This time the outcome had been fatal. Joan then had extraordinary presence of mind to go around the roundabout back to the Mews house and parked in the garage. I went straight up there, arriving around 2 a.m. I found two policemen inside with Joan. Within a minute the doorbell rang and I answered it to a journalist seeking confirmation of Douglas's demise. Joan and I immediately left for Newbury. She was incredibly composed and strong. Apparently Douglas and Joan had returned to Petersham Mews to change out of evening dress before continuing to the farm. Douglas had said that he was tired, so, as planned, Joan was driving. On the way to the Hogarth roundabout he complained of chest pains – and died. At 7 a.m. the following morning an incessant stream of telephone calls and visits from journalists began. As word got out innumerable cards, flowers and telegrams from those who Douglas had moved through his example started to arrive in droves.[24]

David and his brother-in-law, Michael, later visited Douglas's doctor to obtain the Death Certificate:

The doctor told us that while Douglas was only seventy when he died, he had 'walked uphill' for the majority of his life, and that consequently his heart was in fact that of a ninety-year-old. Certainly we all felt that his death was premature and this helped explain that. Obviously since then artificial limb technology has progressed, using lighter and stronger materials – a long way from the heavy limbs that Douglas and many others used. Being a double amputee, Douglas was under especial strain, not least because he never used sticks or crutches.[25]

Group Captain Sir Douglas Bader's subsequent funeral in Kensington was followed by a private cremation restricted to family and very close friends.

Something Douglas said in the speech on the day he died was more than just coincidental; it was this:

How do I want to be remembered when I die? As a fighter pilot? Look, I want to be remembered so that other people, when they talk about me, smile. That's how I want to be remembered. I don't give a damn about being a fighter pilot. The thing is this: I want to leave warmth behind. You know the sort of person you remember. It might have been an uncle or it might have been a chum. But when you think of him, you smile. You say, 'If only so-and-so were here – he'd have loved this.' Something like that. Or some recollection you have. But it's warmth – that's what you want to leave behind you. You don't want to leave any other nonsense. You want people to say 'Look, he was a *chap*, this fellow. He wasn't a "what not".' I'm sure I'm right.[26]

Understandably, after his recent heart attack, death was on Douglas's mind: when he died, the family found all of his affairs up to date and papers in order.

The final line in Douglas's speech that fateful night also provides an appropriate last word to the narration of his own life: 'The people have left the imprint of their personality. History is made by people, not places.'[27]

19

THE BADER LEGACY

While preparing to surprise Sir Douglas Bader with his *This Is Your Life* programme, presenter Eamon Andrews said that he was to 'pay tribute to a real-life legend. One of the greatest, romantic, real-life heroes of our time or any time.'

Wartime propaganda, of course, gave currency to Douglas Bader's exploits as a fighter pilot and leader. Indeed, the heroic deeds of the legless air ace were a rich source of material for the MOI. Brickhill's 1954 best-seller firmly cemented the legend in popular culture – this being further confirmed by the Angel/Gilbert box-office hit of 1956. This potent mixture fused with other similar treatments of various heroes and deeds to mythicize Britain's popular impression and memory of its part in the Second World War. This mighty media machine projected Douglas Bader globally and made him *the* British pilot and personality people associated with the Battle of Britain and, indeed, the RAF. As evidenced by this book, however, more recent research has confirmed that 12 Group's Big Wing tactics were wrong, that the mass formation was not actually anywhere near as effective in combat as believed in 1940 – and nor was 242 Squadron. Indeed, there were those among Churchill's Few who objected to the star-like treatment accorded Douglas Bader. Among them was Wing Commander HR 'Dizzy' Alan DFC, who flew Spitfires with 66 Squadron in 11 Group:

I am constantly bemused why Group Captain Sir Douglas Bader and the Battle of Britain should be considered synonymous. If he had served in the front line of 11 Group, based essentially in Kent and Sussex, he might have realised that the Big Wing concept was balderdash – for the front line anyway, and that was the line that mattered. This is not to denigrate Douglas Bader's sheer determination in getting himself back into the RAF with tin legs, nor his distinguished record on fighter sweeps of 1941. But I do wish that he would not allow himself to be pressed continually as the epitome of the Battle of Britain pilot. That is not his place in history, but he carved his own niche elsewhere.[1]

Brickhill was undoubtedly a Bader fan: 'I agree with all those who class him as the best fighter leader and tactician of the Second World War (and one of the best pilots).'[2] Such a statement is all too easily debunked, however. Not only has the actual value of the Big Wing been proven, but the idea to copy the German *schwarm* and create what the RAF called the 'Finger Four' was not Douglas's idea but that of Flying Officer Hugh 'Cocky' Dundas. There can be no doubt that there are many other fighter leaders well ahead of Douglas Bader in the queue for such a mantle – not least the true father of modern air fighting: *Oberst* Werner Mölders, and not to mention, of course, Air Chief Marshal Sir Hugh Dowding and Air Vice-Marshal Sir Keith Park! Air Vice-Marshal Johnnie Johnson, who was part of the Tangmere Wing's inner sanctum and a close personal friend of Douglas's until the day he died, ended the war as the RAF's top-scoring fighter pilot and undoubtedly the Wing Leader *par excellence* (see *Spitfire Ace of Aces*, also published by Amberley and by this author). Johnnie once told me that when his turn came to lead, he had modelled himself on Bader, 'the great man'.[3] The truth is, however, that Johnson actually did the reverse. Douglas Bader was a product of his social background and education – a snob unable to relate to those of a lower status in the service. Evidence exists, unfortunately, confirming that he could be a bully. Johnson was not from a privileged background but was a police inspector's son; he was not a Cranwellian but a volunteer reservist. There is no doubt that his ordinary origins made Johnson infinitely more able to engage with all those under his command – no matter how lowly their rank or trade. When I put this to him, Johnson's response, loyal to the end, was silence – but he knew that what I said was right.

There can be no doubt that Douglas's greatest contribution to mankind was not as a fighter pilot or leader but as an inspiration to the disabled – for which he was deservedly knighted. Rightly, Brickhill describes his subject as being 'a mixture of modesty and ego. In a swashbuckling way he is given to bragging about his golf scores ... People who don't know him well have resented that, but they have never heard him brag of important things.'[4] Indeed, throughout this book are many examples of surprising humility and modesty – making Douglas Bader a real enigma. The problem is, though, that *Reach for the Sky*, both book and film, concerned his wartime exploits. The book is still often re-printed; the film appears occasionally on television and is widely available as a DVD. Scale plastic and flying models of Douglas's Hurricane and Spitfires abound. Indeed, Douglas Bader even has a page on Facebook, the immensely popular online global social networking site! All of these things combine to keep the Bader myth alive and well in the public consciousness – but as a wartime fighter pilot. Nonetheless, as time marches ever on, the Battle of Britain is passing from living memory – and the survivors are now few indeed. The current generation, therefore, has no personal knowledge of the war, and those born after the 1970s even missed the weekly war films broadcast on television. The chances are that only a small percentage of today's population has any real idea of what the Battle of Britain was, and would be unable to name any of the successful pilots involved – except, perhaps, Douglas Bader. That this is because of a powerful myth is irrelevant – the important thing is that people still hear his name and of the deeds performed in war-torn skies. Increasingly, therefore, Douglas Bader – like the Spitfire – has become an icon, representing all of those who took part. There is no one else, in spite of their august aerial deeds, whose story ignites the popular imagination and interest in this way. That being so, without Douglas Bader, I would argue, the Few would more easily disappear from our consciousness and be consigned to dusty history books. That Douglas Bader's story has significantly helped decelerate this happening, and inspired the international disabled community in the process, is unique.

During the mid-1990s I intensively researched Douglas Bader's RAF career for three earlier books on the man. During this process I led an expedition to the Pas-de-Calais in search of his Spitfire's crash site – which defies discovery even to this day. This search, though, generated immense international media interest – leading to my engagement by Twenty Twenty Television as a consultant to their programme on Douglas for the Channel 4 *Secret Lives* series. The resulting programme, broadcast in 1996, relied heavily upon my research and interviewed numerous of those whose memories I had recorded. Needless to say, the picture presented was very different to that cemented in popular memory and culture by *Reach for the Sky*. Throughout the making of the programme, however, I was concerned that the producers were far more interested in negatives than positives. That was not the right approach. Impartiality and presenting all the facts in equal measure has integrity – a hatchet job does not. The newspapers subsequently delighted in reporting that Douglas Bader was, in fact, a 'very flawed hero'. The evidence confirmed this to be the case, but many, heavily influenced by wartime propaganda and subsequent post-war material, refused to accept the truth – so heavily buttressed was the myth. Indeed, as that great historian Sir Geoffrey Elton once wrote, 'Of course the demolition of comfortable myths causes pain at best and horror-struck revulsion at worst; it can lead to a dangerous over-reaction.'[5]

The myth generated by *Reach for the Sky*, however, is immensely powerful. Television programmes, like that made by Twenty Twenty Television, reach only a small percentage of those who flocked to box offices around the world in 1956; the same is true of this book – which will achieve but a minuscule readership compared with Brickhill's best-seller. A similar case in point is the Normandy campaign of 1944. This was, of course, a combined Allied operation, involving the troops of many nations. In 1998, however, Hollywood director Stephen Spielberg released *Saving Private Ryan* – another enormous global success story.[6] In this film, a team of American Rangers undertook a fictitious mission to extract the sole surviving Ryan brother from the Normandy fighting. It was not, however, intended to be a documentary of D-Day and the liberation of France, as had been Daryl F. Zannuck's star-studded *The Longest Day* of 1962,[7] and was swiftly followed by the similarly popular television series *Band of Brothers*, concerning the experiences of 'Easy Company's' American paratroopers between D-Day and the war's end. The problem is that to many unaware of the actual history involved, the indelible impression of Spielberg's creations is that America solely liberated France and defeated Nazi Germany. In spite of the undeniably huge resources America brought to the war effort, such a view is absurd. Again, more holistic books and films, especially specialist examples, are unlikely to achieve the same circulation – and therefore make little or no impression on the myth Spielberg's work has given global currency. The same is true of *Reach for the Sky* and the Bader myth – which is likely to remain more or less intact, simply because the truth cannot be projected on the same scale as the book and film of that title. Indeed, it is likely that forevermore these myths will remain impervious to whole-scale deconstruction.

Before Douglas died, friends had suggested the idea of a commemorative statue – which he firmly rejected on the grounds that such funds could be better spent elsewhere. Naturally, however, those same friends and family were keen to memorialise him in death. It was decided that this tribute would take the form of a living and working memorial dedicated to helping the limbless lead full and successful lives. So it was that on 27 October 1982 a memorial service was held at St Clement Danes for Group Captain Sir Douglas Bader – and on that day a new charity was launched in his name: the Douglas Bader Foundation. Lady Bader became an active president – for which work Joan was later honoured with a well-earned OBE; David Bickers was chairman, and the original trustees included Dogsbody Section: Johnson, Crowley-Milling and Dundas. The Foundation remains a most active and determined organisation – providing all manner of assistance to amputees. Challenges; grants facilitating the limbless to achieve a variety of goals from education, the arts, sport and recreation to small businesses; the 'Bader Braves' initiative to help children suffering limb loss and other physical disability by offering unique experiences to improve life skills and increase confidence; the Douglas Bader Walking School, which opened in Kuala Lumpur in 2005; Bader Golf and many more projects besides all project Douglas's story as an inspiration to amputees (see www.

douglasbaderfoundation.com). Now this is clearly something that Sir Douglas would have approved of very much indeed.

On 9 August 2001, Lady Bader unveiled a statue of her late husband outside Goodwood Flying Club. The date was, of course, the sixtieth anniversary of Wing Commander Douglas Bader's last operational flight from that very airfield – known as Westhampnett in 1941. Also present was the last surviving member of Dogsbody Section, Sir Alan Smith. The bronze was commissioned by Lord March and created by the sculptor Kenneth Potts, who used as reference several photographs from my collection. Once more, Douglas Bader was in the newspapers – all over the world. This is vitally important, because every time his name is brought to the public's attention it helps keep the memory alive – which is of immeasurable benefit to the continued success of the Foundation. Given the exemplary and extensive good works conducted in his name, Sir Douglas could hardly complain that ultimately a statue in his likeness was erected. More recently, on 31 May 2009, entrepreneur, Virgin tycoon and Bader family friend Sir Richard Branson unveiled an English Heritage Blue Plaque in Douglas's honour at 50 Petersham Mews, Kensington – the Baders' London home. Sir Richard said that Douglas 'overcame his disability and even now you see disabled people coming back from war, doing the marathon, doing some extraordinary activities. I feel pretty sure that somewhere in their backgrounds the name Douglas Bader is something where there's a referral point – he did it and we wish to continue that.'[8] In peace, as in war, therefore, and even many years after his death, Douglas Bader remains significant as a media icon.

Douglas Bader was very much the product of an elitist, white, imperial society and the RAF College, Cranwell. As a young man he was over confident and impetuous to the point of recklessness – for which negative character trait he paid with the loss of both legs. He was headstrong, could be arrogant, rude and impatient – but was as brave as a lion and equally, on occasion and especially towards others like him who were physically challenged, could be incredibly warm and generous. The subject of intense media interest from 1940 onwards, his became a household name all over the world. A British patriot in the Victorian mould, he was always prepared to forcibly speak his mind on any subject – and never suffered fools. Only someone single-minded and obstinate beyond belief could have achieved what he did. Although not the only limbless fighter pilot during the Second World War, he remains the most famous of them all; his was an example others followed. Certainly a fighter pilot and leader of some repute, he was not, however, the great tactician and aerial strategist of myth and legend. A man made for war, it was really in peace that his real mark was made – as a champion of the disabled community. What made Douglas Bader really special was not, in fact, his war record but his incredible ability to ignite the spirit. Many who had lost all hope rediscovered it – because of the legless fighter pilot who refused to give in.

In conclusion, Douglas Bader was a man of his time – one that has long since passed into history. Society and the world are very different today, and unlikely to produce another such character; it is doubtful, therefore, that we will ever see his like again. For all his faults, the fact is that Douglas Bader's story, whether romanticised or factual, *is* inspirational – confirmed all these years later by continued interest in him and the Douglas Bader Foundation's good work in his name. Group Captain Sir Douglas Bader could not have hoped for a better legacy.

NOTES

1 Growing Pains

1. Clapson, M., *Britain in the Twentieth Century*, p. 15
2. Brickhill, P., *Reach for the Sky*, p. 10
3. Brickhill, P., *ibid.*, p. 11
4. Brickhill, P., *ibid.*, p. 11
5. Lucas, P. B., *Flying Colours*, p. 28
6. Brickhill, P., *op. cit.*, p. 12
7. Brickhill, P., *ibid.*, p. 12
8. Brickhill, P., *ibid.*, pp. 15, 258
9. Lucas, P. B., *op. cit.*, p. 29
10. Turner, J. F., *Douglas Bader*, p. 2
11. Somay, J., Commonwealth War Graves Commission, *Bader, Major Frederick Roberts*, E-mail to Sarkar, D., 3 August 2011
12. Turner, J. F., *op. cit.*, p. 2
13. Brickhill, P., *op. cit.*, p. 13
14. Mowat, C. L., *Britain Between the Wars 1918–1940*, p. 520
15. Pugh, M., *We Danced All Night: A Social History of Britain Between the Wars*, p. 86
16. Mowat, C. L., *op. cit.*, p. 480
17. Priestley, J. B., *English Journey*, pp. 397–408
18. Branson, N. and N. Heinemann, *Britain in the 1930s*, p. 168
19. Branson, N. and N. Heinemann,, *ibid.*, p. 168
20. Branson, N. and N. Heinemann, *ibid.*, p. 168
21. Stevenson, J., *British Society 1914–1945*, p. 350
22. Stevenson, J., *ibid.*, p. 351
23. Stevenson, J., *ibid.*, p. 254
24. Stevenson, J., *ibid.*, p. 257
25. Pugh, M., *op. cit.*, p. 207
26. Lucas, P. B., *op. cit.*, p. 29
27. Goodhew, S., *Secret Lives*: 'Douglas Bader' (Channel 4, 1996)
28. James, J., *The Paladins: The Story of the RAF up to the Outbreak of World War II*, p. 135
29. Haig-Brown, A. R., *The OTC in the First World War*, p. 80
30. James, J., *op. cit.*, p. 137
31. James, J., *ibid.*, p. 140
32. Brickhill, P., *op. cit.*, p. 16
33. Brickhill, P., *ibid.*, p. 16
34. Brickhill, P., *ibid.*, p. 20
35. Lucas, P. B., *op. cit.*, p. 30
36. Brickhill, P., *op. cit.*, p. 22
37. Anon., St Edward's School Chronicle, December 1925, p. 278
38. Mackenzie, S. P., *Bader's War*, p. 13
39. Lucas, P. B., *op. cit.*, p. 31
40. Bader, D. R. S., 'Fighter Pilot', in Leyland, E. and T. E. Scott-Chard (eds), *The Boys Book of the Air* (1st edn: London, Edmund Ward, 1957)
41. Cox, S., *Leadership*, E-mail to Sarkar, D., 12 October 2009
42. Brickhill, P., *op. cit.*, p. 24
43. Brickhill, P., *ibid.*, p. 26
44. Brickhill, P., *ibid.*, p. 27

2 Cranwell: Gateway to the Stars

1. Brickhill, P., *ibid.*, p. 28
2. Jefford, J., 'Aircrew Status in the 1940s', p. 57

3. Wells, M. K., *Courage in Air Warfare*, p. 4
4. 'AHE', 'Cranwell and its Traditions', p. 12
5. Lucas, P. B., *op. cit.*, p. 39
6. Brickhill, P., *op. cit.*, p. 32
7. Lucas, P. B., *op. cit.*, p. 37
8. Brickhill, P, *ibid.*, p. 34
9. Lucas, P. B., *op. cit.*, p. 32
10. Brickhill, P., *op. cit.*, p. 31
11. Brickhill, P., *ibid.*, p. 34
12. Oulton, W., *Secret Lives (op. cit.)*
13. Brickhill, P., *op. cit.*, p. 23
14. Brickhill, P., *ibid.*, p. 36
15. Lucas, P. B., *op. cit.*, p. 43
16. Lucas, P. B., *ibid.*, p. 50
17. Lucas, P. B., *ibid.*, p. 32

3 'Bad Show'
1. Lucas, P. B., *op. cit.*, p. 57
2. Brickhill, P., *op. cit.*, p. 38
3. Lucas, P. B., *op. cit.*, pp. 52–53
4. Burns, M., *Bader: The Man and his Men*, p. 18
5. Lucas, P. B., *op. cit.*, p. 60
6. Brickhill, P., *op. cit.*, p. 39
7. Mermagen, H. W., *Secret Lives (op. cit.)*
8. Mackenzie, S. P., *op. cit.*, p. 23
9. Brickill, P., *op. cit.*, p. 42
10. Lucas, P. B., *op. cit.*, p. 66
11. Lucas, *ibid.*, p. 62
12. Turner, J. F., *op. cit.*, p.
13. Bader flying logbook
14. Lucas, P. B., *op. cit.*, p. 64
15. Burns, M., *op. cit.*, p. 24
16. Brickhill, P., *op. cit.*, p. 42
17. Mackenzie, S. P., *op. cit.*, p. 24
18. Lucas, P. B., *op. cit.*, p. 64
19. Brickhill, P., *op. cit.*, p. 42
20. Brickhill, P., *ibid.*, p. 43
21. Lucas, P. B., *op. cit.*, p. 65
22. Mackenzie, S. P., *op. cit.*, p. 24
23. Mackenzie, S. P., *ibid.*, p. 24
24. Lucas, P. B., *op. cit.*, p. 65
25. Brickhill, P., *op. cit.*, p. 46
26. Brickhill, P., *ibid.*, p. 47
27. Brickhill, P., *ibid.*, p. 52
28. Brickhill, P., *ibid.*, p. 52
29. Bader flying logbook
30. Lucas, P. B., *op. cit.*, p. 66
31. Bader, Lady J., *Secret Lives*
32. Oulton, W, *ibid.*

4 'Greenlands': Gateway to the Wilderness
1. Lucas, P. B., *op. cit.*, p. 68
2. Brickhill, P., *op. cit.*, p. 59
3. Turner, J. F., *op. cit.*, p. 11
4. Brickhill, P., *op. cit.*, p. 61
5. Brickhill, P., *ibid.*, p. 64
6. Turner, J. F., *op. cit.*, p. 10
7. Brickhill, P., *op. cit.*, p. 65
8. Mackenzie, S. P., *op. cit.*, p. 24
9. Mackenzie, S. P., *ibid.*, p. 24
10. TNA, Air 43/7, Court of Inquiry report into Pilot Officer Bader's accident

5 'Damn That! I'll Never, *Never* Walk with a Stick!'
1. Brickhill, P., *op. cit.*, p. 68
2. Brickhill, P., *ibid.*, p. 72
3. Brickhill, P., *ibid.*, p. 75
4. Bader papers
5. *Ibid.*
6. Lucas, P. B., *op. cit.*, p. 70
7. Brickhill, P., *op. cit.*, p. 83
8. Bader papers
9. Hodkinson, C., letter to Sarkar, D., 1 May 1996
10. Turner, J. F., *op. cit.*, p. 13
11. Brickhill, P., *op. cit.*, p. 102
12. Brickhill, P., *ibid.*, p. 102
13. Mackenzie, S. P., *op. cit.*, p. 26
14. Lucas, P. B., *op. cit.*, p. 75
15. Burns, M., *op. cit.*, p. 27
16. Mackenzie, S. P., *op. cit.*, p. 27
17. Lucas, P. B., *op. cit.*, p. 85

6 The Wilderness
1. Lucas, P. B., *op. cit.*, p. 80
2. Brickhill, P., *op. cit.*, p. 115
3. Bader papers
4. Calder, A., *The People's War*, p. 27
5. Mowat, C. L., *op. cit.* p. 520
6. Branson, N. and M. Heinemann, *op. cit.*, 167
7. Calder, *op. cit.*, p. 26
8. Clapson, M., *op. cit.*, p. 20
9. Dean, Sir M., *The Royal Air Force in Two World Wars*, p. 41
10. Dean, Sir M., *ibid.*, p. 42
11. Dean, Sir M., *ibid.*, p. 41
12. Dean, Sir M., *ibid.*, p. 49
13. Mitchell, G., *R. J. Mitchell. World Famous Aircraft Designer: From Schooldays to Spitfire*, p. 124

14. Orange, V., *Dowding*, p. 69
15. Brickhill, P., *op. cit.*, p. 132
16. Lucas, P. B., *op. cit.*, p. 102
17. Lucas, P. B., *ibid.*, p. 104
18. Brickhill, P., *op. cit.*, p. 133
19. Lucas, P. B., *op. cit.*, p. 105
20. Mackenzie, S. P., *op. cit.*, p. 29
21. Brickhill, P. B., *op. cit.*, p. 133
22. Brickhill, P. B., *ibid.*, p. 133
23. Calder, A., *op. cit.*, p. 33
24. Brickhill, P., *op. cit.*, p. 134
25. Brickhill, P., *ibid.*, pp. 135–6
26. Mackenzie, S. P., *op. cit.*, p. 29
27. Brickhill, P., *op. cit.*, p. 137
28. Brickhill, P., *ibid.*, p. 137
29. Brickhill, P., *ibid.*, p. 140
30. Woodhall, A. B., 'Introduction', in Sarkar, D., *Duxford 1940: A Battle of Britain Base at War*, p. 11
31. Brickhill, P., *op. cit.*, p. 143

7 Spitfires
1. Morris, R., interviewed by Sarkar, D., 1 October 1986
2. Anon., 'The Spitfire', *The Aeroplane*, 12 April 1940, Vol. LVIII, No. 1507, p. 524
3. Unwin, G. C., interviewed by Sarkar, D., 8 November 1989
4. Bader, D. R. S., *Fight for the Sky*, p. 12
5. Bader, D. R. S., *ibid.*, p. 12
6. Roberts, F. V., letter to Sarkar, D., 10 June 1990
7. French, E., interviewed by Sarkar, D., 6 May 1997
8. Bader, D. R. S., *op. cit.*, pp. 12–13
9. Bader, D. R. S., *ibid.*, p. 12
10. Brinsden, F. N., letter to Sarkar, D., 25 July 1989
11. Lyne, M. D., letter to Sarkar, D., 1 May 1989
12. French, E., interview, *op. cit.*
13. Brickhill, P., *op. cit.*, p. 145
14. Brickhill, P., *ibid.*, p. 146
15. Brickhill. P., *ibid.*, pp. 147–48
16. Burns, M., *op. cit.*, p. 33
17. Orange, V., *Park*, p. 72
18. Brickhill, P., *op. cit.*, p. 148
19. Mackenzie, S. P., *op. cit.*, p. 34
20. Burns, M., *op. cit.*, p. 36
21. Turner, J. F., *op. cit.*, p. 24
22. Brickhill, P., *op. cit.*, p. 149
23. Mermagen, H. W., letter to Sarkar, D., 26 January 1989
24. Woodhall, A. B., *op. cit.*, p. 11
25. Mermagen, H. W., letter to Sarkar, *op. cit.*
26. Lyne, M. D., letter to Sarkar, *op. cit.*
27. Brickhill, P., *op. cit.*, p. 150
28. Bader flying logbook
29. Brinsden, F. N., interviewed by Sarkar, D., 13 September 1990
30. Johnson, R. B., letter to Sarkar, D., 3 March 1989
31. Brickhill, P., *op. cit.*, p. 153
32. Lane, B. J., *Spitfire!*, p. 23
33. Brickhill, P., *op. cit.*, p. 153
34. Lyne, M. D., letter to Sarkar, D., 1 October 1989
35. Burns, M., *op. cit.*, p. 39
36. Orange, V., *Park*, *op. cit.*, p. 86
37. Orange, V., *ibid.*, p. 87
38. Burns, M., *op. cit.*, p. 40
39. Terraine, J., 'The Battle of France' in Probert, H. and S. Cox (eds), *The Battle Re-thought: A Symposium on the Battle of Britain*, p. 15
40. Mermagen, H. W., letter to Sarkar, *op. cit.*
41. Bader, D. R. S., *op. cit.*, p. 15
42. Mermagen, H. W., interviewed by Sarkar, D., 1 September 1989
43. Bader flying logbook
44. Bader, D. R. S., *op. cit.*, p. 15
45. Peach, S. W., 'Air Power and the Fall of France' in Cox, S. and P. Gray (eds), *Air Power History: Turning Points from Kittyhawk to Kosovo*, p. 164
46. Lucas, P. B., *op. cit.*, p. 120
47. Burns, M., *op. cit.*, p. 45
48. Lucas, P. B., *op. cit.*, p. 124
49. Lane flying logbook
50. Bader flying logbook
51. Mermagen, H. W., *Secret Lives*
52. Mermagen, H. W., letter to Sarkar, *op. cit.*
53. Bader flying logbook
54. Woodhall, A. B., *op. cit.*, p. 16
55. Mermagen, H. W., letter to Sarkar, *op. cit.*
56. Mackenzie, S. P., *op. cit.*, p. 40
57. Bader, D. R. S, speech at 'Gathering of Eagles Aircrew Reunion', Winnipeg, Manitoba, Canada, 1970

8 242 (Canadian) Squadron

1. Bader, D. R. S, speech at 'Gathering of Eagles Aircrew Reunion', Winnipeg, Manitoba, Canada, 1970
2. Brickhill, P, *op. cit.*, p. 164
3. Bader flying logbook
4. Bader, D. R. S, Eagles speech, *op. cit.*
5. Crowley-Milling, D., letter to Sarkar, D., 3 May 1995
6. Lucas, P. B., *op. cit.*, p. 136
7. Brickhill, P., *op. cit.*, p. 172
8. Brickhill, P., *ibid.*, p. 174
9. Woodhall, A. B., *op. cit.*, p. 35
10. Evans, D., letter to Sarkar, D., 10 January 1996
11. Brickhill, P., *op. cit.*, p. 176
12. Brickhill, P., *ibid.*, p. 185
13. Mackenzie, S. P., *op. cit.*, p. 50
14. Bader, D. R. S., *op. cit.*, p. 64
15. Unwin, G. C., letter to Sarkar, D., 23 February 1988

9 The System

1. Orange, V., *Dowding, op. cit.*, p. 31
2. Townsend, P., *Duel of Eagles*, p. 176
3. Orange, V., *Dowding, op. cit.*, p. 66
4. Orange, V., *ibid.*, p. 85
5. Quoted by Terraine, J., in "The Dowding System", 'Battle of Britain' (Part One), *The Daily Telegraph Editorial Supplement*, 16 June 1990, p. XI.
6. Wright, R., *Dowding and the Battle of Britain*, p. 40
7. Orange, V., *Park, op. cit.*, p. 44
8. Overy, R., *Air War*, p. 17
9. Anon., *The Battle of Britain*, Air Ministry Pamphlet 156, pp. 4–12
10. Orange, V., *Park, op. cit.*, p. 78
11. Orange, V., *ibid.*, pp. 80–81
12. Wright, R., *op. cit.*, p. 94

10 Battle of Britain

1. Mason, F. K., *Battle Over Britain*, p. 123
2. Brickhill, P., *op. cit.*, p. 180
3. Ramsey, W. (ed.), *The Blitz Then and Now, Volume One*, p. 121
4. Burns, M., *op. cit.*, pp. 54–55
5. Lucas, P. B., *op. cit.*, p. 146
6. Turner, J. F., *The Bader Wing*, p. 22
7. Brickhill, P., *op. cit.*, p. 180

8. Brickhill, P, *ibid.*, p. 181
9. Anon., 'The Extra Bit', *Malvern Gazette*, 23 July 1940, p. 4
10. Burns, M., *op. cit.*, p. 55
11. Cox, D. G. S. R., letter to Sarkar, D., 10 April 1989
12. Cunningham, W., letter to Sarkar, D., 2 February 1988
13. Crowley-Milling, D., letter to Sarkar, D., 1 November 1988
14. Cox, D. G. S. R., letter to Sarkar, D., 10 August 1988
15. Mason, F. K., *op. cit.*, p. 231
16. Cox, D. G. S. R., letter to Sarkar, D., 10 August 1988
17. Morten, E., letter to Sarkar, D., 1 October 1996
18. Woodhall, A. B., *op. cit.*, p. 52
19. No. 11 Group Instructions to Controllers No. 7, 27 August 1940
20. Orange, V., *Park, op. cit.*, p. 121

11 'Tally Ho!'

1. Brickhill, P., *op. cit.*, p. 186
2. 501 Squadron CR
3. 1 Squadron ORB
4. 1 Squadron CR, Sergeant Marchand
5. *Ibid.*, Squadron Leader Pemberton
6. Brickhill, P., *op. cit.*, p. 187
7. Lucas, P. B., *op. cit.*, p. 152
8. 242 Squadron CR
9. 242 Squadron CR, Squadron Leader Bader
10. 242 Squadron CR
11. Bader, D. R. S., 'Dogfights Over England' in *We Speak from the Air*, p. 46
12. Bader, D. R. S., *ibid.*, p. 46
13. 242 Squadron CR
14. Bader, D. R. S., 'Dogfights', *op. cit.*, p. 47
15. 242 Squadron CR
16. *Ibid.*
17. *Ibid.*
18. *Ibid.*
19. Cox, S., 'RAF and Luftwaffe Intelligence Compared' in *Intelligence and Military Operations*, p. 434
20. Bader, D. R. S., 'Dogfights', *op. cit.*, p. 46
21. Berton, P., *Marching as to War*, pp. 322–23
22. Intelligence Report, 'Fighter Tactics v Escort and Bomber Formation', 2

September 1940, Squadron Leader Bader
23. Bader, D. R. S, interviewed by Price, A., date unknown
24. Lucas, P. B., *op. cit.*, p. 152

12 Duxford Wing
1. Johnson, J. E., *Wing Leader*, pp. 41–42
2. Bader, D. R. S., interviewed by Price, A., date unknown
3. Lane, B. J. E., *op. cit.*, p. 107
4. 19 Squadron ORB
5. Sinclair, G. L., letter to Sarkar, D., 9 April 1988
6. Blackwood, D., letter to Sarkar, D., 1 March 1995
7. Cox, S., *op. cit.*, p. 438
8. Air Ministry Pamphlet 248, p. 85
9. Bekker, C., *The Luftwaffe War Diaries*, p. 221
10. Orange, V., *Park, op. cit.*, p. 123
11. 242 Squadron CR
12. Bader, D. R. S., *op. cit.*, p. 78
13. 242 Squadron CR
14. Bader, D. R. S., *op. cit.*, p. 78
15. 242 Squadron CR
16. Evans, D., letter to Sarkar, D., 12 June 1996
17. Bader, D. R. S., *op. cit.*, p. 78
18. Morten, E., letter to Sarkar, D., 1 October 1996
19. Brothers, P. M., letter to Sarkar, D., 10 January 1997
20. Bader, D. R. S, interviewed by Price, A., date unknown
21. Cox, S., *op. cit.*, p. 434
22. Woodhall, A. B., *op. cit.*, p. 48
23. Woodhall, A. B., *ibid.*, p. 49
24. Bader, D. R. S., interviewed by Price, A., date unknown
25. Burns, M., *op. cit.*, p. 81
26. 310 Squadron ORB
27. *Ibid.*
28. CR, Cunningham, P/O W., 19 Squadron
29. CR, Bader, S/L D. R. S., 242 Squadron
30. Bader flying logbook
31. CR, McKnight, P/O W., 242 Squadron
32. Brickhill, P., *op. cit.*, p. 198
33. Brickhill, P., *ibid.*, p. 197

13 Big Wing
1. 19 Squadron ORB
2. Morten, E., letter to Sarkar, D., 12 April 1996
3. *London Gazette*, Issue 34958, p. 5789, 1 October 1940
4. 310 Squadron ORB
5. Bader, D. R. S., 'Dogfights', *op. cit.*, p. 48
6. CR, 242 Squadron, S/L Bader, D. R. S.
7. Lane, B. J., *op. cit.*, p. 118
8. 310 Squadron ORB
9. Lane, B. J., *op. cit.*, p. 113
10. Bader, D. R. S., 'Dogfights', *op. cit.*, p. 48
11. CR, 242 Squadron, S/L Bader, D. R. S.
12. Lane flying logbook
13. Overy, R., *The Battle*, p. 87
14. Cox, D. G. S. R., letter to Sarkar, D., 10 June 1988
15. Jones, R. L., letter to Sarkar, D., 1 July 1990
16. Cox, S. and H. Probert (eds), *The Battle Re-Thought*, p. 71
17. Bader flying logbook
18. 310 Squadron ORB
19. Newton, Dunn, B., *Big Wing*, p. 74
20. 310 Squadron ORB, 18 September 1940
21. 12 Group CR, 18 September 1940
22. 242 Squadron CR, 18 September 1940
23. *Ibid.*
24. *Ibid.*
25. Bader, D. R. S., 'Dogfights', *op. cit.*, p. 48
26. Park, A. V. M. K, Report on German Attacks on England, 11 September–2 November 1940
27. 242 Squadron ORB
28. 242 Squadron CR, Squadron Leader Bader
29. *Ibid.*
30. 310 Squadron CR, Sergeant Komineck
31. 242 Squadron CR, Squadron Leader Bader
32. Jones, R. L., letter to Sarkar, D., 12 November 1994
33. Jones flying logbook
34. Orange, V., *Park, op. cit.*, p. 124

35. Park, A. V. M. K., Points for Air Ministry Conference, 6 October 1940
36. Brickhill, P., *op. cit.*, p. 218
37. 242 Squadron ORB
38. Brickhill, P., *op. cit.*, p. 219
39. Wright, R., *op. cit.*, p. 219
40. Wellum, G., letter to Sarkar, D., 2 February 1993
41. 11 Group Intelligence Report, 29 October 1940
42. Orange, V., *Park, op. cit.*, p. 132
43. Overy, R., *Battle, op. cit.*, p. 120
44. Wright, R., *op. cit.*, p. 232
45. Lucas, P. B., *op. cit.*, pp. 184–85
46. Bader, D. R. S., interviewed by Price, A., date unknown
47. Lucas, P. B., *op. cit.*, pp. 365–67

14 Winter of Content
1. Mowat, C. L., *op. cit.*, p. 1
2. Calder, A., *op. cit.*, p. 21
3. Bialer, U., *The Shadow of the Bomber*, p. 2
4. Report of a subcommittee on plans for re-establishing the MOI, 27 July 1936, CAB 4/23
5. Francis, M., *The Flyer*, p. 1
6. Anon., 'The Greatest Hero of Them All', *Mirror*, 15 July 1940, p. 1
7. Anon., 'Identity of Legless Pilot', *Telegraph*, 16 September 1940
8. Campion, G., *The Good Fight*, p. 145
9. 19 Squadron CR, Flight Lieutenant Lawson
10. Lane flying logbook
11. Wells, P., interviewed by Foreman, J., date unknown
12. Douglas, ACM W. S., 'Air Operations by Fighter Command from 25 November 1940–31 December 1941', *London Gazette*, 14 September 1948, p. 5025
13. Brickhill, P., *op. cit.*, p. 224
14. Brickhill, P., *ibid.*, p. 226
15. Brickhill, P., *ibid.*, p. 226

15 Tangmere Wing: Bader's Bus Company
1. Brickhill, P., *op. cit.*, p. 229
2. Smith, Sir A., letter to Sarkar, D., 2 April 1995
3. Johnson, J. E., interviewed by Sarkar, D., 5 August 1995

4. Twitchett, F., interviewed by Sarkar, D., 10 January 1996
5. Ward-Smith, P., letter to Sarkar, D., 2 October 1995
6. Morton, R., interviewed by Sarkar, D., 15 March 1986
7. *Ibid.*
8. Casson, L. H., letter to Sarkar, D., 1 June 1995
9. Allom, J., letter to Sarkar, D., 3 November 1995
10. Smith, Sir A., letter to Sarkar, D., 2 April 1995
11. Johnson, J. E., interviewed by Sarkar, D., 5 August 1995
12. Dundas, Sir H. S. L., letter to Sarkar, D., 1 May 1986
13. Dundas, Sir H. S. L., *Flying Start*, p. 63
14. Dundas, Sir H. S. L., letter to Sarkar, D., 1 May 1986
15. Johnson, J. E., interviewed by Sarkar, D., 5 August 1995
16. Crowley-Milling, Sir D., letter to Sarkar, D., 3 February 1996
17. Brickhill, P., *op. cit.*, p. 237
18. Johnson, J. E., interviewed by Sarkar, D., 5 August 1995
19. Rayner, R., interviewed by Sarkar, D., 1 May 1994
20. Bader, Wg Cdr D. R. S., 616 Squadron CR
21. Cox, S., *op. cit.*, p. 434
22. Morton, R., interviewed by Sarkar, D., 15 March 1986
23. Brickhill, P., *op. cit.*, p. 237
24. Bader, Wg Cdr D. R. S., 616 Squadron CR
25. *Ibid.*
26. *Ibid.*
27. *London Gazette*, Issue 35219, p. 4063, 15 July 1941
28. Reid, G., letter to Sarkar, D., 2 February 1996
29. Clowes, H., letter to Sarkar, D., 4 January 1996
30. Jacks, H., letter to Sarkar, D., 2 January 1996
31. Twitchett, F., interviewed by Sarkar, D., 1 October 1995
32. Casson, L. H., interviewed by Sarkar, D., 12 September 1992
33. Johnson, J. E., interviewed by Sarkar, D., 5 August 1995

34. Crowley-Milling, Sir D., interviewed by Sarkar, D., 2 June 1992
35. Rayner, R., interviewed by Sarkar, D., 19 August 1994
36. Johnson, J. E., interviewed by Sarkar, D., 4 October 1995
37. *Ibid.*
38. Bader, Wg Cdr D. R. S., 616 Squadron CR
39. *Ibid.*
40. *Ibid.*
41. *Ibid.*
42. *Ibid.*
43. *Ibid.*
44. 610 Squadron ORB
45. 616 Squadron ORB
46. Winskill, Sir A., letter to Sarkar, D., 3 March 1996
47. Rayner, R., interviewed by Sarkar, D., 19 August 1994
48. Brickhill, P., *op. cit.*, p. 237
49. Winskill, Sir A., letter to Sarkar, D., 3 March 1996
50. Johnson, J. E., interviewed by Sarkar, D., 24 February 1996
51. Beardsley, R., letter to Sarkar, D., 15 October 1995
52. Johnson, J. E., interviewed by Sarkar, D., 24 February 1996
53. Brickhill, P., *op. cit.*, pp. 252–53
54. *Ibid.*, p. 253
55. RAF Tangmere ORB

16 'BREAK! For Christ's Sake, BREAK!'
1. Dundas, Sir H. S. L., *op. cit.*, p. 73
2. Johnson Papers
3. *Ibid.*
4. 610 Squadron CR
5. Johnson Papers
6. *Ibid.*
7. *Ibid.*
8. Johnson, J. E., interviewed by Sarkar, D., 5 August 1995
9. Johnson Papers
10. Casson, L. H., letter to Bader, D. R. S., date unknown, 1945
11. Schöpfel, G., letter to Sarkar, D., 9 September 1995
12. Johnson, P/O J. E., 616 Squadron CR
14. Johnson, J. E., interviewed by Sarkar, D., 5 August 1995

15. Crowley-Milling, D., letter to Sarkar, D., 26 April 1996
15. Bader, D. R. S., *op. cit.*, p. 31
16. *Ibid.*, p. 32
17. *Ibid.*, p. 33
18. Johnson, J. E., interviewed by Sarkar, D., 5 August 1995
19. John flying logbook
20. Burton flying logbook
21. Roberts, D., letter to Sarkar, D., 13 May 1996
22. Dundas, Sir H. S. L., *op. cit.*, p. 75
23. Dundas, Sir H. S. L., *ibid.*, p. 75
24. Dundas, Sir H. S. L., *ibid.*, p. 76
25. Galland, A., *The First and the Last*, p. 85
26. Galland, A., *ibid.*, p. 85
27. Galland, A., *ibid.*, p. 86
28. Galland, A., *ibid.*, p. 85
29. Schöpfel, G., letter to Sarkar, D., 9 September 1995
30. Reid, G., letter to Sarkar, D., 2 February 1996
31. Crowley-Milling, D., letter to Sarkar, D., 26 April 1996
32. Schöpfel, G., letter to Sarkar, D., 9 September 1995
33. *Ibid.*
34. 616 Squadron ORB
35. Galland, A., *op. cit.*, pp. 84–85
36. Bader, Wg Cdr D. R. S., POW repatriation report, April 1945
37. Hepple, Pilot Officer P. W., 616 Squadron CR
38. Finucane, B., Flight Lieutenant, 452 Squadron CR
39. Truscott, Flight Lieutenant, 452 Squadron CR
40. Lucas, P. B., *op. cit.*, p. 241
41. Lucas, P. B., letter to Sarkar, D., 19 February 1996
42. Johnson, J. E., letter to Sarkar, D., 25 April 1995
43. Dundas, Sir H. S. L., letter to Sarkar, D., 2 May 1995
44. Crowley-Milling, Sir D., telephone conversation with Sarkar, D., 4 May 1995
45. Casson, L. H., telephone conversation with Sarkar, D., 1 June 1995
46. Lucas, P. B., *op. cit.*, p. 241
47. Burns, M., *op. cit.*, p. 191
48. Mackenzie, C. J., 'A Day of

Memories for Tin Legs', *Sydney Daily Mirror*, 15 March 1981, pp. 1–2
49. Bader, D. R. S., letter to Mayer, M., 5 August 1981
50. Mackenzie, C. J., letter to Sarkar, D., 31 August 1995
51. *London Gazette*, Issue 35270, p. 5217, 9 September 1941

17 An Unappeasable Prisoner
1. Dubreu, A., interviewed by Sarkar, D., 28 March 1996
2. Brickhill, P., *op. cit.*, p. 276
3. Galland, A., *op. cit.*, pp. 86–87
4. Crowley-Milling, Sir D., letter to Sarkar, D., 12 May 1995
5. Lubbock, D., Bader Papers
6. Mackenzie, S. P., *op. cit.*, p. 140
7. Boulding, R. J. E., interviewed by Sarkar, D., 2 August 1988
8. Tuck, R. S., letter to Sarkar, D., 1 March 1986
9. MacDonnel, D., *Dogfight to Diplomacy*, p. 103
10. Fox, P. H., interviewed by Sarkar, D., 11 August 1994
11. Mackenzie, S. P., *op. cit.*, p. 148
12. Linlithgow, Lord C., Bader Papers
13. Pardoe, P., Bader Papers
14. Lucas, P. B., *op. cit.*, p. 254
15. Ross, A., *Secret Lives* (*op. cit.*)
16. *Ibid.*
17. Mackenzie, S. P., *op. cit.*, p. 150
18. Brickhill, P., *op. cit.*, p. 322
19. Crowley-Milling Papers
20. *Ibid.*
21. Brickhill, P., *op. cit.*, p. 293
22. Brickhill, P., *ibid.*, p. 320
23. Brickhill, P., *ibid.*, p. 325
24. Brickhill, P., *ibid.*, p. 327
25. Brickhill, P., *ibid.*, p. 328
26. Mackenzie, S. P., *op. cit.*, p. 152
27. Francis, M., *op. cit.*, p. 93
28. Galland, A., *op. cit.*, p. 87
29. Galland, A., *ibid.*, p. 87

18 Reach for the Sky
1. Turner, J. F., *Bader, op. cit.*, p. 135
2. Dawson, G., 'History-Writing on World War II' in Hurd, G. (ed.), *National Fictions: World War Two in British Films and Television*, p. 1
3. Turner, J. F., *Bader, op. cit.*, p. 155
4. Lucas, P. B., *op. cit.*, p. 288

5. Lucas, P. B., *ibid.*, p. 288
6. Medhurst, A., '1950s War Films' in Hurd, G., *op. cit.*, pp. 35–38
7. Lucas, P. B., *op. cit.*, p. 306
8. Crowley-Milling, Sir D., interviewed by Sarkar, D., 8 March 1990
9. Lucas, P. B., *op. cit.*, p. 310
10. Mackenzie, S. P., *op. cit.*, p. 166
11. Turner, J. F., *The Bader Tapes*, p. 171
12. Mackenzie, S. P., *op. cit.*, p. 161
13. Mackenzie, S. P., *ibid.*, p. 166
14. Mosley, L., *Battle of Britain*, p. 141
15. Mosley, L., *ibid.*, p. 142
16. Mosley, L., *ibid.*, p. 143
17. Mosley, L., *ibid.*, pp. 144–46
18. Mosley, L., *ibid.*, p. 146
19. Bader Papers
20. Bader, D. R. S., *op. cit.*, p. 26
21. Bader Papers
22. *Ibid.*
23. *Ibid.*
24. Bickers, D., The Douglas Bader Foundation
25. *Ibid.*
26. Turner, J. F., *Bader, op. cit.*, pp. 248–49
27. Turner, J. F., *ibid.*, p. 249

19 The Bader Legacy
1. Bader Papers
2. Brickhill, P., *op. cit.*, p. 341
3. Johnson, J. E., interviewed by Sarkar, D., 3 August 1995
4. Brickhill, P., *op. cit.*, p. 340
5. Elton, Sir G., 'Return to Essentials' in Jenkins, K. (ed.), *The Post Modern History Reader*, p. 177
6. Spielberg, S., *Saving Private Ryan* (Dreamworks Pictures and Paramount Pictures, 1998)
7. Zannuck, D. F., *The Longest Day* (20th Century Fox, 1962)
8. Anon., 'Blue Plaque for War Hero' [Online], http://news.bbc.co.uk/1/hi/uk/8075270.stm, [03 June 2012]

BIBLIOGRAPHY

Primary Sources

General
The Bader Papers, The Douglas Bader Foundation
Air Vice-Marshal J. E. Johnson Papers
Air Marshal Sir Denis Crowley-Milling Papers
Dilip Sarkar Archive, correspondence and interviews

Flying Logbooks
Air Marshal Sir Denis Crowley-Milling
Air Vice-Marshal J. E. Johnson
Group Captain Sir High Dundas
Group Captain Sir D. R. S. Bader (RAF Museum, Hendon)
Group Captain H. F. Burton
Squadron Leader B. J. E. Lane (TNA, AIR 4/58)
Flight Lieutenant R. L. Jones
Flight Lieutenant R. Rayner

The National Archives

AIR 43/27	Court of Inquiry report into flying accident, Pilot Officer D. R. S. Bader
AIR 16/956	11 Group Combat Report (CR), 30 August 1940
	242 Squadron CR, 30 August 1940
AIR 16/281	Report on Fighter Tactics, Squadron Leader D. R. S. Bader, 2 September 1940
AIR 16/635	Report on German Attacks on England, 11 September–2 November 1940, Air Vice-Marshal K. Park
AIR 16/957	12 Group CR, 7 September 1940
AIR 16/957	310 Squadron CR, 7 September 1940
AIR 27/1	1 Squadron Operations Record Book (ORB)
AIR 27/252	19 Squadron ORB
AIR27/528	56 Squadron ORB
AIR 27/601	66 Squadron ORB
AIR 27/1371	222 Squadron ORB

AIR 27/1471   242 Squadron ORB
AIR 27/1661   302 Squadron ORB
AIR 27/1680   310 Squadron ORB
AIR 27/1949   501 Squadron ORB
AIR 27/2109   611 Squadron ORB
AIR 27/2126   616 Squadron ORB

AIR 50/92   Douglas Bader's CRs
AIR 50/10   19 Squadron CRs
AIR 50/18   41 Squadron CRs
AIR 50/62   145 Squadron CRs
AIR 50/116   302 Squadron CRs
AIR 50/122   310 Squadron CRs
AIR 50/155   452 Squadron CRs
AIR 50/162   501 Squadron CRs
AIR 50/172   610 Squadron CRs
AIR 50/173   611 Squadron CRs
AIR 50/176   616 Squadron CRs

Films and Programmes
Gilbert, L., *Reach for the Sky*, Directed by Lewis Gilbert (Rank Organisation, 1956).
Secret Life of Douglas Bader, Directed by Simon Berthon (Twenty Twenty Television, 1996).
This Is Your Life: Group Captain Sir Douglas Bader, Presented by Eamon Andews (Thames Television, 1982).

Websites
www.douglasbaderfoundation.com: Website of the charity founded in Sir Douglas Bader's name to promote his example to inspire and assist amputees.
www.dilipsarkarmbe.co.uk: Dilip Sarkar's personal website.

Published Sources

'AHE', 'Cranwell and its Traditions', *Journal of the Royal Air Force College* (1930), pp. 12–15
Anon., *The Battle of Britain*, Air Ministry Pamphlet 156 (1943).
Anon., *The Rise and Fall of the German Air Force 1939–1945*, Air Ministry Pamphlet 248 (1948).
Bader, D. R. S., 'Dogfights Over England' in *We Speak from the Air: Broadcasts by the RAF* (1st edn, London: HMSO, 1943).
Bader, D. R. S., *Fight for the Sky: The Story of the Spitfire and Hurricane* (1st edn, London: Sidgwick & Jackson Ltd., 1973).
Bekker, C., *The Luftwaffe War Diaries* (6th edn, London: Corgi, 1972).
Berton, P., *Marching as to War: Canada's Turbulent Years* (2nd edn, Canada: Anchor, 2001).
Bialer, U., *The Shadow of the Bomber: The Fear of Air Attack and British Politics, 1932–1939* (1st edn, London: Royal Historical Society, 1980).
Branson, N. and M. Heinemann, *Britain in the 1930s* (1st edn, London: Weidenfeld & Nicholson, 1971).

Brickhill, P., *Reach for the Sky: The Story of Douglas Bader DSO DFC* (1st edn, London: Collins, 1954).

Burns, M. G., *Bader: The Man and His Men* (2nd edn, London: Cassell & Co., 1998).

Calder, A., *The People's War: Britain 1939 –45* (13th edn, London: Pimlico, 2008).

Caldwell, D., *The JG 26 War Diary, Volume One: 1939-1942* (1st edn, London: Grubb Street, 1996).

Campion, G., *The Good Fight: Battle of Britain Propaganda and The Few* (1st edn, Basingstoke: Palgrave MacMillan, 2010).

Clapson, M., *The Routledge Companion to Britain in the Twentieth Century* (1st edn, Abingdon: Routledge, 2009).

Connolly, M., *We Can Take It! Britain and the Memory of the Second World War* (1st edn, London: Pearson Longman, 2004).

Cox, S., 'RAF and Luftwaffe Intelligence Compared' in Handel, M. I. (ed.), *Intelligence and Military Operations* (1st edn, Abingdon: Frank Cass & Co. Ltd, 1990).

Cox, S., and H. Probert (eds), *The Battle Re-Thought: A Symposium on the Battle of Britain, 25 June 1990* (1st edn, Royal Air Force Historical Society, 1990).

Dean, Sir M., *The Royal Air Force in Two World Wars* (1st edn, London: Cassell & Co., 1979).

Dundas, Group Captain Sir H. S. L., *Flying Start: A Fighter Pilot's War Years* (1st edn, London: Stanley Paul, 1988).

Foreman, J., *RAF Fighter Command Victory Claims of World War Two, Part One: 1939-1940* (1st edn, Walton-on-Thames: Red Kite, 2003).

Francis, M., *The Flyer: British Culture and the Royal Air Force 1939–1945* (2nd edn, Oxford University Press, 2011).

Galland, A., *The First and the Last* (4th edn, Bristol: Cerberus Publishing Ltd., 2001).

Haig-Brown, A. R., *The OTC in the Great War* (1st edn, London: Country Life Publications, 1915).

Hurd, G. (ed.), *National Fictions: World War Two in British Film and Television* (1st edn, London: BFI Books, 1984).

James, J., *The Paladins: The Story of the RAF up to the Outbreak of World War II* (2nd edn, London: Futura Publications, 1990).

James, T. C. G., *The Battle of Britain* (1st edn, London: Frank Cass & Co. Ltd, 2000).

Jefford, J., 'Aircrew Status in the 1940s', *Royal Air Force Historical Society*, 42 (2008), pp. 57–93.

Jenkins, K. (ed.), *The Post Modern History Reader* (1st edn, London: Routledge, 1997).

Johnson, J. E., *Wing Leader* (1st edn, London: Chatto and Windus, 1956).

Johnson, R., *Hitler and Nazi Germany: The Seduction of a Nation* (1st edn, Bishop's Lydeard: Studymates, 2004).

Lane, B. J. and D. Sarkar (ed.), *Spitfire! The Experiences of a Fighter Pilot* (3rd edn, Stroud: Amberley Publishing, 2009).

Leyland, E. and T. E. Scott-Chard (eds), *The Boys Book of the Air* (1st edn, London: Edmund Ward, 1957).

Lucas, P. B., *Flying Colours: The Story of Douglas Bader, World War II's Most Renowned Hero of the Air* (2nd edn, London: Granada Publishing Ltd., 1985).

MacDonnell, A. D., *Dogfight to Diplomacy* (1st edn, Barnsley: Pen and Sword, 2009).

Mackenzie, S. P., *Bader's War: 'Have a Go at Everything'* (1st edn, Stroud: Spellmount, 2008).

McLaine, I., *Ministry of Morale: Home Front Morale and the Ministry of Information in World War II* (1st edn, London: George Allen and Unwin Ltd., 1979).

Mason, F. K., *Battle Over Britain* (2nd edn, Bourne End: Aston Publications, 1990).

Mitchell, G., *R. J. Mitchell. World Famous Aircraft Designer: From Schooldays to Spitfire* (1st edn, Olney: Nelson and Saunders, 1986).

More, K., *More or Less* (1st edn, London: Hodder & Stoughton, 1974).

Mosley, L., *Battle of Britain: The Story of a Film* (1st edn, London: Pan Books, 1968).

Mowat, C. L., *Britain Between the Wars 1918–1940* (1st edn, London: Taylor & Francis Ltd., 1968).

Newton Dunn, B., *Big Wing: The Biography of Air Chief Marshal Sir Trafford Leigh-Mallory* (1st edn, Shrewsbury: Airlife, 1992).

Noakes, L., *War and the British: Gender and National Identity 1939–1991* (1st edn, London: I. B. Taurus, 1998).

Orange, V., *Park: The Biography of Air Chief Marshal Sir Keith Park* (2nd edn, London: Grubb Street, 2001).

Orange, V., *Dowding of Fighter Command* (1st edn, London: Grubb Street, 2008).

Overy, R., *The Air War 1939–1945* (1st edn, London: Europa Publications Ltd, 1980).

Overy, R., *The Battle* (2nd edn, London: Penguin, 2001).

Paris, M., *From Wright Brothers to Top Gun: Aviation, Nationalism and Popular Cinema* (1st edn, Manchester University Press, 1995).

Peach, S. W., 'Air Power and the Fall of France' in Cox, S., and P. Gray (eds), *Air Power History: Turning Points from Kittyhawk to Kosovo* (1st edn, London: Frank Cass & Co. Ltd., 2002).

Priestley, J. B., *English Journey* (1st edn, London: Victor Gollancz, 1934).

Probert, H., and S. Cox (eds), *The Battle Re-thought: A Symposium on the Battle of Britain* (1st edn, Shrewsbury: Airlife, 1991).

Pugh, M., *We Danced All Night: A Social History of Britain Between the Wars* (1st edn, London: Bodley Head, 2008).

Ramsey, W. (ed.), *The Blitz Then and Now, Volume One* (1st edn, London: After the Battle, 1987).

Ramsey, W. (ed.), *The Blitz Then and Now, Volume Two* (1st edn, London: After the Battle, 1988).

Ray, J., *The Battle of Britain: Dowding and the First Victory, 1940* (6th edn, London: Cassell & Co., 2009).

Rosenstone, R., *History on Film: Film on History* (1st edn, Harlow: Pearson Education Ltd., 2006).

Sarkar, D., *Spitfire Squadron: No 19 Squadron at War, 1939–41* (1st edn, New Maiden: Air Research Publications, 1990).

Sarkar, D., *Bader's Duxford Fighters: The Big Wing Controversy* (1st edn, Worcester: Ramrod Publications, 1997).

Sarkar, D., *Group Captain Sir Douglas Bader: An Inspiration in Photographs* (1st edn, Worcester: Ramrod Publications & The Douglas Bader Foundation, 2001).

Sarkar, D., *Duxford 1940: A Battle of Britain Base at War* (1st edn, Chalford: Amberley Publishing, 2009).

Sarkar, D., *How the Spitfire Won the Battle of Britain* (1st edn, Stroud: Amberley Publishing, 2010).

Sarkar, D., *Spitfire Ace of Aces: The True Wartime Story of Johnnie Johnson* (1st edn, Stroud: Amberley Publishing, 2011).

Stevenson, J., *British Society 1914–1945* (1st edn, London: Penguin, 1984).

Townsend, P., *Duel of Eagles* (3rd edn, London: Fontana, 1972).

Turner, J. F., *Douglas Bader: A Biography of the Legendary World War II Fighter Pilot* (1st edn, Shrewsbury: Airlife, 1995).

Turner, J. F., *The Bader Tapes* (1st edn, Bourne End: Kensal Press, 1986).

Turner, J. F., *The Bader Wing* (2nd edn, Shrewbury: Airlife, 1990).

Webster, W., *Englishness and Empire 1939–1965* (1st edn, New York: Oxford University Press, 2005).

Wells, M. K., *Courage in Air Warfare: The Allied Aircrew Experience in the Second World War* (1st edn, London: Frank Cass & Co. Ltd., 1995).

Wright, R., *Dowding and the Battle of Britain* (2nd edn, London: Corgi, 1970).

Wynn, K., *Men of the Battle of Britain* (1st edn, Norwich: Gliddon Books, 1989).

ACKNOWLEDGEMENTS

Firstly I would like to thank my friends of many years now, Lady Bader OBE, Keith Delderfield and David Bickers of the Douglas Bader Foundation; Professor Paul MacKenzie, Chris Johnson (eldest son of the RAF's top-scoring fighter pilot of the Second World War, the late Air Vice-Marshal Johnnie Johnson), and Ken Potts.

All of those I corresponded with or interviewed are mentioned in my references, so their names are not duplicated here; I thank them all.

I would also like to thank Christopher Cunliff for kindly supplying several films for my research.

My wife, the artist Karen Sarkar, is always ready to offer constructive advice and criticism, and generally suffers my various obsessions with good grace!

OTHER BOOKS BY DILIP SARKAR
(IN ORDER OF PUBLICATION)

Spitfire Voices: Heroes Remember
The Battle of Powick Bridge: Ambush a Fore-thought
Duxford 1940: A Battle of Britain Base at War
The Few: The Battle of Britain in the Words of the Pilots
The Spitfire Manual 1940
The Last of the Few: Eighteen Battle of Britain Pilots Tell Their Extraordinary Stories
Hearts of Oak: The Human Tragedy of HMS Royal Oak
Spitfire Voices: Life as a Spitfire Pilot in the Words of the Veterans
How the Spitfire Won the Battle of Britain
Spitfire Ace of Aces: The True Wartime Story of Johnnie Johnson

SPITFIRE
ACE OF ACES

The Wartime Story of Johnnie Johnson

'An exceptional record of a leader of men'
THE SPITFIRE SOCIETY

DILIP SARKAR

Available from all good bookshops or to order direct
Please call 01453-847-800
www.amberleybooks.com